The American Journalists

FOUR YEARS IN SECESSIA

Junius Henri Browne

ARNO
&
The New York Times

Collection Created and Selected
by Charles Gregg of Gregg Press

Reprint edition 1970 by Arno Press Inc.

LC# 72-125681
ISBN 0-405-01656-5

The American Journalists
ISBN for complete set: 0-405-01650-6

Manufactured in the United States of America

FOUR YEARS IN SECESSIA:

OUR CAPTURE BEFORE VICKSBURG.

FOUR YEARS IN SECESSIA:

ADVENTURES

WITHIN AND BEYOND THE UNION LINES:

EMBRACING A GREAT VARIETY OF

FACTS, INCIDENTS, AND ROMANCE OF THE WAR.

INCLUDING

THE AUTHOR'S CAPTURE AT VICKSBURG, MAY 3, 1863, WHILE RUNNING THE REBEL BATTERIES; HIS IMPRISONMENT AT VICKSBURG, JACKSON, ATLANTA, RICHMOND, AND SALISBURY; HIS ESCAPE AND PERILOUS JOURNEY OF FOUR HUNDRED MILES TO THE UNION LINES AT KNOXVILLE.

BY

JUNIUS HENRI BROWNE,

SPECIAL WAR CORRESPONDENT OF THE NEW YORK TRIBUNE.

With Illustrations.

HARTFORD:
O. D. CASE AND COMPANY.
CHICAGO: GEO. & C. W. SHERWOOD.
LONDON: STEVENS BROTHERS.
1865.

TO

THE PRIVATE SOLDIERS OF THE UNION,

THE UNRECORDED AND FAMELESS HEROES

OF THE WAR,

WHO DESERVE THE ETERNAL GRATITUDE OF THE REPUBLIC THEY

HAVE PRESERVED,

THIS UNPRETENDING VOLUME

IS ADMIRINGLY INSCRIBED.

PREFACE.

Most first books either are, or assume to be, written at the request of that apochryphal class known as Friends. Having a very limited acquaintance with that somewhat intangible portion of the community, I would state that this unpretending volume owes its unfortunate parturition to the urgent solicitation of my publishers, who, unsolicited, offered me such terms as a Gentleman of very slender income (his valuable estates in Castile being entirely inconvertible in Wall Street) and somewhat expensive habits could ill afford to refuse.

The contents of "Four Years in Secessia" are merely poor pieces of patch-work clumsily stitched together with a needle that grew very rusty in the long dampness of Rebel Prisons. The little labor on the book has been, under very adverse circumstances, irregularly and hurriedly performed, not extending beyond a fortnight's duration, and this, though no excuse, may be some reason for the poverty of its contents.

If my readers are half as much wearied in its perusal as the author was in its preparation, he can only entreat them to remember the Spaniard's advice to men about to choose a wife: "Shut your eyes, and commend your soul to God."

THE AUTHOR

NEW YORK, *May* 1, 1865.

ILLUSTRATIONS.

CONTENTS.

CHAPTER I.

THE WAR CORRESPONDENT.

CHAPTER II.

THE FREMONT CAMPAIGN.

CHAPTER III.

CAMP-LIFE AT SYRACUSE, MO.

CHAPTER IV.

A NIGHT WITH THE FLEAS.

CHAPTER V.

ROMANCE AND REALITY IN CAMP.

CHAPTER VI.

ON THE MARCH.

CHAPTER VII.

WILSON'S CREEK.

CHAPTER VIII.

ZAGONYI'S RIDE TO DEATH.

CHAPTER IX.

THE RETROGRADE MOVEMENT.

CHAPTER X.

SECESSION IN MISSOURI.

CHAPTER XI.

BATTLE OF DONELSON.

CHAPTER XII.

AFTER THE BATTLE.

CHAPTER XIII.

OCCUPATION OF COLUMBUS.

CHAPTER XIV.

BATTLE OF PEA RIDGE.

CHAPTER XV.

PROSE AND POESY OF WAR.

CHAPTER XVI.

INDIAN ATROCITIES.

CHAPTER XVII.

BENIGHTED ARKANSAS.

CHAPTER XVIII.

DOWN THE MISSISSIPPI.

CHAPTER XXV.

MAYING IN ARKANSAS.

CHAPTER XXVI.

COMMODORE FOOTE'S FAREWELL.

CHAPTER XXVII.

NAVAL ENGAGEMENT AT FORT PILLOW.

CHAPTER XXVIII.

FALL OF MEMPHIS.

CHAPTER XXIX.

THE EXPEDITION UP WHITE RIVER.

CHAPTER XXX.

THE BRAGG-BUELL CAMPAIGN.

CHAPTER XXXVI.

THE LIBBY PRISON.

CHAPTER XXXVII.

THE LIBBY PRISON.

CHAPTER XXXVIII.

THE KITCHEN CABINET AT THE LIBBY.

CHAPTER XXXIX.

CELL-LIFE IN RICHMOND.

CHAPTER XL.

CASTLE THUNDER.

CHAPTER XLI.

EXECUTION OF A LOYAL TENNESSEAN.

CHAPTER XLII.

SALISBURY PENITENTIARY.

CHAPTER XLIII.

PHOTOGRAPHS OF HORROR.

CHAPTER XLIV.

TUNNELS AND TUNNELING.

CHAPTER XLV.

MUGGING.

CHAPTER XLVI.

DESPERATE ESCAPE.

CHAPTER XLVII.

UNION BUSHWHACKERS.

CHAPTER XLVIII.

THE ESCAPE.

CHAPTER XLIX.

THE MARCH TO FREEDOM.

CHAPTER L.

THE HAVEN OF REST.

CHAPTER LI.

THE MARCH ONWARD.

CHAPTER LII.

THE HEGIRA IN EAST TENNESSEE.

FOUR YEARS IN SECESSIA.

CHAPTER I.

THE WAR CORRESPONDENT.

His Anomalous Position.—A Ruralist's Idea of a Bohemian.—How the Name was obtained.—Genesis and Purpose of the War Correspondent.—His Duty and Obligation.—The Difficulty of his Task.—His Habits, Peculiarities, and Defects.—What he requires of the Service.—His Just Claims, &c.

During the few days I have passed in the Free States since the breaking out of the Rebellion, I have been so often questioned about the province, purpose, and habits of a War Correspondent, that I deem it well, in the initial chapter of this volume, to state what manner of animal he is, and what are his peculiarities.

That the War Correspondent is a hybrid, neither a soldier nor a citizen; with the Army, but not of it; is present at battles, and often participating in them, yet without any rank or recognized existence, has mystified not a few, and rendered his position as anomalous as undesirable.

"Do you belong to the Army?" inquired a bumpkin, riding up beside myself and a couple of journalistic companions, as we were moving toward Fayetteville during the Bragg-Buell campaign in Kentucky, in the autumn of 1862. "Yes," was the answer. "Are you soldiers?" "No." "Are you officers?" "No." "Are you sutlers?" "No." "What are you, then?" "War Correspondents." "Oh, that's what you are, is it?" and after this comment on our response, he seemed lost in reflection the most profound. Fully a minute must have passed, when his face brightened, and he seemed to have solved some mental problem. "Oh, well, boys, you're all right. War Correspondents, eh? Why, they're the fellows that fought in the Revolution!"

Droll idea that of the Bohemians, as they have been christened, from their nomadic, careless, half-literary, half-vagabondish life; but not much more so than far more intelligent persons entertain of them. What they are, and what they do, I will endeavor to explain.

The War Correspondent is the outgrowth of a very modern civilization; though Xenophon and Julius Cæsar were early examples of the profession. They, however, told the story of their own deeds, and the nineteenth-century Bohemians narrate the acts of others; make their name and fame without themselves gaining any glory.

They are the outgrowth of the great and constantly augmenting power of the Press, and were first fully developed and their influence felt during the Crimean contest. There were War Correspondents before that day: in the Napoleonic struggle for universal domination, and in our own little affair, as it now appears, with Mexico; but, until the time mentioned, it had not become a regular and recognized department of military-civic life.

Since the first gun discharged at Fort Sumter awoke the American world to arms, War Correspondence on this side of the Atlantic has been as much an avocation as practising law or selling dry goods. Every newspaper, of prominence in the metropolitan cities, has had its Correspondents in the field and with the Navy. No army in the East or West but has had a journalistic representative. No expedition of importance has set out without its writing medium between it and New York, Philadelphia, Boston, Cincinnati, Chicago, and St. Louis.

The War Correspondent is the proper and natural medium between the Army and Navy and the people at home, and ought to be, and is generally, the purest, because the only unprejudiced medium between the military and civil phases of existence. He only has, as a general thing—and there should be no exceptions—no friends to reward, and no foes to punish. He is at his post to relate what he sees; to applaud valor and merit wherever found; to point out abuses and blunders that would not otherwise be reached, save through the endless duration of military investigations and courts-martial. His duty is to illustrate the situation so far as is prudent; to describe the movements, actions, and combinations of the forces; in a word, to photograph the life and spirit of the combatants for the benefit of the great Public, united to them by blood and sympathy, and who thrill and suffer with the gallant warriors, and mourn over and honor the heroic dead.

Such being the duty and obligation—and it should be a solemn one—of the Correspondent, he has as much place and fitness in the field as the Commander-in-Chief; and is as much entitled to consideration. That he is not what he should be often, is true of him, as it is of every other class; and that many of his profession have, by unworthy conduct, reflected discredit upon its members, is equally true. The misfortune is, that the unworthy, by their assurance, carelessness, and lack of principle, give such false impressions of the entire tribe, that I marvel not a most wholesome prejudice exists against them on the part of many officers.

The ill-starred Bohemian has a most delicate and difficult task to perform. He must do his duty, and yet offend no one. He must praise, but not censure. He must weave chaplets of roses without thorns for the brows of vanity, and applaud modest merit without wounding pompous conceit. Every thing is expected of him—impossibilities and virtues more than human. Few give him commendation; yet many are willing to denounce him. What he does well passes in silence; what he does ill is blazoned to his shame.

War Correspondence is a most thankless office. The Correspondent may do, and dare, and suffer; but who yields him credit? If he die in the service by disease or casualty, it is thought and declared by many that he had no business there. The officers frequently dislike him, because they have not received what they conceive to be their meed of praise; and the people do not appreciate him. So, on the whole, he is always between Sylla and Charybdis, and never avoids one without encountering the other.

No disposition have I to laud my profession; but I do think its members are unkindly and ungratefully treated.

I have known many of them intimately, of course; and while I have been called to blush for some, I can testify to the high and noble qualities of more.

As a class they are brave, loyal, talented, and honorable gentlemen; a little too prone, perhaps, to recklessness of conduct and statement, and unduly sensitive about their own dignity and the importance of the Press. They believe implicitly in the aphorism: *Cedant arma togæ*, and do not always understand that the customs of Peace are incompatible with the exigencies of War. Yet, in the main, they perform their duty conscientiously, and deserve more kindly of the Army, the Navy, and the general Public, than they receive.

The worst feature of their profession is—and they deplore it as much as any one—they are compelled, from the great competition in respect to news, to write up their accounts so rapidly, and forward them so early, that correctness of statement and excellence of style are often precluded. When they write their letters, as I have seen them, in the midst of action; on their knee and upon the ground; in crowded railway cars and on thronged transports; under every variety of adverse circumstance, I have wondered, and still wonder, at their fluency, propriety, and exactness. They certainly accomplish marvels, considering their surroundings and facilities, and at least suggest what they might do if leisure and opportunity were given them.

The Correspondents have figured in the casualties again and again; have been killed, and wounded, and captured; have, perhaps, had quite their share of the accidents of war. Yet, on the whole, they have been rather fortunate, for they go so recklessly hither and thither on the march and in action, wherever their humor or fancy prompts, that it seems strange a larger number have not lost life, limb, and freedom.

They have splendid opportunities for observation, being a privileged body, under no orders, and consequently at liberty to roam when and where they please. They have probably seen more of the romance of the War than any other class of men in the Army—much of which they have not given to the public, and which they cannot give conveniently or prudently until the struggle is over.

They usually enter some officer's mess, on taking the field; have their own horses; pay their proportion of the expenses; and live exactly as the officers do, except that they are not subject to orders. During a battle they can go where they list—to the skirmish line or to the rear; to the right or left wing; with the infantry or artillery.

If they have any fondness—and many of them have—for fighting, they can always be accommodated. I have more than once seen them in the field, musket in hand, and frequently trying their skill as sharpshooters. They very often act as voluntary aides on the staff of General Officers, and have, in numerous instances, played a conspicuous and important part in engagements. They have again and again joined hazardous expeditions for which volunteers have been called; have gone on perilous raids and scouts; run batteries, and taken risks purely from a love of adventure—to have the experience—which is a very natural desire with the poetico-philosophic temperament. They have done a number of what many would call very foolish and reckless, though certainly courageous, acts—all the more courageous because they had no inducement of glory, and would not at all have been honored as an officer or a soldier would if they had fallen, as they sometimes have, in what would be considered obedience to a freak or feeling, instead of a conviction of duty.

"Why do they not enter the service regularly?" I presume has been often asked, "and so do some good?" They perform their part as Correspondents, would be a fair answer. They do good, though in a different way, just as much as the Captain of a battery, or the Lieutenant of cavalry, or the Major of an infantry regiment does. They are, in my judgment, as much a portion of the Army or Navy as any of the officers of the Army or Navy, and render perchance as essential, though less interested and heralded, service.

Moreover, I suspect the Bohemians, from a certain impatience of restraint and a Shelley-like hatred of obedience, are often opposed to entering the ranks or accepting a commission. They want more freedom than a regular connection with the Army or Navy gives them; but that such fantastic scruples are not infrequently removed is shown by the number who have entered both branches of the service.

The profession of War Correspondence has, it seems to me, declined somewhat during the past two years. Or it may be that I see no more the names of those who were in the field when I passed out of it into a Rebel Prison, and fancy the new men inferior to the old campaigners because I do not know them. This supposition is quite probable, and I am very willing it should be regarded as the cause of the apparent decadence.

One thing is certain, however. There has been so much

inharmony between the Officers and Correspondents, so many unpleasant jarrings and misunderstandings, that most of the gentlemen who were in the field, when I had any knowledge of it, have resigned their positions and taken new ones. There are some of my retired intimates who insist that a gentleman cannot be a Correspondent without detracting from his dignity, or abrogating a portion of his proper pride. I have not found it so in the Past; I trust I shall not in the Future. I am aware there are officers—some of very high standing—who are absurdly and causelessly prejudiced against the Bohemians; but I cannot perceive why the two should not be *en rapport*, and administer to each other's advantage.

That the Correspondent ought to have some fixed and recognized position in the Army and Navy, or be expelled from both, there can be little question. There is no middle ground. Either he has full right there, or he has not. Then recognize or remove him. He is always in the field, and always will be; but he is really regarded, so far as the Regulations go, as a kind of camp-follower or hanger-on. Our readers remember, no doubt, the trouble that occurred between General Halleck and the Bohemians before Corinth in the summer of 1862, which seemed very unwise and unnecessary on that officer's part, and which, I am glad to say, has never been repeated.

If the Correspondent had a defined position, it would be far more agreeable to him; for, however well he may be treated, it is rather unpleasant to know that he is, to a certain extent, merely tolerated. The Bohemians with whom I have associated have always been politely received by the officers, often courted and flattered;

but still that does not remove the objection of which I have complained. Accept them entirely, or suppress them utterly. They have complete right there, as I have said ; but their right must be established before the genuine gentlemen of the profession can feel altogether at one with themselves and perfectly at their ease.

The Bohemians have faults not a few, as has been stated ; but they are the best abused class of which I have any knowledge. They are too much inclined to publish their information before prudence and patriotism permit ; but that is the fault of their employers, and ought to be wholly discouraged. The man who can forget the duty he owes his country in his desire to serve the journal he represents, ought to be disgraced and punished.

The Bohemians generally give the facts about as they are, and to few of their letters from the field are exceptions taken unless by those officers—alas, how many !—who insist that their company, regiment, brigade or division, did all the fighting, and saved the fortunes of the day.

It is well known to all veteran campaigners that every soldier and commander has a different story to tell, but each regards it as his religious obligation to praise his own company or corps, at the expense of all others. Such jealousy, envy, and heart-burning as are in the service, are painful to any and every true patriot, and prove that, after all that has been said, "Our Special" or "Our Own" is more trustworthy, and has less motive for misrepresentation than any other individual on land or sea.

We should look leniently on the Bohemian, and will, I apprehend, when we reflect how extremely difficult his duty is, and how utterly impossible it is to give general satisfaction. Let us yield him some credit, if not for what he does, for what he refrains from doing; and if we look into his life and avocation, we will find he is far more sinned against than sinning, and less a journalist than a patriot; that he undergoes hardship, and exposes himself to dangers because he is earnest and loyal, and truly devoted to our great and glorious cause.

CHAPTER II.

THE FREMONT CAMPAIGN.

Life in Jefferson City, Mo.—Effect of the Sudden Changes from Metropolitan Life.—A Contrast to the Glory of War.—A Romantic Soldier.—A Camp Picture.—The Original Bohemian Brigade.

THE Fremont campaign was the first in which I fairly took the field, and, consequently, many things impressed me then, that, later in the War, would not have affected me at all.

The prominent features of that campaign have passed into history, and would not bear repetition here. Therefore I shall merely give my personal impressions and observations when I reached Jefferson City, early in September, 1861, fresh from the pursuits of peace and the comforts of metropolitan life.

I arrived at the capital of Missouri some weeks before General Fremont quitted St. Louis, when Jeff. C. Davis, then Colonel, commanded the post. There was very little doing there then in the military way, and very sudden transplanting to that rude frontier town made me merely vegetate in that most uncongenial atmosphere.

I put up at a miserable hotel, and for a fortnight I was so lonely and wretched, that, if there had been an agreeable woman in the place, I should have fallen in love with her from sheer desperation.

Safe enough was I, however, in that particular. There were no women of any kind, not to speak of lovable ones, visible in the streets, through which I sauntered listlessly and gloomily, wondering when my brother Bohemians, whom I had left in St. Louis, would make their appearance at the dreary capital.

I had no books with me, and could get none in the town worth reading. I did not know how to pass the hours. I was extremely miserable. I am not ashamed to confess it now—I was home-sick; and, if it had not been for pride, I should have resigned my position of War Correspondent, and hurried back to peaceful avocations and metropolitan life, with a keener appreciation than I had ever known before.

Having little to occupy me, I was a great observer, and grew a trifle sentimental, perhaps, as indolent and unhappy persons usually do.

One saw just then much of "the pomp and circumstance of glorious war." While cavalry companies were constantly dashing through the streets, regiments marching to the inspiring strains of martial music, officers hurrying to and fro on prancing steeds, artillery rumbling along, bugle-notes and drum-rolls rising from the adjacent camps, a funeral cortége passed my window.

A rude car contained a coffin, enveloped in the American colors; a squad of soldiers followed, with reversed arms; a bugle played a mournful dirge; but no one noticed the sad procession. All had too much of life to care for the dead.

No one paused to think of the poor fellow in the coffin, who sickened and died afar from home and friends, in a military hospital.

No kind sister had spoken comfort to him; no mother's

hand had smoothed his pillow; no nearer and dearer friend—kindred only in heart—had bathed his brow or moistened his fevered lips, or received his last word, or sigh, or kiss.

He had not even had the consolation of dying in battle, poor fellow! Disease had struck him down; but his death was not therefore less glorious.

Happy soldier! his troubles were over. He had suffered, and was at rest. Nor care, nor pain, nor strife could reach him evermore.

No one noticed the funeral cortége, I have said.

Yes, there was one.

A young man stood on the sidewalk, with head uncovered, his face beautiful with sympathy, and his eye moist with pity and with love.

Men are not all careless and selfish, even there.

He who pitied and who felt, whate'er his creed or station, must have been, in the largest sense, a Christian and a gentleman.

One night, as I was at the railway dépôt, I observed a young man, with an unusually intelligent and comely face, standing sentry, in the uniform of a private.

I had rarely seen such a face in the ranks, and I stopped a minute near him, gazing at the stars, which were unusually bright and numerous.

"A beautiful night this," he said. "External nature is charming, but human nature is ever melancholy. How calm and beautiful the stars are! They seem silently to rebuke the scene of arms on which they gaze."

My impression of his superiority to his station was corroborated.

Few private soldiers think or talk as he had done; and at once we fell into conversation, which continued for an hour.

I learned from him—for he at once unbosomed himself—that he had been in love with a beautiful girl, the only daughter of a wealthy merchant of Cincinnati, and been affianced to her.

During three months' absence in the East, she had been flirting desperately with another young man, and my soldier-friend, learning, on his return, that the two were engaged, concluded to call on her no more.

The girl wrote to him, and he answered, informing her of what he had heard. She acknowledged the truth, but declared her affair with his rival merely a flirtation; that she loved the youth she addressed, and never could love any one else.

This was not satisfactory. The enamored youth was wretched and desperate, and, declaring all women false, volunteered as a private, and went to Missouri.

He informed me that, but for the war, he would have committed suicide; that he was anxious to fall in the first charge, for life had for him no further charms.

I smiled at his infatuation, and told him that nearly all women were fickle; that his "Louisa" was less so, probably, than most of her sex; that he should have more philosophy than to think of dying for a silly girl, and that he should congratulate himself on his escape from matrimony.

He thought me jesting, at first, and then wondered how one at my age—I was far younger than now—had become so cynical.

"Through observation and reason," I answered; and, assuring him he would soon forget "Louisa," and fancy he loved some other woman, bade him good-night.

He vowed I was mistaken; that I would hear of his death in his first battle.

I never did.

He will go through the war unhurt, no doubt, and live long enough after to laugh at his boyish passion, and experience, perhaps, that Love, as young hearts imagine and poets paint it, is a myth that Reason immediately removes.

About the 1st of October we went into camp, and on the evening of the 4th, all was activity, and the scene was quite picturesque.

The sky was dark with clouds, and the lightning in the southern horizon, and the low-muttering thunder, blending with the neigh of horses, the rattling of sabres trailing on the ground, the "good-by" of officers, as they rode off to join their commands, already in advance, the hoarse cry of the artillerymen and teamsters, the music-swell of the National bands, coming in waves over the slopes and through the trees, with the illuminated tents, the camp-fires reddening the oaks and beeches—all gave a strange but attractive wildness to the mezzotinto landscape before our eyes.

With all its monotony, all its painful suggestions, there is a kind of charm in camp-life—in its freedom from ordinary restraint, its out-door existence, its easy, reckless tone, its devil-may-care indifference, and utter disregard of the formal barbarians the enlightened world calls "Society."

3

"The Bohemian Brigade" was the name the little corps of army correspondents and artists that soon assembled at Jefferson City had received. They were only seven or eight in number: Albert D. Richardson, of the New York *Tribune*, Thomas W. Knox, of the *Herald*, Franc B. Wilkie, of the *Times*, Richard T. Colburn, of the *World*, Joseph B. McCullagh, of the Cincinnati *Commercial*, Geo. W. Beaman, of the St. Louis *Democrat*, Henri Lovie, artist for Frank Leslie, and Alex. A. Simplot, for *Harper's Weekly;* with several other scribblers and sketchers, who were there for a few days, but grew tired or disgusted, and did not accompany our expedition to the South-West.

Of course, we had considerable leisure, and amused ourselves as best we could, in the absence of books, which were very scarce. We smoked pipes, played whist, discussed Poetry, Metaphysics, Art, the Opera, Women, the World, the War and its future, and various themes on which we then could merely speculate. Most of our Brigade were bachelors—unless Michelet's idea of bachelordom, as represented in "L'Amour," be correct —and enthusiastic members of the anti-matrimonial school of philosophy.

The unwedded bore camp-life resignedly and cheerfully; but the Benedicks seemed delighted with it, because, as the most confirmed celibates declared, they then had an excuse for absenting themselves from their domestic hearths, and, to use that exquisitely satirical phrase, the "blessings of connubial life."

CHAPTER III.

CAMP-LIFE AT SYRACUSE, MO.

Effects of Camp-Life.—Sentimental Reflections on War.—A Modern Penthesilea. —Woman's Military Influence Beautifully Exemplified.—The Rural Females of Missouri.—Their Unpoetic Appearance.

In the early days of October, 1861, Fremont's army began to move from Missouri's capital, for the purpose of intercepting, if possible, and certainly of giving battle to, Price's forces, who had from some mysterious cause been allowed to take Lexington, and then retreat southward without opposition or hindrance. Whose the fault was, I will not here attempt to show. I will simply accompany Fremont to Springfield, describing such noteworthy incidents of the camp and march as have not already become familiar to the general reader.

When the correspondent of the *Herald* and myself reached Syracuse, Mo., about the 13th or 14th of October, I was becoming accustomed to camp-life, though I could hardly say I liked it, nor did I believe I ever should.

It was certainly a change, and on that account I sought it. It was very different from existence at the Fifth Avenue or Metropolitan—about as different as a transfer from Paris to Canton, or from the equator to the north pole. I had not expected to find agreeableness in camp-life, but rather its opposite; and therefore I was not to be disappointed.

Residence in camp has a decided effect in removing the romantic idea of War, which, by the by, I have ever regarded as the most prosaic and unattractive of actualities. No spirit of poesy, no breath of sentiment enters into War; no æsthetic principle animates it. War bristles with facts—is terribly real, repulsively practical.

War may be beautiful on the historian's page, and through the idealization of time and distance; but to the spectator or the actor it is divested of its charms, and becomes a reign of horrors and a civilized monstrosity. And yet it has its fascinations, as drunkenness, licentiousness, murder, journalism, and the stage have theirs.

What is War, after all, but scientific assassination, throat-cutting by rule, causing misery and vice, and pain and death by prescribed forms? It seems high time War had ceased to be. It is a palpable anachronism, and yet it continues, and will until the mental millennium arrives; until this sphere is spiritualized, and mankind have grown philosophers.

So I thought then; but my duty was to write of, not against, War; and, stretched on the earth beside my tent, in the shade, on a warm, bright, beautiful day, full of the loveliness of October, I proceeded to discharge my journalistic obligations as best I could, reserving my sentimental opinions about War for the private ears of my sentimental friends.

A great deal of disharmony and trouble occurred about that time in a Missouri cavalry regiment, which threatened then to, and eventually did, break it up completely. About the 1st of October, the commander had placed a number of the inferior officers under arrest at Tipton, and a detachment at Jefferson refused to obey his orders, and were insubordinate because they were not armed. Much of this trouble was reported to have arisen on account of the interference of the wife of the Colonel with the affairs of the regiment, in which she took the most lively interest.

I was told she threatened to horsewhip some of the refractory officers, drew revolvers upon others, and adopted the most masculine measures to restore order out of chaos. Of course, a woman's interference was resented by the officers, who murmured loudly against petticoat domination, and were extremely anxious to get rid of her. The Madame, however, would not be gotten rid of, and continued to play the part of Penthesilea with a degree of boldness and perseverance which, in the days of the Amazons, would have made her their queen.

She bore dispatches, rode through storm and tempest, faced curses and opposition, met insult with maledictions and menaces, and evinced an energy, a resolution, and a courage, that rendered it a pity she was not born of the opposite sex.

Notwithstanding her feminine gendership, she was said by those who knew her to be most masculine in character, and that she would be very effective in leading a cavalry charge, or attacking a death-dealing battery. From all accounts, she seemed unfortunate in her genesis—to have been created physically a woman and mentally a man.

The virago finally demoralized the regiment, caused its disbandment, and her husband's removal from the army.

She had her way ; but she ruined her liege-lord, who, the last I heard of him, had taken to superlative potations and the exhibition of seven-legged calves and Irish giants, still accompanied, and haunted, and tortured by the pursuing Nemesis of his life, the precious friend whom we have honored with the fragment of a chapter.

After my arrival in the rural regions of Missouri, and my association with the army, I often wondered how men fond of women managed to endure ; indeed, I, who had always regarded the softer sex as works of art—and are they not such ?—from the level of cold criticism or pure æsthetics have been compelled to commiserate, though I could not sympathize with, those countless amorous Alfonsos.

Fine women did not appear indigenous to the disloyal soil of Missouri.

They were in the rough, as sculptors phrase it ; lacking the refining chisel of Art and Culture to fashion them into loveliness.

A lover of the beautiful looked in vain for the classic features, the spiritual expression, the soul-reflecting eye, the charming symmetry, the voluptuous proportions, the elegant drapery, the delightful but airy nothings that appeal to the Imagination more than the Sense.

In their stead, he saw brown and brawny women, that offended his taste, and chilled his gallantry ; that repressed his chivalrous sentiment, and falsified his memories of the blue-eyed "Belles" and hazel-haired "Heroes" he had met, and made them seem the angels of a dreamy Past.

CHAPTER IV.

A NIGHT WITH THE FLEAS.

Unanticipated Attack.—Inexplicable Sensations.—Prosaic Revelation.—Our Intense Suffering.—A Novel Remedy.—Extraordinary Ride through a Tempestuous Night.—Finale of the Tragi-Comedy.

UNTIL I began to follow the camp, I had never known, save by auricular evidence, of those unpoetical insects known as fleas; but one night in Syracuse, Mo., "our mess" experienced the cruelty and savageness of the diminutive foes of man, to our bodies' extremest dissatisfaction.

We were all lounging in the tent, reading, undreaming of enemies of any kind, when we all became restless, and the interest of our books began seriously to diminish.

There were various manual applications to various parts of the body, multifarious shiftings of position, accompanied with emphatic expletives that sounded marvelously like oaths.

"What is the matter?" was asked by one of us of another. "What renders you so uneasy?"

"Heaven knows!" was the answer; "but I itch like Satan."

"My body seems on fire," observed one.

"I wonder," said another, "if I have contracted a loathsome disease!"

"Confound it! what ails me?"

"And me—and me—and me?" was echoed from my companions.

One hand became insufficient to allay the irritation of our corporeality. Both hands became requisite to the task, and our volumes were necessarily laid aside.

No one yet appeared aware of the cause of his suffering. If we were not all in Tophet, no one could deny we had gone to the old Scratch. We seemed to be laboring under an uncontrollable nervous complaint. We threw our hands about wildly. We seized our flesh rudely, and rubbed our clothes until they nearly ignited from friction.

One of the quartette could stand it no longer. He threw off his coat and vest spasmodically, and even his under garments, and solemnly exclaimed—

"Flee from the wrath to come!"

The mystery was explained—the enigma solved.

The martyr's person was covered with small black spots, that disappeared and reappeared in the same instant.

To be practically expressive, he was covered with fleas.

The rest of us followed his example, and converted ourselves into model artists.

We were all covered with fleas.

Fleas were everywhere. Tent, straw, books, blankets, valises, saddles, swarmed with them.

The air scintillated with their blackness.

We rushed out of the tent.

They were there in myriads.

The moonlight fell in checkered beams through their innumerable skippings.

They made a terrible charge, as of a forlorn hope, and drove us back.

We roared with anger and with pain, and loud curses made the atmosphere assume a violet hue.

Three of the flea-besieged caught up canteens of whisky and brandy, and poured the contents over their persons and down their throats; scratching meanwhile like a thousand cats of the Thomas persuasion, and leaping about like dancing dervises.

The more the fleas bit, the more the victims drank; and I, having no taste for liquor, began to envy them, as, in their increasing intoxication, they seemed to enjoy themselves after a sardonic fashion.

The fleas redoubled their ferocity on me, and I surrendered at discretion; and at last became resigned to their attacks, until, a few minutes after, a storm that had been gathering burst with fierce lightning, heavy thunder, and torrents of rain.

A happy idea seized me.

I caught up my saddle and bridle, and placed them on my sable steed "Festus," which stood neighing to the tempest, a few feet from the camp.

I mounted the fleet-footed horse, and, nude as the Apollo Belvidere, cried "go" to the restive animal; and off we sped, to the amazement of the sentinels, through the darkness and the storm.

Every few moments the lightning blazed around us with a lurid sheen, as we went like the wind through the tempestuous night.

"Festus" enjoyed it, as did his rider; and six swift-speeding miles were passed ere I drew the rein upon the neck of the panting beast, covered with white flecks of foam.

I paused, and felt that the fleas had been left behind.

The pelting rain and rushing blast had been too much for them; while the exercise had made my attireless body glow into a pleasant warmth.

"Festus" galloped back, and soon I was in the tent, rolled so closely in a blanket that no new attack of the fleas could reach me.

My companions, overcome with their exertions, sufferings, and potations, had lain down; but the fleas were still upon them, and they rolled and tossed more than a rural tragedian in the tent scene of "Richard the Third."

They were asleep, and yet they moaned piteously, and scratched with demoniac violence.

In spite of my pity for the poor fellows, I could not refrain from laughing.

With the earliest dawn I awoke, and the tent was vacant.

Horrid thought!

Had the fleas carried them off?

I went out to search for them; and, after a diligent quest, found them still in nature's garb, distributed miscellaneously about the encampment.

In their physical torture they had unconsciously rolled out of the tent.

One lay in an adjacent ditch; a second under an artillery wagon; and the third was convulsively grasping the earth, as if he were endeavoring to dig his own grave; believing, no doubt, that, in the tomb, neither Fortune nor fleas could ever harm him more. The unfortunate two were covered with crimson spots, and looked as if recovering from the small-pox.

I pulled them, still stupid from their spiritual excess, into the tent again, and covered them with blankets, though they swore incoherently as I did so, evidently believing that some giant flea was dragging them to perdition.

When they were fully aroused, they fell to scratching again most violently, but knew not what had occurred until they had recalled the events of the previous night.

They then blasphemed afresh, and unanimously consigned the entire race of fleas to the Bottomless Pit.

The fleas still tried to bite, but could find no new places, and my companions had grown accustomed to them.

They felt no uneasiness for the coming night; they were aware that the new fleas would retire from a field so completely occupied, and that the domesticated creatures were in sufficient force to rout all invaders.

So ended that memorable Noche Triste, an exemplification of the Scriptural declaration,

"The wicked flee when no man pursueth."

CHAPTER V.

ROMANCE AND REALITY IN CAMP.

Conversion of a Fair Secessionist.—Disadvantage of Securing a Guard.—A Grand Mule Concert.—Sonorous Imitations of the Opera.—High-Art Jackassical Performances.—Terror excited by the Unique Entertainment.

A CAPTAIN on one of the general's staff in McKinstry's division, while we were at Syracuse, sent a guard to protect the house of a secessionist in this neighborhood, who felt very needless alarm about his property; and learning that the rebel had a pretty and interesting daughter (remarkable circumstance in Missouri), paid frequent visits to her domicil, and assumed the deepest interest in the protection and welfare of the family.

This was, as may be supposed, the effect of the attractiveness of the daughter, whose acquaintance, of course, the officer made on his first visit. He found the fair girl a violent advocate of that meaningless phrase, "Southern Rights;" but, like a sensible man, he was the more attracted to her therefor.

Here let me state what Brantôme and Crébillon, and the other French writers on women and their peculiarities, have failed to mention.

The man of perseverance, who eloquently opposes a woman's ruling opinion, excites her love through her hate.

So it proved with the Captain.

The girl was furious at first; declared him an abolitionist and an assassin; vowed she would not marry a Yankee if her soul's salvation depended on it, and so on to the end.

The Captain blended vehement Unionism with his passionate gallantry, and in a week the girl struck her Secession colors, and is now warmly in favor of the Government, and betrothed to the young officer.

Her father knows not the change of his daughter's sentiments.

When he does, he will regret asking a guard for his property. He should rather have requested a guard for "Helen's" heart, which was hopelessly lost, even to a rebel lover she had in Tennessee.

What is called "winning a woman's heart" is generally a melancholy business.

It is often less difficult to get it than to get rid of it; and is, on the whole, a very uncomfortable and unremunerative acquisition.

We had an amusing entertainment one night at Syracuse, and an entertainment of an original character.

I am passionately fond of music; could listen to sweet music, I think, until my hair turned gray, and be unaware of the passage of time.

I have heard all the great vocalists and artistes that have visited this country; but never, until the night in question, had my melody-longing ears been greeted with so unique a performance as a mule concert.

It was irresistibly droll to hear, though it can not be described, and would have made Heraclitus laugh.

My army-correspondent companions and myself were

talking about the prospects of the campaign, while rolled in our blankets in the tent, when our voices were drowned by the loudest and shrillest and most space-penetrating bray I remember to have heard.

A moment passed, and the bray was repeated in a baser key; then another, and another, and another, each with a different modulation.

All the mules in the camp volunteered for the operatic rôle, and the atmosphere quivered with the cacophonous notes.

Sometimes all the mules but one would cease; and he would execute the solo part, the rest coming in most energetically by way of chorus. All voices were represented, to the extent of a mule's capacity.

We had the soprano, mezzo and pure; the first and second tenore; the baritone the basso profundo and secondo; the alto and falsetto.

One mule would attempt a florid passage, and in the midst of a roulade would break; when the others, either in applause or ridicule, would indulge in a species of mule music that was positively infernal.

Ten thousand tom-cats, a million of screaming babies, a billion of rusty saws carelessly filed, with four trillions of intoxicated Teutons, endeavoring to play "Hail Columbia" with the wrong end of a cornet, might give a faint idea of the sound.

If we could obtain that noise in a concentrated liquid form, and pour it out on the battle-field, it would frighten the Rebels out of their senses, and make the moon blink with terrified amazement.

Indeed it would.

For at least four hours the mules kept up their infernal noise.

The soldiers started from their slumbers; the sentinels turned pale; those of the Catholic faith crossed themselves, and said an "Ave Maria;" the horses neighed wildly; and the general impression seemed to be that Hades had broken loose, and emptied itself into Camp McKinstry.

I thought I had heard unpleasant noises, but I confess I was in error.

No man can justly declare he knows what perfect discord is, until he has listened to a mule concert of the high art style.

I have often been told mules were vicious, but now I am convinced they are totally depraved; that they are possessed of a devil, and that they let him out through their mouths on the night of the ever-to-be-remembered jackassical entertainment.

CHAPTER VI.

ON THE MARCH.

Brutality of Officers.—Shameful Treatment of a Woman.—Change of Base.—A Model Missouri Hotel.—Resumption of the March.—Bohemian Philosophy.—Its Necessity in the Field.

THE injustice and brutality with which private soldiers are often treated by their officers, is enough to render any sensitive nature cynical. I have seen repeated instances of this, and I wonder some shoulder-strapped ruffians are not often assassinated, as they deserve to be, by the men they so grossly abuse.

As an instance: One day, at Syracuse, a private who had a canteen of liquor, and had been drinking, was knocked down, beaten, and kicked in the most brutal manner, before a dozen Captains, Colonels, and Majors, all of whom, doubtless, professed to be gentlemen, and yet not one of them remonstrated against the outrage, or interfered to prevent it.

Gentlemen, indeed! They were not even human.

Not a voice was raised against the cowardly and ruffianly officers, except that of a woman, whose instincts of humanity could not be repressed.

When she spoke of the grievous wrong, she was insulted by the "military gentlemen" who had failed to prevent the cruelty the weak woman only had courage to rebuke.

THE BOHEMIANS AS HOUSEKEEPERS.

Another instance: Two soldiers, who had been in the hospital in St. Louis, and who, extremely anxious to join their regiment, had left their beds before they were able, arrived one day at Syracuse; and, still pale and wan, but with patriotism and enthusiasm flashing from their eyes, went up to the Colonel, and said:

"Well, Colonel, we are about again. We got up against the Surgeon's orders; but we were afraid we'd be left behind, and we always want to be with the brave Seventh."

The Colonel, contemptible puppy as he was, looked angrily at the poor, brave fellows, and said, in the most angry tone:

"Well, G—— d—— you, go and report yourselves, and don't trouble me."

After seeing and hearing the brutality of a portion of the officers to their men, I do not wonder the former are so often killed in battle, though I presume they often fall by other hands than those of the enemy.

It must be a sweet satisfaction, as well as a species of poetic justice, to shoot the brutal tyrants, for whose loss Humanity is better, and the World improved.

After tarrying for eight or ten days at Syracuse, waiting in vain for McKinstry's division to move, several of the Bohemians determined to join Fremont at Warsaw, and therefore rode through the country, infested as it was by guerrillas, without any accident or event of interest.

The only hotel, so called, in Warsaw, was an antique frame tenement, somewhat larger than a dry-goods box, without its cleanliness, however, that rejoiced in the name of the Henry House—apt enough in one respect; for whoever boarded there no doubt thought he had gone to the old Harry. It was said, moreover, to be kept in the same recherché, though rather profane manner that characterized the Bonifacial administration of Mr. Henry Achey, formerly of Cincinnati. The proprietor of the Henry being asked if he could prepare dinner for the "Bohemian Brigade," said he would do so with pleasure if we would furnish him with flour, butter, beef, coffee, sugar, potatoes, salt, and mutton; but that those small superfluities were just now lacking in his larder.

Such was life, then, in the Secession regions of Missouri; and I apprehend it is not much better now.

We did not remain long in Warsaw. As soon as the bridge over the Gasconade was completed, we pushed on towards Springfield, whither it was reported Price was moving in all haste.

We had few incidents of consequence to relate on our march, and the "Bohemian Brigade" was barren of news for its war correspondence, though its personal experience and observations might furnish a rather racy chapter of gossip by itself.

At Quincy we took possession of a Rebel deserted mansion, I was about to say, but cabin is the word; and from a most desolate abode we made it quite endurable in half an hour by our own diligence.

We laid aside our metropolitan ideas, cut and gathered wood, carried furniture from adjacent unoccupied houses, collected corn for our horses, swept up the floor, lighted the fire and our pipes, and made ourselves very comfortable under the circumstances.

With our books and correspondence and conversation

we contrived to pass away half a dozen hours, that would ordinarily have been most tedious and monotonous.

At Yort's Station we appropriated the negroless slave quarters attached to a Secession domicil to our own use, and for a day placed ourselves in quite a cosy condition, and had begun to feel somewhat at home, when the order to march came, and we bade adieu to our extemporized dwelling-place.

We adopted the true Bohemian code of doing the best we could for our comfort, and of laughing away the multifarious annoyances that were inseparable from camp-life, even in its best and most endurable forms.

No one complained, no one grumbled; though I doubt not more than one of us wished the war and its wagers to the devil, and resolved in his own heart that military existence was a Behemothian bore.

A man must become philosophical in camp, if he would not follow the example of Cato and Brutus, or perish in a fit of choler.

One looks for his blankets, and they have been stolen; for his books, and they are gone; for his spurs, and they have been borrowed; for his pipe, and it is broken; for his boots, and one is missing; for his gauntlets, and they are in the fire.

So it goes, day after day.

Make what effort you will, you can find nothing when you want it most; and I very much question if St. Paul would not have been very profane, if he had ever attached himself to the Army.

CHAPTER VII.

WILSON'S CREEK.

Visit to the Battle-Ground.—Its Appearance.—Cause of Sigel's Discomfiture.—Scenes on the Field.—Ghastly Spectacles.—The Sleeping Camp.—A Skyey Omen.

After our arrival at Springfield, Mo., I paid a visit to the battle-ground of Wilson's Creek, some ten miles from that place, and found a number of persons wandering over the hard-fought field.

I can imagine few more disadvantageous localities for a battle. The country is very rolling, sloping down to the little stream, now made historic, and is covered with timber and underwood, so that troops can readily conceal themselves when the foliage is as thick as it must have been in August.

The ridges are quite steep, and it is difficult to move cavalry or artillery over them. The battle must have raged over four or five miles of space, and General Sigel began the attack far down the creek, while Lyon, and Totten, and Sturgis, with the Iowa, Kansas, and Missouri regiments, and the regulars, fought at the upper end of the field.

During my sojourn in Springfield, I learned the cause of Sigel's discomfiture in the early part of the engagement. He was ordered to go to a certain point, where he was to meet a part of our forces; and seeing a regiment from Louisiana advancing, he supposed from their gay uniforms that they were the Iowa troops; nor did he discover his mistake until within thirty yards of them, when the Rebels opened a tremendous fire upon his command, throwing them into a confusion from which they could not recover.

I saw the spot where the noble Lyon fell; where every officer of distinction fought and died; where Totten drove back with fearful slaughter the Rebel cavalry; where every memorable act of that eventful day occurred.

I beheld, too, the traces of the August battle in fragments of clothing; in occasional cups and canteens; in the rude and unmarked graves; in the skeletons of horses and mules, and in the whitening bones of some of the soldiers whose bodies had not been found, and were therefore deprived of sepulture.

Out of the short grass and among the brown and yellow and crimson leaves looked more than one grinning skull—a grim satire on the glory of War, and the pomp of the hollow world.

One skeleton in particular impressed me.

It lay in a bent position on the back, with outstretched arms, as if begging for mercy, or seeking to protect itself from an advancing foe.

The flesh was all gone; but the woollen socks were still on the feet; the pantaloons upon the bones where once the legs had been; while the eyeless sockets, the prominent and gleaming teeth, the bony horror of the skull, seemed to rebuke the pretensions of Life and make a mockery of Death.

In a tree, at the foot of which the skeleton lay, the birds were singing, and out of the clear sky a flood of warm and genial sunshine was falling, as if Nature, in its largeness and goodness, failed to recognize the strifes and errors of Man, and paved with splendor even the once sanguinary spot where her laws had been profaned.

In a few days, not far from there—then I thought—that dreadful scene will be re-enacted; and hearts that now beat high with Hope and Love and Ambition, and lips that are yet moist with memories of sacred kisses, will, ere long, be moldering in the dust, and the Autumn winds singing their requiem in the vast cathedral of this whirling sphere.

Looking out of the tent as I so reflected, all was formless before my baffled eyes.

I heard no sound.

A hush as of death rested over the canvas city of the outspread plain.

How many were dreaming there of Home and Happiness, of Honor and Success, that would never know them beyond the domain of Dreams, or have the longings of their spirit satisfied until the angel of the Ideal rests its flight upon the rough marble of the Actual, and with the magic shadow of its wings makes the Real seem the Beautiful and True.

The sky that night was dark and mysterious—deepening with blackness in the North—no star visible—no watching moon—as if out of that quarter were coming an element of wrath to punish the perfidious and tyrannic South.

May the omen be verified! my heart murmured then; and the omen has been since, my knowledge now declares.

CHAPTER VIII.

ZAGONYI'S RIDE TO DEATH.

Charge of the Fremont Body-Guard.—Its Desperate Character.—The Heavy Loss.—Scene of the Engagement.—Description of the Battle.—Progress of the Ride.—Flight of the Foe.—After the Struggle.

THAT terrible charge, which has been aptly named "Zagonyi's Ride to Death," was the theme of conversation at Springfield weeks after its occurrence; and, though many censured the act as entirely unnecessary, and therefore unmilitary—a needless sacrifice of life, in a word—all agreed in pronouncing it one of the most daring and brilliant achievements in the annals of modern warfare.

While, from a mere military point of view, every one must condemn the charge; while it shows no more generalship than would an order for a squad of raw troops to charge in the face of a hundred death-belching batteries, no one can fail to admire the perfect dare-devilism and magnificent recklessness with which one hundred and fifty young men, entirely inexperienced in war, swept like a whirlwind, through a most murderous fire from a double column they could not reach with their sabers, upon fifteen hundred determined troops, and, in spite of preparation and position, put them to a most inglorious flight.

All things taken into consideration, I doubt if that martial feat has ever been surpassed on the field. The Fremont Body-Guard were all young and uninitiated, scarcely one of them having been before under fire; without any food worthy of mention, or rest, for forty-eight hours, or a cavalry drill on horseback, and having ridden over seventy-eight miles previous to the engagement; and yet, under all these overwhelming disadvantages, they did not hesitate to attack, with all the odds against them, a force of fresh troops nearly fourteen times greater than their own.

Large as their loss was—ascertained to be seventeen killed, twenty-eight wounded (two mortally), and ten missing, with sixty horses killed, and one hundred and forty more or less wounded—it seems incredible that their loss was not much greater; that every other man did not perish on the field.

I have visited the scene of the terrific engagement several times, and the more I learned of the charge, the more I wondered it could have been successful. Surely it was horribly grand, sanguinarily glorious.

Even now I see the charge as plainly as if it were passing before my eyes. Ghastly, but glorious picture!

My heart would have sunk if it had not swelled; my blood would have curdled if had not tingled, as the wild panorama flashed before my mental vision!

On that warm, bright, beautiful, autumnal afternoon, the breezes voluptuously dallying with the golden and crimson leaves of the drowsy trees, and the birds singing a glad hymn to lovely though pensive October, a gallant troop of cavalry go prancing down the brown and dusty road, their voices sounding merrily, and their sabers clattering harmoniously at their sides. On they go, and suddenly, out of a thick wood, where the birds are still singing, and Nature seems performing her silent myteries in the ancient groves, five hundred muskets rain their leaden messengers upon the little band.

The horses plunge and neigh, and four brave riders reel upon their saddles and fall without a groan heavily to the ground.

No enemy is visible through the trees; but a glance to the east, over the little hill, shows fifteen hundred foemen, with deadly weapons in their hands and a deadly glitter in their eye, ranged on each side of the narrow road through which they must pass.

Inevitable death seems to stare them in the face.

The floating clouds above their heads seem like their descending shrouds.

The bright sun seems shining the last time for them.

All their past rushes in a moment through their mind.

Forsaken scenes of home, of friends, of those beloved, rise in painful contrast to their swimming view.

But with the seconds speed recollection and regret. The dread present stands there, inexorable, and demands to be answered.

The commander's voice rings out like a clarion: "Follow me, my brave boys!" "Fremont and the Union!" "Victory or death!"

No hesitation now; no pause.

Determination flashes from every eye. The Will has triumphed, and Nature has succumbed.

The cry is caught up, and along the entire line echoes and re-echoes: "Fremont and the Union! Victory or death!"

The horses plunge forward as the rowels are buried in

their sides, and, yelling like savages, the cavalry rush down the road through a continuous and deadly fire.

Here a rider tumbles; there a noble steed falls. On this side, a Guard clasps his hand to his breast, as a ball strikes home. On the other, a stream of blood starts from the temple of a youthful warrior; his limbs relax; his saber falls from his nerveless hand; his eye glazes; his head sinks upon his horse's neck; he is dead upon his bounding steed.

The dust and smoke arise in clouds, and commingle, and the din of battle swells; and the noise of musketry shatters the surrounding silence of the charming afternoon. Still goes on the ride of the horsemen—the ride to death. Their carbines and pistols are in their hands, and they return the galling fire, and many a Rebel dies ere he can ask Heaven's pardon for his sins. While an absent mother or sister is praying for his safety, there he lies dead, with a bullet through his heart.

Now the fearless cavalry have ridden through the fire of death, and paused before one of the fences separating them from their malignant foes.

The fence must be let down, and four brave fellows are soon dismounted, and, under a heavy fire, perform their task as coolly as if they were executing an every-day labor. At this point four or five of the Guard are shot down, and in a moment all who are unhurt are dashing through the opening into the adjacent field, where the Rebels are formed in a hollow square.

The Body Guard form in a double column, and spread out, fan-like, to the north and south, and with tremendous cries of "Hurrah for Cincinnati!" "Old Kentucky forever!" "Remember the Queen City, boys! do nothing she will be ashamed of!" they charge upon the Rebels with a terrible energy.

The foe endeavor to sustain the shock, and for a minute stand their ground; but the Body Guard, Major Zagonyi at their head, fight like devils; and cutting with their sabers to the right and left, and riding over the enemy, and trampling them under their horses' feet, the Secessionists give way, and, breaking their square, retire to a central position.

Here the Guards are again upon them, and their energy and ferocity seemed to increase as the fight continues, and the Rebels, unable to resist their furious attack, break into small bodies, and run in every direction, seeking shelter in the bushes and behind the trees; firing, as rapidly as they can load, upon their pursuers.

The Rebels are soon dislodged from their place of shelter, and those on horseback place a safe distance between themselves and harm, and seek the adjacent country through the woods.

The infantry fly to the corn-fields and down the road leading to Springfield, and are closely followed by the victorious Guards, who, with pistol, carbine, and saber, continue the work of destruction until their blades reek with blood, and their tired arms hang heavy at their sides.

Up and down the streets of the town fly the affrighted Rebels, still retaining their weapons.

Women and children stand pale with fear, gazing, with the strange fascination that courage excites, through closed windows at the horrid spectacle.

Here a youth lies with his skull cloven to his cheek;

there the life of an aged man ebbs away through a purple wound.

Before that peaceful dwelling an expiring Rebel glares with powerless hatred upon an unhorsed Guard whose eyes are swimming in death.

In the public square, two foes are breathing their last in each other's arms—the embrace of those who grapple at one another's throats while falling into the grave.

At the entrance of the Court-house, a son lies dead upon the corpse of a father he had sought to save in vain; and in the bend of yonder lane two brothers of the Guards are striving to gasp out last words to each other, before this World fades forever from their glassy eyes.

After a dreadful hour, that must have seemed a minute to some, to others an age—the battle, the rout, the slaughter is over.

The sinking sun looked with a crimson glow upon the gory battle-field, upon the piles of lifeless chargers, upon the wounded, the dying, and the dead—Unionists and Rebels—who had sealed their devotion with their blood.

A melancholy offering was that upon the altar of patriotism. Human victims lay upon the disputed ground; loud, agonizing groans and cries of pity, and even bitter curses, went up together to the peaceful heaven, bending in blue beauty over all—upon the Northman and the Southron alike, upon the friend of the Union and its foe.

And, long after the voiceless midnight, the moon glided up the clear sky, like a celestial nun, telling her rosary of stars, and praying silently for the gallant spirits that had so bravely fought, so bravely died.

CHAPTER IX.

THE RETROGRADE MOVEMENT.

The Return to Rolla.—A Ghastly Jest.—A Brace of Fair Bohemians.—The Discrediting Effect of Camp Attire.—A Night in a Barn.—Potency of an Army Pass.

EVERY one knows how Fremont was removed at Springfield, and that Hunter, after succeeding him, made a grand retrograde movement to Rolla. The excitement produced by that event I do not care to particularize, nor to express at this late day any opinion of the justice or injustice of the measure.

Fremont is out of the service; and let the dissensions to which his enthusiastic friends and his bitter enemies gave rise die with the causes that made them.

At that time hardly any of the War-Correspondents had witnessed a battle worthy of the name; and when they turned their back upon Springfield, where they had fully expected to chronicle a decisive engagement, and share in some of its hazards, they were vexed, chagrined, and disappointed, as was the whole Army—I have never seen a better one of its size—on its countermarch to Rolla.

The Correspondent of the St. Louis *Democrat*—for three years past an officer in the Navy—and myself brought up the rear, and journeyed leisurely with General Wyman's brigade over the Ozark Mountains back toward St. Louis.

On our retrograde movement in Laclede County, on the night of November 11th, a very sudden death occurred at Camp Plummer, proving that the skeleton-king oft comes when least expected—passing from the blazing battery to strike his victim in the midst of security and peace.

A young man, Henry Holt, bugler of Major Power's cavalry, attached to the Thirteenth Regiment, was complaining of feeling rather ill, when the Quartermaster, Captain Henderson, who had a passion for aught like fun, proposed to bury the musician; and, in the spirit of merriment, seized a spade, and, after measuring the complainer, dug a grave of his exact proportions.

The bugler laughed, as did his companions, at the humor of the officer, and soon after went away to discharge some duty with which he had been intrusted.

About nine o'clock the same evening, Holt was sitting, with seven or eight of his company, about a camp fire, within a few feet of the grave, when some one pointed to it and remarked, in a tone of badinage,

"Come, Harry, get ready for your funeral!"

The youth looked over his shoulder at the gloomy cavity in the earth, put his hand to his head, and fell from his stool.

His companions laughed at the little piece of acting, as they supposed it, and were surprised that he did not rise from the earth.

They went up to him, asking, "Are you asleep, Harry?"

He made no answer, and yet his eyes were open.

They shook him in vain.

His friends grew alarmed. One placed his hand upon Harry's heart. It was still: he was dead!

He had perished of a stroke of apoplexy, and was buried at midnight, in the grave made for him in jest by a merry-hearted friend.

And so the droll jest was drowned in the hollow sound of the earth falling upon a rude coffin, and solemnly waking the stillness of the night-morn amid the solitude of a broad prairie of the Southwest.

During the last two or three days of our march, its monotony was relieved by the companionship of two young and cultivated women who were on their way to St. Louis, under the protection of the army. With a positive passion for Beauty, Nature, Poetry, and Romance, their conversation beguiled the weary hours, and often their light-hearted laugh made the desolate mountain silences echo with gladness.

Quite Bohemianish, and certainly fond of adventure, were those fair girls, who frequently regretted they were not men, that they might be emancipated from the narrowness Society imposed upon them, and follow the bent of their large inclinations.

My journalistic companion and myself explained to them the character of the Bohemian Brigade, and with their full permission elected them honorary members of that unique society.

The girls and we duo of Bohemians had a good deal of amusement in riding, walking, fording creeks and rivers, and exploding, to our satisfaction, the multifarious shams of modern society and present-day custom.

Our journeying was romantic, and certainly agreeable,

after our long absence from feminine society. We parted with the fair girls, not, I believe, without mutual regret, and never probably to see them more.

They were Bohemians then; but Society and Custom have perhaps ere this made them conform.

They are still young and romantic; but a few years will doubtless find them deteriorated into domestic drudges, shut out forever by household necessities from the land of Bohemia and the realm of the Ideal.

Arriving near Rolla on Saturday, the correspondent of the *Democrat* and myself concluded to go to town and stop at a hotel, hoping to become accustomed ere long to civilized life once more.

We did so in our campaign costume; and before the landlord learned who we were, he evinced great distrust of our honesty, and asked us, in a very polite manner, just as we were about to take a walk after dinner, if it would be convenient for us to pay for our meal.

We laughed, and told him our profession, and that our baggage was in his house—a fact of which he was unconscious—when he apologized, and said he thought we might have forgotten so small an amount of indebtedness, as we doubtless had many more important things to remember.

This little incident proves the truth of Herr Teufelsdroch's opinion respecting the power of clothes.

Had we been attired as we would have been in the city, he would have danced attendance on us all day; but, fresh from camp, he imagined us suspicious characters, designing to swindle him out of the poor price of a most wretched meal.

That is a fine sentiment Shakspeare put in the mouth of old Polonius:

> "It is the mind that makes the body rich;
> And as the sun breaks through the darkest cloud,
> So honor peereth in the meanest habit."

But I fear the sentiment is not at all true with the great mass of the people, who believe there is an inseparable association between dishonesty and damaged attire.

When night came we found every particle of hotel space in the miserable village of Rolla occupied; and as a last resource we repaired to the barn, never before having had the pleasure of sleeping in such a place; expecting, however, we might be a little *hoarse* in the morning.

We carried our blankets to the barn, where we found several other bed-despairing individuals, and were soon ensconced in a self-made couch composed of woolen and hay.

As there was a heavy storm during the night, the rain on the roof and the wind sighing through the loose weather-boarding conjured up poetic pictures to the imagination, and transformed the desolate old barn into an Aladdin's palace of fancy.

About daylight, one of the sleepers discovered he had fallen into a hay-rack; another was awakened by a hostler endeavoring to put a halter around his neck; and a third by the thrusting of a pitch-fork within an inch of his head, which had been mistaken for a part of a bundle of oats.

We paid our bill to the rural Boniface, including fifty cents for lodging in the barn—that was cheap, considering that more was charged for reposing in the shadow of the town-pump—and we are soon on the eve of departure for St. Louis by the railway, which appears odd enough after long weeks of nothing but equine journeys.

An incident occurred the evening after our arrival in St. Louis, at one of the dancing halls in the city, of rather an amusing nature.

Two of the Bohemian Brigade were admiring the dancing of a pretty girl on the stage, when one of them determined to go behind the scenes and pour his tale of burning passion into what he conceived would necessarily be her all-attentive ear.

He accordingly presented himself at the stage-door, and was very naturally refused admission; whereupon he drew out an army pass, and said that gave him the privilege of going anywhere, at any time, in the territory of the United States, and that whoever disobeyed the order would be arrested at once.

This very bold statement was accompanied by such a magnificent manner of authority and importance that the guardian of the portal, without reading the pass, allowed the holder to enter, and in a few minutes the adroit Bohemian was seeking to convince the Terpischorean divinty that he had never believed in love until he had seen her an hour before, and that for the future the earth would be desolate unless revivified by her smile.

CHAPTER X.

SECESSION IN MISSOURI.

The Feminine Secessionists of St. Louis.—Their Parrot-like Raving.—Their Resemblance to Barnaby Rudge's Raven.—Harmlessness of Petticoated Traitors.—Sale of Rebel Property.—Curious Scene.—A Mysterious Article.

THE principal element of Secession in St. Louis, early in the War, was, and probably is still, in the women, who, having the privilege of saying what they pleased, were often loud in their denunciations of the Government, and profuse in their expressions of sympathy with the South. They talked an infinite deal of Rebel fustian; but it meant nothing, and did no harm.

There, as in the other Slave State cities, Secession was the mode, and that, combined with what was then the newness of the doctrine, was sufficient to make almost any woman its exponent.

Many silly girls in St. Louis thought they would not be fashionable unless they talked treason; and they did it systematically, just as they wore a certain kind of mantle or a peculiar style of bonnet.

Brainless women spoke of the outrages of the North and of the wrongs of the South, without having any more idea of the meaning of the words than a parrot that has caught the sound has of a metaphysical phrase of Fichte or Hegel, and screams it out to every passer-by.

The political conversation of many of the feminine

Secessionists in that town reminded one of the raven, Grip, in "Barnaby Rudge," on the night when that sagacious bird endeavored to recollect the valuable admonition to a popular though mysterious Polly, respecting the preparation of the evening meal.

Grip could recollect "Polly put the ket——," but there his memory failed, and drowsiness overcame him. At last he caught the remainder of the quotation, and uttered:

"Polly put the kettle on,
And we'll all take tea.
I'm a devil! I'm a devil! I'm a devil!
Fire, fire, fire! Never say die!
I'm a kettle on! I'm a fire!
Never say kettle on, we'll all take Polly.
I'm a fire—kettle—on devil—I'm a ——."

and he fell asleep again.

All that would have been necessary to complete the comparison between the women and Grip would have been for him to declare himself a Secessionist, for certainly his speech was no more mixed and irrelevant than the arguments of the petticoated traitors.

All they could tell you was that they were Secessionists; but what that meant, or why they were so, or what they wanted, or how they were injured, was beyond their power of representation.

Secession women are amusing, at any rate, and, so long as they confine themselves to talking, do no harm, unless to some false reputation they may have acquired for understanding.

Women, at best, are what men make of them. They shine by a borrowed light, and see through the eyes of their last lover.

Let me know a woman's nearest friend, and I will tell you what are her opinions and her tastes.

I have been not a little entertained at the conversation I have had with some of the pretty Rebels in the South, who, with their little doll faces, express the most sanguinary sentiments, and hope the "Yankees" will all be killed, in the blandest of tones, and with the sweetest of smiles.

Their efforts to perform the rôle of desperate traitors appear like the endeavor of a rose-bud to convert itself into a Paixhan gun or a sub-marine battery.

But enough of those dear little know-nothings, all of whom would not mar the peace of the most sentimental school-boy that ever moistened with his tears the pages of the "Children of the Abbey."

The sale in St. Louis, during February, 1862, of the goods seized from assessed Rebels, by a Fourth street auctioneer, attracted a very dense crowd of the most miscellaneous character.

So great was the curiosity excited, that the thoroughfare before the building was blocked, the street-cars compelled to stop, and the serried mass on the track dispersed, before the conveyance could advance.

Several of the war correspondents then sojourning in that city, waiting for coming events, witnessed the sale of the confiscated pianos, tables, buggies, mirrors, center-tables, vases, rugs, lamps, chess-boards, and other articles of household furniture and ornament, and were amused at the grotesque appearance of the pressing, jostling, excited, anxious crew of bidders and lookers on.

Old and young women, peddlers and pickpockets, Jews and journalists, bar-keepers and book-worms, stevedores and strumpets, printers and pugilists, authors and actors, loafers and littérateurs, were there in profusion and confusion.

Here was a venerable, desiccated proprietress of a Broadway boarding-house—who, for a lover of paleontology, would have been an interesting study—in close contact with a youthful and pretty woman, whose elegance of toilette was surpassed only by her vapidity.

Here was a stalwart shoulder-hitter peeping over the glossy hat of an elaborately done-up dandy, who had braved the inclement weather to purchase his "darling Julia's pianah-stool," if it cost him, as he heroically expressed it, the last drop of his blood.

Near the awning-post leaned a begrimed artisan upon the shoulder of a flashily-attired gambler; and, a few feet off, a juvenile vender of matches was pushing his basket into the parabolic apron of a feminine figure, in a manner that would have delighted a disciple of Malthus.

Some article of furniture, said by the auctioneer to have been the property of the beautiful Miss ——, but which I could not see, created a sensation, and was immediately inclosed by a living wall of young men, as if they wished to act as a body-guard, fearful that some other and more enterprising citizen would carry off the mysterious what-not.

The bidding was very animated, and it appeared a point of honor and a piece of gallantry to obtain it at any price.

"Five—ten—fifteen—twenty dollars," said the auctioneer; "will you see this wonder of art, this glorious instrument, sacrificed at such a rate?

"No man of feeling but would give twice the sum. Be generous, gentlemen ; this is a rare opportunity.

"The owner of this is not poor, but she is beautiful. Bid now, like men who are true to themselves, but truer to the sex."

Thirty, forty dollars was offered, and finally fifty was named, and the apocryphal article sold.

I here made another desperate but unsuccessful effort to obtain a glimpse of the furniture, and still marveling what it could have been, even after I had heard a fellow say : "It was not worth one-tenth so much, but I suppose it was valuable from association."

The sale of seized property was, I learned, quite profitable, and certainly attracted a large crowd, who enjoyed the auction exceedingly, and carried off the various articles as if they had been trophies of war, instead of the most harmless instruments of peace.

CHAPTER XI.

BATTLE OF DONELSON.

March from Fort Henry to the Field.—Troubles of the Correspondents.—Difficulty of Subsistence.—Courage of our Soldiers.—Examples of Sacrifice and Heroism.—Gallant Charge.—Amateur Sharpshooting.—Mortification of the Enemy after the Surrender.—Desperation of the Rebels.—Repudiation of the Five to One Boast.—Ghastly Wounds.—Touching Incidents.

THE army correspondents had no power, through love or largess, to obtain horses on their February campaign in Tennessee, the second year of the War.

The talisman of the Press had lost its equine potency, and most of the war-pursuing Bohemians were compelled to go to the field from Fort Henry over a rough and miry road in a pedestrianizing capacity.

Philosophers complain of nothing; but, to a vivid imagination, the prospect of the approaching fight was more unique than fascinating.

I fancied the Bohemians wandering over the field knee-deep in mud, liable, without uniforms or any badge of distinction, to be mistaken by each side for foes, and, in the event of a defeat, to be ridden down and shot at, under suspicion of being Rebels, in the most miscellaneous and magnificent manner.

So I fancied; and my fancies were more than half realized.

No one cares for a Bohemian, I hope, and no true Bohemian cares who cares for him.

If, to speak typographically, he is set up leaded with a

BOHEMIA AS A BELLIGERENT.

shooting-stick, or his form is knocked into everlasting pi by a shell, no column-rule will be turned for him. There will be merely one journalist less in the World, and one more phase of boredom exhausted.

For any ill-fated quill-driver who may breakfast with Proserpine one of these dull mornings, I have composed an epitaph, which nothing but regard for my readers, and the memory of the deceased that is to be, prevents me from inserting here.

Well I remember how we of the Press wandered about that hard-fought field, half-starved and half-frozen, having left our blankets and india-rubbers behind, and brought no rations with us; supposing, as did every one in the army, that the capture of Donelson would be a simple before-breakfast recreation.

Few of us, as I have said, had horses; and, being without tents, provisions, or sufficient clothing—particularly after the sudden change, on the day of our arrival, from Spring-life softness and warmth to raw, biting, penetrating wind and storm, followed by sleet, snow, and severe wintry weather—we suffered greatly, but, fortunately for us, not long.

At Fort Henry an explosion of a box of ammunition had dashed a piece of cartridge-paper into one of my optics, which soon inflamed the other through sympathy, and made me nearly blind.

For three days I groped over the frozen and snowy ground, and, with my companion of the New York *World*, followed, from time to time, army wagons, to pick up pieces of hard bread which were jolted out semi-occasionally over the rough roads.

I thought that difficult to endure then; but, since my long apprenticeship in Rebel prisons, I regard by comparison all previous experience of my life, however unpleasant and painful, as a path of roses and a stream of joy.

The battle of Donelson, or siege of Fort Donelson, as it is often called, was continued by land and water for four days, February 12th, 13th, 14th, and 15th; though, from the position of the Rebel works on the river, our gunboats were enabled to do little toward the obtainment of the victory.

The country about Donelson was very uneven, being surrounded by high hills, and covered in many places with trees and undergrowth, so that nothing could be seen of the main work from any point of land that our men were able to reach.

Although I was wandering over the field all four days, I did not see the fort proper myself, nor meet a single person who had seen it, though the outworks were visible from various places, and the Rebels working the guns.

On Saturday, the 15th inst., our troops, though most of them had never been under fire, fought like veterans, under the most disadvantageous circumstances, having been without sleep for two or three nights, and without food for twenty-two hours.

All the officers acted coolly and gallantly, and encouraged the soldiers by word and example.

A lieutenant seized the colors of one of the regiments, after the ensign had been shot down, and bore them for a quarter of an hour in the thickest of the fight.

A captain of one of the companies received two balls through his hat and three through his coat without being conscious of his narrow escapes until after the battle.

Three or four of the officers had the hair of their head and their faces grazed by musket-balls; and, in two instances, the skin was removed from the ear by the leaden messengers of the Rebels.

An orderly sergeant, seeing a Rebel pointing a rifle at the captain of his company, threw himself before his beloved officer, received the bullet through his breast, and fell dead in the arms of the man he had saved.

The sergeant, I learned, had been reared and very generously treated by the father of the captain, and had declared, when he first enlisted, that he would be happy to die to save the life of his benefactor's son.

Most nobly and gloriously did he redeem his promise.

The severest and the decisive contest was on the left at the close of Saturday. General C. F. Smith, with his division, composed of Indiana, Iowa, and Illinois regiments, marched up to the breastworks, and engaged the enemy in the most spirited manner.

The Iowa Second was the first regiment that scaled the breastworks, performing the hazardous and brilliant movement in masterly style, after the manner of the veterans who immortalized themselves in the wars of Napoleon.

They never hesitated, they never faltered, but with firm step and flashing eye, passed, without firing a gun, into the Rebel works.

In a few seconds other regiments followed, and a terrible strife ensued between the contending parties. The

Secessionists seemed resolved to drive the Unionists back, and the latter equally determined not to surrender the advantage they had obtained.

For at least two hours the rattling of musketry was unceasingly heard, and the armed masses surged to and fro. Fortune appeared to favor now one side, and now another.

Ever and anon, a loud cheer went up for the Union, and that was caught up at a distance and echoed by our soldiers, and joyously re-echoed by the surrounding hills.

Many a brave warrior heard that glorious shout as his senses reeled in death, and his spirit went forth embalmed with the assurance that he had not fallen in vain.

A large Rebel gun every few seconds would pour its iron hail against our struggling heroes; but generally, as the sequel proved, the firing was too high. Of that fact we were not aware at the time, and the booming gun caused much uneasiness and alarm.

The correspondent of the St. Louis *Republican* and myself were on the summit of a hill near the hostile breastworks, indulging in a little amateur pugnacity with Birge's sharpshooters, who had very kindly loaned us two of their Enfields. They were trying in vain to pick off the Rebel gunner, whom we could not see, though we could determine, by the puff of the smoke from the vent, about where he stood.

"Are you a good shot?" inquired one of Birge's men of me. "If you are, here is as good a rifle as ever killed a Rebel; and if you'll pepper that fellow over there at that gun, I'll give you any thing I've got."

I made no promises, for I have very little skill as a marksman, but quietly accepted the Enfield, with the air of Leather Stocking; and, waiting until the gun went off again, I fired at the very moment the blue smoke puffed above the earthworks.

For some reason or other, the gun was not fired for nearly five minutes.

The sharpshooter looked at me with wonder and admiration, and saying, "I think you fixed him that time," received back the rifle I handed him as if there would be no more use for it in the future.

"I shouldn't be surprised," I remarked to my companion, and walked dignifiedly away while my laurels were green.

That sharpshooter will believe to his last hour I killed that Rebel gunner.

I hope as he believed.

Soon after that incident, a loud report was heard, and the woods reverberated with a Union cry of joy, for the soldiers recognized it as the thunder of a Yankee gun, gotten into position at last, and believed it would do much to decide the battle.

Again and again that gun sounded, and the national banner waved, and the Rebels were driven from their redoubt.

The Union regiments received orders to hold their position during the night, and renew the strife in the morning.

The morning came, but there was no need of further contest; for in the morning the enemy surrendered, and Donelson was ours.

Our foes sought to save their pride and conceal their mortification by declaring they were betrayed by Pillow and Floyd; that they had no idea of surrendering, and would not have surrendered until reduced to the last extremity, if the question had been left to them.

That was all bosh, however.

No such course would have been adopted, if the enemy had believed himself capable of holding out longer, or if braggadocio and bluster could have been made to answer for stout hearts and brave deeds.

Every one asked, What made nearly twenty thousand able-bodied soldiers surrender, with plenty of provisions and ammunition, intrenched as they were behind breastworks that made them equal to any odds?

How could they, after all their insolence, arrogance, and assumption of superiority, yield to a force very little more than their own, and to men whose courage they questioned, and whose manliness they affected to despise?

The sole answer was, and is, that boastfulness is rarely the parent of valor, and insolence seldom the companion of magnanimity.

In conversation with one of the Rebel Captains, after the surrender, he asked me how our boats had contrived to escape all the torpedoes placed in the Tennessee and Cumberland Rivers, and which, he had thought, would blow our fleet to atoms.

When told the torpedoes were usually harmless, and that some of them had been taken up and exhibited as specimens of ineffectual malignity, he declared it was very hard to kill a Yankee; that, if you baited a hook with the Devil, a Yankee would steal the hook without the Devil's knowing it.

Several of the Rebels showed, during the engagement, a recklessness of life that proved their desperation.

One of them mounted the breastworks in full view of our forces, and defied the "d——d Yankees." But hardly had the defiance passed his lips before he fell pierced by a score of bullets.

Another remained outside of the rifle-pits after all his companions had retreated behind them, and fought with his sword against half a dozen of the Unionists who had surrounded him, and were anxious to take him prisoner.

They asked him several times to surrender; but he declared he would rather die: and die he did, on the point of a Union bayonet; but not before he had slain one, and wounded three of his adversaries.

One of the prisoners afterward gave me the history of that desperate Secessionist.

He had inherited a large fortune; married a wife in Tennessee; squandered his means in riotous living and dissipation; separated from his spouse; become reckless; joined the army, and declared his intention to live no longer than the first battle.

He redeemed his word, and closed his wild career a needless martyr to an unholy cause.

A third Secessionist, a private in a Mississippi company, left his companions in arms, and, with a horrid imprecation, rushed into the midst of one of our regiments, aiming a blow with his musket at an Indiana Captain, who shot him dead with his revolver before the desperado could inflict any injury.

Three members of the 8th Illinois rushed over the rifle-pits after the enemy had retreated into them, and perished fighting against a thousand foes.

On Saturday, a young soldier, James Hartley, who had lost a brother the previous day, swore he would be revenged; and in one of the *sorties* by the Rebels, he attacked six of them single-handed, killed three, and then lost his own life.

Corporal Mooney, an Irishman, seeing that the staff of one of the regimental flags was shot away, picked up the Stars and Stripes, and, wrapping them round his body, rushed over the parapet, and crying, "Come on, my brave boys!" was blown to pieces by a shell.

A Lieutenant-Colonel in an Iowa regiment, during the fierce contest of Saturday afternoon, had nine bullets put through his coat, and yet sustained no injury.

Peter Morton, of the 13th Illinois, had the case of his watch, which he wore in his upper vest pocket, immediately over his breast, torn away by a canister-shot, and the chronometer still continued to keep time.

The life of Reuben Davis, of the 5th Kentucky, was saved by a silver half dollar in his waistcoat pocket.

He had borrowed that amount from a companion some days before, and offered to return it before going into the engagement; but his companion told him to keep the coin, as he might stand in need of it before night.

He had the greatest need of it. A rifle-ball struck the coin in the centre, and destroyed the figure of Liberty on its face, but harmed not the Kentuckian.

Within the Fort a small Secession flag was planted; and twice the pole supporting it was shot away.

Some one picked it up, saying, "That is a bad omen. If it is brought down again, we will be defeated." Hardly had he spoken before a shell burst above his head, and a fragment shivered the staff, and crashed through the speaker's skull.

On Monday, the day after the surrender, I talked a great deal with the Rebel officers; asking some from South Carolina and Mississippi their opinion about the capacity of a Southerner to whip five Northerners.

"It's all d——d nonsense," was the reply. "Whoever says so is a d——d fool."

"Your newspapers have so stated, time and again," I remarked.

"Probably they have. If the editors think so, let them try it. It is enough for us soldiers to whip one Yankee at a time. When we get done with him, we think we've done about all that we desire."

Many of the enemy found upon the battle-field, after we had obtained possession of a part of the intrenchments on Saturday afternoon, were horribly wounded, mostly by our Minié rifles and Enfield muskets, and usually in the face or on the head.

Poor fellows lay upon the ground with their eyes and noses carried away; their brains oozing from their crania; their mouths shot into horrible disfiguration; making a hideous spectacle that must have haunted those who saw it for many days.

I saw an old gray-haired man, mortally wounded, endeavoring to stop, with a strip of his coat, the life-tide flowing from the bosom of his son, a youth of twenty years.

The boy told his father it was useless; that he could not live; and while the devoted parent was still striving feebly to save him who was perhaps his first-born, a shudder passed over the frame of the would-be preserver.

His head fell upon the bosom of the youth, and his gray hairs were bathed in death with the expiring blood of his misguided son.

I saw the twain half an hour after; and youth and age were locked lifeless in each other's arms.

A dark-haired young man, of apparently twenty-two or three years, I found leaning against a tree, his breast pierced by a bayonet. He said he lived in Alabama; that he had joined the Rebels in opposition to his parents' wishes; that his mother, when she had learned that he would go into the army, had given him her blessing, a Bible, and a lock of her hair.

The Bible lay half opened on the ground, and the hair, a dark lock, tinged with gray, that had been between the leaves, was in his hand.

In the lock of hair, even more than in the Volume, Religion was revealed to the dying young man. I saw him lift the tress again and again to his lips, as his eyes looked dimly across the misty sea that bounds the shores of Life and Death, as if he saw his mother reaching out to him with the arms that had nursed him in his infancy: to die, alas! fighting against his country, and the counsels of her whose memory lived latest in his departing soul.

A Secession soldier of the 10th (Irish) Tennessee regiment, I believe, was lying just inside of the fortifications.

His glazing eyes gave assurance that life was embraced in minutes. He held a rosary and crucifix in his hand, and his moving lips were doubtless offering a prayer. He had evidently endeavored to kneel, but was too weak.

One of our soldiers saw and hurried to him, to assist him in his attitude of prayer ; and while engaged in that kind office, a shot from a Rebel cannon struck and killed them both.

CHAPTER XII.

AFTER THE BATTLE.

Extracts from my Note-Book.—Sensations of a Reasoning Man Under Fire.—A Novel in Brief.—A Faithless Woman and a Sacrificed Lover.—A Juvenile Hero.—Difficulty of Dying on the Field.—Ultra-professional Correspondents. —Ludicrous Incidents of their Journalistic Devotion.

In two instances, at Donelson, I noticed wounded foes lying near, who were offering water to each other from their canteens. So humane and gentle were our living to the wounded and dying enemy, that one would have supposed they were the nearest and closest friends.

One fierce Rebel, a Mississippian, refused all aid, though badly wounded, and endeavored to shoot a member of one of the Ohio regiments, who had approached to render him assistance; which so outraged the good-hearted soldier, that he lifted his musket to blow out his enemy's brains.

A moment's reflection made him magnanimous, however, and he left the Mississippian to care for himself.

The many instances I might relate of daring, suffering, and heroism, on both sides, prove how mysteriously what we call Good and Evil is commingled in Humanity; that even through the dark clouds of War the sun of Justice and Mercy streams; that on the most barren heath fair flowers are breathing out their sweetness ever, though all unseen.

Few persons but have some curiosity about battle-fields, and a positive wish to know how men feel under fire, especially before custom has made them indifferent. Most of those at Donelson must have had that experience, as the field was such that few could go to any part of it without incurring more or less risk.

Hardly any one could see the Rebels or their guns; and, consequently, the first intimation of their presence was the falling of a shell, or the rattling of shot or balls in his immediate vicinity.

I am not aware that I have any courage, moral or physical; but the sensations under fire, judging from my experience, are different from what is anticipated.

A reasoning man, with a love of adventure, at first feels alarmed; and his impulse is to run away; and if he has no motive to stand, he probably does run. But at each additional exposure he grows less timid, and after hearing canister and grape about his ears a dozen times, begins to think he is not destined to be hurt.

He still feels rather uneasy, perhaps; but the danger acquires a sort of fascination; and, though he does not wish to be hit, he likes to have narrow escapes, and so voluntarily places himself in a position where he can incur more risk.

After a little while, he begins to reason the matter; reflects on the Doctrine of Probabilities, and how much powder and lead is necessarily wasted before any man is killed or wounded.

Why should he be, he thinks, so much more unlucky than many other people? So reasoning, he soon can bear the whizzing of bullets with a tolerable degree of equanimity, though he involuntarily dodges, or tries to dodge, the cannon-balls and shells that go howling about his immediate neighborhood.

In the afternoon, he is quite a different creature from what he was in the morning, and unwittingly smiles to see a man betray the same trepidation which he himself exhibited a few hours before.

The more he is exposed to fire, the better he can bear it; and the timid being of to-day becomes the hero of to-morrow.

And he who runs from danger on his first battle-field, may run into it on the next, and court the hazard he once so dreaded.

Thus courage, as it is styled, is little more, with most men, than custom; and they soon learn to despise what has often threatened without causing them harm.

If wounded, they learn wounds are less painful to bear than they had imagined; and then the Doctrine of Probabilities teaches them once more, they are less likely to be wounded again.

So the mental process goes on, until the nerves by degrees become the subjects of the Will; and he only fears who has not the will to be brave.

* * * *

A young man belonging to one of the Tennessee regiments—he held the rank of first lieutenant in his company—was very dangerously wounded at Donelson, in Saturday morning's strife, and was not expected to live when I left Dover. where he lay in much pain.

The young man stated he was a native of Harrisburg, Pennsylvania, and had resided there until the Autumn of

1859, when he went to Columbia, Tennessee, and there engaged in the practice of the law, with considerable success. While in that State, he became acquainted with, and enamored of, a woman of culture and position —a distant relative of General Pillow—and was soon engaged to marry her.

The love-stream of the young couple flowed smoothly enough until the fall of Sumter, and the secession of Tennessee, when the affianced husband, being a strong Unionist, returned home, designing to wed after the troubles were over.

The betrothed pair corresponded regularly; but, some weeks after her lover had gone to Harrisburg, the girl, who had suddenly grown a violent Secessionist, informed him she would not become his wife unless he would enlist in the Rebel service, and fight for the independence of the South.

The young man was exceeding loth to take such a step, and remonstrated with his love to no purpose. At last, in the blindness of his attachment, and in the absorbing selfishness of passion, he informed his parents of his intention to win his mistress on the tented field.

In vain they endeavored to dissuade him from his resolution. He returned to Tennessee, raised a company, received the congratulations of his traitorous friends, and the copious caresses of his charming tempter.

In December, 1861, the lieutenant proceeded to Donelson, with his company; and, a few days before the battle, he heard his betrothed was the wife of another.

His heart had never been in the cause, though in another's keeping; and, stung by remorse, and crushed by the perfidy of his mistress, he had no desire to live any longer in a world that had become hateful to him.

Unwilling to desert, or resign, on the eve of battle, lest he might be charged with cowardice, he resolved—so he said, at least—to lose the existence that had become unbearable to him; and, in the thickest of the fight, seeking death, without desiring to inflict it, he received a mortal wound.

The misguided and betrayed lover must soon have ceased to think of her who had so cruelly deceived him; for, twenty-four hours after the wound, the Lethean stream of Death was flowing round the Eternity-bound island of his soul.

The double traitress, no doubt, learned all; for her lover dictated a letter to her on his couch of pain.

Could she have been happy, even in the rosy hours of her early marriage, when the thought of the dead adorer, slain by her hand, darkened, like a portentous cloud, the fair horizon of her life?

Must not his pale corpse, with its bleeding wounds, have glided between her and her husband's arms, and banished contentment forever from the profaned sanctuary of her spirit?

Pshaw, that is sentiment!

She was a woman of a more practical kind. Her heart was made of sterner stuff. She could laugh and mock, no doubt, though her sacrificed lover had stood beside her in his winding-sheet, asking her absolution for the sins she had caused him to commit. Was not the old English poet correct?—

> "When Woman once to Evil turns,
> All Hell within her bosom burns!"

* * * *

A mere boy, of about fifteen years, from Darke County, Ohio, being in Illinois, had enlisted in one of the regiments raised in the southern part of that State; but, as he was in very delicate health, his father was extremely anxious to have him released from the service, though the youthful soldier greatly desired to remain in it.

While at Forts Henry and Donelson, the boy was very ill, but still insisted upon performing his duty. His father arrived at Donelson on Friday, the 14th inst., intending, if possible, to take him home.

* * * *

While looking industriously for him among his companions, he learned, to his surprise and horror, that the poor boy, after fighting gallantly on Thursday, had died from exposure, lying, without fire or shelter, upon the frozen ground, on that bitter and desolate night.

* * * *

A lieutenant of a company in one of the Ohio regiments, while preparing for a charge, had his pipe shot from his mouth. He laughed, and lighted it again; and, soon after, its fire was extinguished by a Rebel rifle-ball, which killed a man three feet from him; and, while wondering at his escape, he received a shot through his cap, and another struck his scabbard.

The lieutenant has since thought, no doubt, he was not born to die on the battle-field.

The proverb that lightning does not strike the same tree twice must be truer than that balls do not design to do mischief to soldiers more than once during the same engagement.

A number of our soldiers were wounded five, or six, and even seven times, at Donelson, none of the wounds proving serious; and yet the variation of a quarter of an inch would have proved fatal in many of the instances. Truly—to change the aphorism—in the midst of death we are in life.

The head of one of the enemy—a member of the Alabama Rifles—was shot off, the second day of the fight, by a Parrott rifle-gun—First Missouri Battery—at a distance of nearly two miles, while he was peeping above the breastworks.

A lieutenant, in an Illinois regiment, was shot with a musket in the left cheek, the ball passing through his mouth, which was open at the time, and, knocking out three false teeth, carried two of them into the thigh of his sergeant, who was at his side; making a painful, but not serious, wound.

* * * *

Curious stories were told, at Donelson, of some ultra-professional journalists on the field, who never for a moment forgot their calling, or the disagreeable duties it imposed. They never moved out of range until they had completed their notes, though the shot and shell fell like hail; and conducted their business as calmly as if they were reporting a political speech.

One of the Correspondents is said to have locked General S. B. Buckner in a room at Dover, and kept him there, in spite of threats, until he had taken a pencil sketch of his person.

Another—so rumor says—declared to General Bushrod K. Johnson, that he would give him shameful antecedents, unless he furnished materials for a brief biography.

Johnson blustered, at first; but when the newspaper-scribbler began putting down and reading, in a loud voice: "B. K. Johnson, a native of Massachusetts, formerly one of the editors of Lloyd Garrison's anti-slavery journal, but compelled to fly to Tennessee, on account of having been detected in a forgery of his father's name," etc., Bushrod became a suppliant, and gave the irrepressible fellow the main events of his life.

The representative of a New York journal is stated to have run up to a wounded officer of distinction, who believed himself mortally hurt, and begged him not to die yet, for the sake of the ——, which he had the honor to represent; remarking, if he had any last words to utter, that they should appear in the best form, in the earliest possible issue of his widely circulated and highly influential journal.

The officer turned away his head in abhorrence and disgust, and some of his friends compelled the painfully persevering correspondent to retire; but the professor of the quill insisted he could make a better speech for the wounded soldier than he could make for himself, and expressed the hope that he would not give any member of the Press the least hint of his dying sentiments, under any circumstances whatever.

I am very anxious to believe, for the honor of journalism, such stories are untrue; but I fear they have some foundation, as there are men in our profession, who, in the discharge of their duties, forget they are any thing but machines, and, to the furtherance of their duties, sacrifice every sentiment of humanity and every prompting of sensibility.

They do not know that the mistaken journalist, who loses sight of what belongs to a gentleman, may earn success in his vocation, but must forever despair of the respect and esteem that render his profession not only useful but honorable.

CHAPTER XIII.

OCCUPATION OF COLUMBUS.

The Departure for the Rebel Stronghold.—Uncertainty of the Situation.—Doubts and Apprehensions.—Pleasant Discovery.—Enthusiasm on Board the Flotilla.—Abortive Defenses of the Enemy.—Evidences of Excessive Orthodoxy.—Superstition and Swagger.—Pikes and Long Knives in Abundance.

For some days before the Union Flotilla left Cairo, there were reports that Columbus had been evacuated; and though there were many external signs to corroborate the impression, no one knew what the condition of affairs was at the Rebel stronghold.

Commodore Foote determined, on the 4th of March, 1862, to acquire that important information; and before dawn every thing was in readiness, and the gunboats and transports steamed down the river, their officers profusely speculating whether they would have a fight or a peaceful occupation.

The Tribune Correspondent was on the *Illinois*, and, as we moved down the Mississippi, it was amusing to hear the conversation and questions in the pilot-house, where another Bohemian and Colonel Buford were also standing, all with glasses in their hands.

The gunboats were just in advance of us, steaming very slowly and cautiously, for they feared the Rebels, as had been often declared, had laid a trap for the "barbarous Yankees."

We were in direct range, below the island opposite the fortifications, and glasses were anxiously sweeping the Eastern and Western horizon.

We thought we descried large guns plainly, and some one said, "I see men behind the breastworks. The Rebels are about to fire. Those immense guns will sink us like an eggshell."

That cheering intelligence caused silence for a few seconds; but some one laughed, and said: "Let the Rebels fire, and be d——d."

They did not fire; but I am quite sure they will be d——d, if the Calvinistic theology be true.

"Do you see that flag?" was inquired. "Those are Rebel colors." "I see more cavalry." "The Rebels are coming down the bluff." "The battle is about to begin."

"Wasn't that a cannon?" "They are running—see them on the hill." "Are those their tents?" "They are burning them—do you see the fire?"

"A few minutes, and we'll know all about it, boys," observed the bluff old pilot. "Beauregard's a cunning fox." "He is there, you may be sure. He wouldn't desert such a stronghold. He's only waiting to get us under his guns, and open on us." "I'll bet there are thousands of the enemy behind those breastworks." "Yes, indeed, you'll see them soon enough." "I want our mortar-boats to begin. They'll give the rebels the devil—won't they?"

Such were the fragments of conversation on the transport, as she proceeded slowly down the river in the rear of the gunboats.

The morning was rather pleasant, but hazy, and while we were straining our eyes to penetrate the attractive distance, a soft breeze, which we felt bathing our faces with early Spring, lifted the flag upon the Kentucky bluffs, and the glorious old Stars and Stripes shone out bright and clear.

Columbus had already been occupied by a regiment of our cavalry which had proceeded there by land. At that moment our hats were off, and three cheers for the Union rang out across the silent bosom of the Mississippi.

The cry was caught up from the gunboats, and the distant bluffs echoed the joyous shout.

Our bands played "Dixie"—that detestable air which I am sorry Secessia has not been allowed to monopolize —and with waving hats and banners, we were soon passing the Rebel fortifications, whose guns had been dismounted—and steaming into the landing of the famed and fearful town.

As soon as the distance rendered it possible, I leaped on shore, and struggled hurriedly up the lofty bluff on which the chief works of the enemy were located.

For five or six hours I occupied myself in walking over the enemy's works, through their deserted barracks and the town, up and down the ravines, over the fallen timber, climbing the bluffs, stumbling through the rayless magazines, and seeing, in a word, all that it was possible for me to see.

Two heavy iron cables were thrown across the Mississippi, and secured at each end by immense anchors ; but both had been broken.

Any quantity of torpedoes had been sunk in the river,

but they were as harmless as a pretty school-girl who does the tragedy at a literary exhibition

About one hundred of these submarine failures were piled up on the banks, with accompanying buoys and anchors, and they looked as innocent as unrewarded virtue. They must have been rejected members of the Peace Society ; and if one would have tied a white cravat about them, they would have passed for the meekest of clergymen.

The enemy at Columbus must have been extremely jocose. I found a number of Valentines the troops had sent each other, with droll letters, showing their fondness for, and appreciation of, humor.

We found a number of stuffed figures of President Lincoln, General McClellan, Horace Greeley, and others, represented in the most grotesque form, and always associated in some way with the gallows and with negroes. They were "gotten up" with bottles in their hands in every instance, and some ultra-Abolition sentiment invariably ascribed to them. Some of their jests would have been sufficiently apt a few weeks before, but then they were inappropriate enough.

In the deserted camps and abandoned barracks we found various letters and documents, all breathing the most fervent spirit of orthodoxy, the loftiest appeals to Providence, the largest faith in its determination to overthrow the wicked Yankees, who would not let the saintly Rebels alone in the enjoyment of their rights.

Not satisfied with the most ardent irrational appeals to the strongest prejudices and worst passions of their blind followers, the Rebels seek to impress them with the mockery that God is in their favor and fighting their battles for them; that He sometimes preserves, as Kentucky tried to do, an armed neutrality, to humble their pride, and prove how little they can effect without His all-powerful aid.

What a jest is that! What a gross impiety it must seem to some!

The idea of the Almighty arraying Himself on the side of Treason, Oppression, Cruelty, and Slavery, would be monstrous, if it were not ridiculous.

Murderers might as well pray to Him to shield them from harm during the progress of their assassinations, or profligates ask His assistance in the betrayal of an innocent maid, as *they* invoke the protection of Heaven, or claim its sympathy with their unholy cause.

Knowing that many, perhaps most, men have a strong religious bias, and believe in special providence, the demagogues of the South endeavor to profit by such mental conditions.

They turn to Superstition when Reason fails, comprehending that early teachings and inflammatory appeals are more potent in the bosom of most mortals than acquired knowledge and dispassionate argument.

If we were to believe the Southern press, we would be compelled to acknowledge God as the vicegerent of the "Confederacy," and the chief, though invisible, member of its traitorous cabinet; Abraham Lincoln and the devil as sworn friends, who had formed a plan to destroy the "last remnant of liberty on earth."

If God is with the Rebels, say I, let us accept the devil as a loyal citizen, with his tail, horns, hoofs, and his large interest in the brimstone trade, that the Calvinists have assigned to his sulphurous majesty.

* * * *

A large number of pikes, and of those murderous-looking knives with which the Rebels were to strike at once terror and death to the hearts of the North, were found at Columbus, and seized as trophies.

On every battle-field, and in every evacuated position, these knives have been picked up by our victorious soldiers. It would seem the enemy manufactured them not for use, but show; intending to prove, by their exposure, with what a terrible set of fellows the North had to deal.

In ancient days, the valor of a nation was determined by the shortness of its weapons; but I opine the nation did something more than throw them away at the approach of real danger.

I have never known an instance in which the Rebels used, or attempted to use, those knives, so savage in semblance; and I must conclude they were designed to produce a moral effect.

The pikes they have never employed, either, against their foes; nor will they, from present appearances, for some time to come.

They do not seem to comprehend their proper use; though, if we had believed the Southern papers, they were to be among the chief means of liberating secession from the yoke of its oppressors.

They proved serviceable to our men in climbing the steep bluffs of Columbus, though they did not deem them adapted to the sanguinary pursuits of war.

CHAPTER XIV.

BATTLE OF PEA RIDGE.

The Three Days' Fighting.—Desperate Struggle for the Possession of the Train.—Sigel's Heroism.—Tremendous Contest for the Guns.—Hand to Hand Combats.—An Epic of War.—Triumph of the Republic.—Retreat of the Rebels.

THE Rebels, before they began the now memorable battle of Pea Ridge, in Benton County, Arkansas, on Thursday morning, March 6th, 1862, were entirely confident of success, and their chief concern was only how to destroy or capture our whole force.

General Curtis anticipated an attack on the South, and accordingly had the train placed on the North side, under the protection of General Sigel, with a body of eight hundred men—the principal Union encampment and main lines being to the eastward, near the head and on both sides of Sugar Creek.

Meantime, the Rebel forces were moving in full strength from Bentonville, whence they had proceeded from Cross Hollows, and with rapid marches were endeavoring to cross the creek, and, by placing themselves on the North, to cut off any attempt on our part to retreat.

An advance of about two thousand cavalry reached the desired position, and made a fierce onslaught on Sigel, hoping to take possession of our large and valuable train.

Sigel proved himself the right man in the right place. He gallantly met the enemy, and, while he repelled his charge, prevented him from seizing our wagons.

The brave and accomplished officer seemed ubiquitous. He rode rapidly here and there, giving orders and observing the point of attack and the situation of the enemy, at the same time cheering and encouraging his troops.

Often he was in the thickest of the fight, and yet he was always cool, calculating, and skillful, exposing himself as a common soldier, and yet preserving the calm judgment of a commander-in-chief.

Sigel's desire was to keep the communication open between himself and the main camp, while the enemy's design was to cut off that avenue for the obtainment of re-enforcements.

The Rebels closed round him with tumultuous shouts, and believed they had accomplished their purpose, when Sigel rushed in upon them with his brave followers, and compelled them to give way.

Sigel could not abandon the train; and so he fought on, and exhorted his men to renewed hope and courage by his example.

For two hours the strife went on with great ardor on both sides, but it seemed as if the Unionists would soon be compelled to yield.

There seemed no hope for them; that they must become exhausted; and doubtless they would have done so, had their destiny been in less powerful and experienced hands than Sigel's.

The waves of opposition rolled around Sigel's courageous band once more; and again the traitorous shout went up to the sky, and swept like a note of victory along the rising hill.

Many a stout loyal heart doubtless sank when that cry was heard; but Sigel had no thought of failure.

He was fighting for his adopted country and the salvation of his little band; and, ordering three companies of his men to charge bayonets, the Rebel cavalry were dispersed, and the way was open once more.

Still no re-enforcements came, and our gallant soldiers appeared contending for a forlorn hope.

About the trains the din of strife rose louder than before, and the rattle of musketry and the boom of cannon awoke the surrounding echoes.

The enemy was losing ground. He rallied, and fell with redoubled force on our heroic band, two hundred of whom had already sealed their patriotism with their blood.

The combat was hand to hand. Horsemen were dismounted and struggling with the infantry, while the officers were sometimes seen defending themselves against the advancing bayonets of the common soldiers.

A superhuman effort on the part of the enemy, and a third time the Unionists were surrounded.

Firmer and firmer were the Rebels closing round the five or six hundred braves, who were evidently going to the wall.

The sun of Hope seemed sinking, though that of Nature was shining clear from out the quiet sky.

Sigel saw the smile of Heaven only, and would not despond. His eye flashed and his form expanded as the shouts of the enemy rose above the din of the struggle.

Only one way was left.

"Follow me!" thundered Sigel, and his proud steed trampled an approaching Rebel under his fiery feet.

A deep, strong, earnest cry from the Unionists, and they met the foe with the rush of determination and the energy of despair.

The Secession line could not endure the shock. It recoiled, was thrown into confusion, and retired from a position that had been deemed as secure as the Alpine peaks. And Sigel was victorious, with the sun still beaming clearly out of the quiet sky.

The train was saved.

The first day was won.

The prestige of success was established, and the Future looked blue with hope as the violets of the early year.

The enemy, during the night and early the following morning, March 7th, poured in from the Bentonville road, and gathered in heavy force to our rear; sweeping round to the right, and occupying both sides of the Keetsville road—a position from which it was absolutely necessary to dislodge him, or surrender all hope of success.

Truly, before the second day's engagement began, the prospect was very dark. Defeat seemed to stare us in the face, and the sole thing possible appeared a struggle to prevent too disastrous a discomfiture.

The way to Missouri was defended by thirty thousand of the enemy, and we had little more than one-third the number to dispute the perilous passage.

On the South were the Boston Mountains. To the East

or West we could not go. Were we not hemmed in by nature and the enemy?

Could we longer resist? Could we say we were contending only for victory, when the shadows were lengthening and deepening on our hearts?

General Carr was sent by General Curtis to force the enemy from his position, and about ten o'clock in the morning the battle was renewed with increased ardor, and soon the batteries from both sides were replying to each other with death-dealing voices.

The main action in the morning was to the right of our encampment, and for seven hours the field was hotly contested.

General Carr made a spirited and heavy charge upon the enemy under McCulloch and Price.

The musket and rifle firing was very sharp, and every few seconds the boom of the batteries burst across the country, and the iron hail swept down the stream of life, and filled the surging, noisy waves with spectral corpses.

The Rebels reeled as we went against them, but their column did not break.

The charge was repeated.

Still the foe stood firm, opening a galling fire from two batteries whose presence had not before been known.

Our troops were thrown into confusion, and three companies of infantry and Colonel Ellis's cavalry were ordered to silence the destructive guns.

Like lightning our men leaped forth prompt to the word, and raged about the Rebel batteries as ravenous wolves around a sheep-fold. Everywhere the strife roared; everywhere the smoke crept; everywhere the ground shook.

The sunbeams glanced off from the swords and bayonets, but they ceased to shine for many eyes on that blood-stained day.

Carr's column advanced and fell back, and advanced again; and beyond them, up the hill, the cavalry and infantry were struggling to capture the detested guns.

The regiment which protected the batteries met them fairly and freely, and for half an hour the two combatants were so commingled that they almost failed to recognize one another.

"Our men have the batteries!" was announced, and the Unicnists made the welkin ring with their huzzas.

Yes, it was so!

Through the blue curling vapors our men could be seen dragging the guns after them.

Ere they had gone a hundred yards, the Rebels were behind them; struggling like Hercules for the repossession of the pieces.

Blood streamed anew, and shouts, and groans, and prayers, and curses went up with the gigantic forms of smoke into the upper air.

Appropriate incense to waft the elements of battle to the skies.

No noise now. All is silent, as when men are holding their breath for a deadly struggle.

The suspense is awful. It cannot last.

Do you not hear a thousand hearts beat across the plain? Anxiety has made the roar of battle almost inaudible—so keenly is the sense upon the rack.

Countless throats are roaring with triumph.

Brief triumph ! The batteries are lost. Our men have been overpowered by numbers. They retire, and blood marks their progress, and many dead are abandoned.

The recaptured guns are revenging themselves. Their shot and shell are plowing up the ground, and tearing open brave bosoms, and making history, and peopling graves.

The batteries are sought once more. We win them back with blood. We are hurrying them off. The Rebels stare like demons out of malignant eyes, and curse through firm-set teeth.

Triumph is about to crown our efforts, when a large force of the enemy, repulsed by General Davis from that section of Pea Ridge known as Leetown, throng to the rescue.

A dozen combats over the guns, and the contest is still undecided, when the darkness gathers, and through the night the enemy is seen bearing off his twice-captured, twice-recaptured guns.

Nature is no longer an impartial witness.

She draws the curtain ; and the camp-fires blaze along the roads, and light up the trees.

Man's Pandemonium is profaning the holy Night.

Midnight comes, and the scattered words of the sentinels are heard ; and the Unionists and Rebels are sleeping on their arms ; dreaming, it may be, of the time when they were friends and brothers, and America had not become one vast military camp.

The stars, too, are keeping watch on the battlements of Heaven.

They challenge no one. They seem to say to all the weary and worn, "Come hither! Here is peace."

Speak they, or be they forever silent, there are many spirits in the air seeking peace that is not of Earth.

At six o'clock on the morning of the 8th, our guns opened on the enemy, and our fire was returned from twenty pieces.

The firing did little harm. The enemy's shot passed over our heads. Our cause was growing darker. That day must win or lose the battle.

As yet, the fortunes of war incline to neither side. We have reason to be alarmed; but hope and courage are firm counselors, and add strength to weak arms.

General Sigel observes new positions for our operations. We plant six batteries at different points commanding their principal forces. A fire of ball is shattering the space with its roar.

The enemy's list of mortality is swelling. He does not understand our great advantages; he turns pale, and hesitates to advance.

No time is given him for reflection; he is in the midst of his soul's perplexity, while judgment tosses in fevered sleep.

Our entire infantry is engaged. The Rebels meet our dreadful volleys of musketry for a quarter of an hour; but their firing slackens.

Still our batteries are forcing the verdict of the outraged nation into their startled souls.

The cannon answers the musketry; the musketry replies to the cannon.

Every inch of ground appears alive with troops;

every twig and dry leaf seems ablaze. The balls are falling like the large drops of a summer shower. The Pentecost of war is descending.

The Rebels can endure no longer the sheet of flame, out of which go Death and Pain in a thousand forms.

They have lost their faith in their bad cause and themselves. They are panic-stricken. They fly, and a roar of victory follows them, as the waves of the river the lean and hungry shore.

They turn not back. Two of their Generals have received their mortal wounds, and the word is: "Save himself who can."

The Unionists have beaten them, and their star has set over the verdureless ridge of that hard-fought field.

The birds twitter overhead. The sun shines warmer and clearer.

The atmosphere of blood is purified by the feeling that it was shed in a sacred cause.

The Spring greets the victors, and kisses their burning brows with the same pure lips that call forth the early flowers.

Nature rejoices over the triumph of principle; for Nature is the Order and the Law.

The Unionists pursue the broken columns; and the breezes come wafting the victorious shouts; and the incense of the youthful March, revealing that all is well, and that the Future is secure.

* * * *

Concerning the death of Generals McCulloch and McIntosh, there seems to be but one opinion. Both of them were mortally wounded on Friday, during the heavy fighting by General Jeff. C. Davis against the center column of the enemy. It will be remembered the Rebels gave way, and the two Southern chieftains made the most determined efforts to rally them in vain.

McCulloch was struck with a Minié rifle-ball in the left breast—as I am assured by one who says he saw him fall, and after he was taken from the ground—while waving his sword and encouraging his men to stand firm. He died of his wounds about eleven o'clock the same night; though he insisted that he would recover, repeatedly saying with great oaths that he was not born to be killed by a Yankee.

A few minutes before he expired, his physician assured him he had but a very brief time to live. At this Ben. looked up incredulously, and saying, "Oh, Hell!" turned away his head, and never spoke after.

The Southern papers no doubt have put some very fine sentiment into his mouth in his closing moments; but the last words I have mentioned are declared by a prisoner to be correct. They are not very elegant nor very dramatic, but quite expressive, and, in McCulloch's case, decidedly appropriate.

It is reported that McIntosh was struck near the right hip with a grapeshot, while giving an order to one of his aids, and hurled from his horse.

The wound was a ghastly one, and though it must have been very painful, McIntosh uttered no groan, but calmly gave directions for his treatment. A few minutes after, he fell into a comatose state, from which he never recovered—passing through Death's dark portal while his attendants supposed he still lay beside the golden gates of Sleep.

CHAPTER XV.

PROSE AND POESY OF WAR.

Facts and Fancies from Pea Ridge.—The Preservative Power of Tobacco.—A Song-Book doing the Work of aBible.—Mysterious Instance of Sympathy.—Another Fabian dei Franchi.—Painful Fate of a Union Lieutenant.—A Reckless Indianian.—A Magnanimous Rebel.—A Gallant Iowa Colonel.

A NUMBER of singular and interesting incidents occurred on the field of Pea Ridge, some of which are worth relating, even at this late day.

A private of the Twelfth Missouri was advancing toward the head of the Hollows, on Saturday, with his regiment, under a heavy fire from the enemy stationed on a hill above, when he was struck by a musket-ball near the heart, and thrown heavily to the earth.

The poor fellow thought no doubt his last moment had come; but after lying for some time on the ground, and feeling no pain, he thought he would see, if possible, where he was hit.

He rose, and opened his vest, and discovered a bullet half imbedded in a large, thick, moist layer of tobacco which he had stolen the day before, and placed under his garment for concealment.

The moist condition of the tobacco had prevented the leaden messenger from fulfilling its fatal mission.

The tobacco was all that had interfered between him and Heaven.

Had he cause to lament or rejoice?

Who knows?

What philosopher can determine whether it be better to live or die?

The soldier, not being a philosopher, rejoiced.

Most men would have done likewise; for not many of us mortals have time to die; and in America few can afford it, though we indulge in the luxury at a most ruinous rate.

Let no one say hereafter there is no virtue in stealing.

There the act preserved a brave fellow's life to his country.

For the sake of the time-honored tradition and all Sunday Schools, I am sorry to say I have heard of no instance in which a life was saved by a Bible; and I am bound to believe the fact is owing to the great scarcity of the sacred volume in the army, rather than to any want of preserving power in the Holy Book itself.

* * * *

Of a secular song-book, rather ribald in character, I fear, I can relate a different story.

One of the Thirty-Sixth Illinois troops carried a volume of the sort in his cap, and a small rifle-ball passed through the cloth and stunned him. He afterward found the bullet had gone through one of the corners of the book, and when he removed it, the metallic fate fell from the leaves.

I can only account for the phenomenon by supposing that the verses of the songs were so execrable, that the ball, like any reader of good taste, could not, by any possibility, get more than half way through the contents.

Can it be said hereafter of the Illinois volunteer that his life was not worth a song?

* * * *

The subtle and mysterious power of sympathy, sentimental metaphysicians have sought fruitlessly to unravel, and Dumas, in the "Corsican Brothers," has pictured the phenomena in its fullness.

A very strange example of the influence of sympathy is reported to have occurred during the battle on Friday.

Hiram P. Lord, of the Twenty-fifth Missouri, Colonel Phelps, while charging up a ravine, fell as if dead, and his companions ran to him and asked if he was hurt.

He did not answer, for he had swooned.

On reviving, he said he must have been struck by a ball, for he felt a pain in his left side, and had distinctly experienced the stunning sensation that results from a gun-shot wound.

His person was examined, and no mark or indication of injury was perceptible.

He could not comprehend the mystery, but soon after resumed the fight, and forgot the sensation until he had returned to the camp, when he learned, to his surprise and sorrow, that his twin brother George was among the dead.

George had been in another part of the field, and had been shot in the same part of the body, and at the same time, that Hiram had believed himself mortally wounded.

The sympathy between the two brothers had ever been complete, and the illness of one was usually accompanied by the sickness of the other.

Strange, if true, say many; but the stranger, the truer, declare the students of Nature.

A melancholy incident occurred to a lieutenant (whose name I was unable to learn) in one of the Iowa companies, that I cannot forbear mentioning.

He had been shot in the leg, and had fallen. He rose, and supporting himself upon a stump, urged his company, whose captain had been killed, to push on in the then important crisis toward the re-enforcement of General Carr.

While the lieutenant was waving his sword, an artillery wagon was driven madly along the road, by the side of which he was standing. The wheel struck him, threw him to the ground, and the heavy carriage passed over his neck, causing his instant death.

Poor fellow! I saw rude men weep over his corpse, and they proved themselves braver and truer for their tears.

*   *   *   *

A private in the Eighteenth Indiana had been left behind for some reason, when his regiment was ordered to the upper part of the Ridge. Before it reached there, it became engaged with the Rebels, and was cut off.

The Indianian resolved to join his companions in arms. though persuaded not to do so, as it was madness to make the attempt.

He heeded not counsel, but hurried forward, and was last seen contending with a score of foes.

His fate is unknown, but he must have perished.

*   *   *   *

Where there was so much valor, there were some individual instances of its opposite, but very, very few; for timidity is a quality little known to American soldiers, fighting in the cause of freedom, and the Republic they have sworn to protect.

A soldier, whose nerves, poor fellow, were weaker than his will, climbed into a tree during the severe fight of Friday; and while there a round shot accidentally struck him, and hurled him, a bloody and irrecognizable mass, to the ground.

Had the soldier remained where his duty ordered, he would probably have been living still. The poet sang truly :—

"The coward often finds the death he shuns,
In that his drunken fear his sober judgment clouds."

* * * *

Even Secession cannot crush the noble instincts of the heart. Even a Rebel often has the generous qualities of Nature, ånd the lofty instincts of a gentleman.

A Colonel of one of the Louisiana regiments saw a poor private, a Unionist, lying wounded alone by the roadside, and begging for a drink.

The Colonel dismounted, and, taking the soldier's canteen, went to the creek and filled it, gave him a drink, and placed him in an easier position; and all that while our bullets were flying thick in his immediate vicinity.

I am very sorry I do not know the gallant Colonel's name. He never did a nobler act on the battle-field. He has some reason to boast of chivalry, though I doubt if he does so.

If the South comprehended chivalry as he comprehends it, their assumption of that high attribute would not render it a subject of jest and an object of scorn.

* * * *

Lieutenant-Colonel Herron of the Ninth Iowa, now Major-General, was wounded in the battle and taken prisoner, though he lost his liberty through no fault of his, as he seemed determined to die rather than fall into Rebel hands. He was surrounded by ten or twelve of the enemy, and his surrender demanded in vain.

He killed one and wounded three of the Rebels, and was making every resistance with his sword, when his arms were seized, and his opposition rendered impossible. He would have been slain most assuredly, had not a Southern major saved his life, and shot an Indian dead who was trying to butcher him after his arms were bound with a handkerchief.

CHAPTER XVI.

INDIAN ATROCITIES.

Aboriginal Outrages and Barbarities at Pea Ridge.—Minds of the Savages poisoned by the Rebels.—Whisky and Gunpowder Stimulant.—The Indians Scalp Friend and Foe Alike.—Slaughter of the Red Men by their own Allies.

THE three thousand Cherokee, Choctaw, Creek, and Seminole Indians, under Colonel Albert Pike, a renegade son of Connecticut, committed the greatest atrocities on the field of Pea Ridge; not only plundering and maiming the dead, but actually murdering and scalping the wounded as they lay helpless and suffering on the ground.

More than one hundred and twenty of our brave men were thus barbarously treated by the savage foe, who had been wrought to a pitch of frenzy by the Rebels, through passionate appeals, and declarations that the "Yankees" designed to enslave them, and force them, with chains and whips, to do the vilest drudgery in their aristocratic homes in the North.

Not only did the enemy thus poison their minds, but every day, before the savages went into action, it is reported, they received large potations of whiskey mixed with gunpowder, which rendered the naturally fierce sons of the forest perfect demons.

Under such extraordinary stimulant, they forgot their usual caution, and, exposing themselves after the American fashion, were killed in great numbers.

Still, they were very formidable, and often attacked the Unionists in the rear, as they were passing some bend in the road or piece of wooded land, and did much execution.

They yelled, and danced, and brandished their knives, and acted like madmen; but when they grew partially sober, became more prudent, and fought after their time-honored fashion, from behind trees and fallen timber.

When our troops discovered on the second day that the Indians were using the scalping-knife, their rage knew no bounds, and they made sad havoc in the ranks of the red devils, slaying them without mercy whenever and wherever they could reach them.

In one instance, the Second Iowa Battery, which had four of its members scalped, obtained the range of a body of four or five hundred of the savages, and fired several charges of cannister and shell upon them in rapid succession, at a distance of not more than a quarter of a mile.

The effect upon the aborigines was terrible. They were cut down like grass, and the dusky demons who were unhurt ran howling from the field, and could not be rallied again on that day (Friday), though Colonel Albert Pike, it is said, shot several with his own hand, and bawled at them until he was hoarse.

Some ten or twelve of the chiefs were killed, whose names I can not undertake to give.

One of them, a Seminole, was very famous as a warrior in his tribe, and, though over fifty years of age, was athletic and daring to an extraordinary degree.

He is said to have fought with the celebrated Red Jacket in Florida during the Seminole war, and bore upon his person no less than twenty wounds.

It is said the Indians, in the engagement of Friday, became so excited by the alcohol they had drank and the scenes they witnessed, that they turned their weapons upon their own allies, and butchered and scalped the Rebels and Unionists with the most charming indifference.

An instance of that was given by one of our prisoners, a member of one of the companies that suffered from what the Southerners believed to be the treachery of the savages.

Four companies of Arkansas infantry, belonging to Ben McCulloch's division, were marching up one of the ridges north of Sugar Creek, on Saturday, to strengthen the enemy, who was hardly pressed by General Sigel.

The Arkansans had come in sight of about three hundred Creeks and Choctaws, who stood on the brow of an adjacent hill, and were within about one hundred and fifty yards of the savages, when the latter opened fire on them.

The Rebel Major who commanded the battalion cried out to them, that they were killing their friends; but the Indians did not heed what he said, and again discharged their pieces.

"The d——d rascals have turned traitors," cried the Major. "Upon them, Arkansans, and give them no quarter."

The Southerners needed no second order.

They attacked them with great energy, and for nearly

an hour a desperate battle was waged on the Ridge ; the Indians fighting with blind fury, and scalping all who fell into their hands, whether living, wounded, or dead.

That was described as one of the severest actions of the entire battle, and the Indians, who were finally routed, are said to have lost one hundred and twenty-five in killed and wounded.

CHAPTER XVII.

BENIGHTED ARKANSAS.

Semi-Barbarism of the People.—Benton County as an Example.—Extent of the Conscription.—Modern Harpies in the Shape of Women.—The Loyal Sentiment of the State.—Chivalrous Mode of its Suppression.

THE semi-barbarous condition of Arkansas has become proverbial in this country; and yet no one who has not traveled in the State can have any just idea of the ignorance and immorality that prevail there.

If a foreigner were set down in that Patagonia of places, and told that it was one of the component parts of the Great Republic, famous for its school-houses, railways, and newspapers, he would not believe a story so apparently self-contradictory.

In Benton County, in which Pea Ridge was fought, one sees very few indications of civilization, and it would seem an anomaly if loyalty ever could have flourished on such barren soil.

The population was not then, and is not now, over eighteen hundred, though it once boasted of four thousand. The dwellings were usually miles apart, and made of logs and mud, presenting a most cheerless and squalid appearance. No one was at home save women and children, and the old men, and very few of them; even those of sixty years, who were not diseased, having been impressed into the Rebel army.

The women were only such in name; their sex, in their absence of physiological demonstration, requiring to be taken on faith.

Tall, meagre, sallow, with hard features and large bones, they would have appeared masculine if they had not been too attenuated to suggest the possibility of health or strength.

They drank whisky and smoked as freely as men; often chewed tobacco, and went about swearing in discordant tones, and expectorating skillfully, and were as hideous as any Tophetian trollops that the most depraved mind could imagine.

Very few of the common people—and Heaven knows they were common enough—could read or write; and it was not unusual to find but one or two in a township so blessed beyond their kind.

Ignorance and crime were inseparable companions, and it was no wonder vice there assumed many of its lowest and most disgusting forms.

The life led was one of brutalized sense and dissipation. Practical amalgamation, gambling, and fighting were the end and aim of Arkansas existence. Not many of the people had been out of the State—just think of a being that had no idea beyond or above that Bœotia—and they lived, if I may employ so inappropriate a verb, and died there unpenetrated by a ray of Beauty; unlifted by a hope of Advancement; undeveloped by a thought of Change.

Among some of the farmers in that county were men of considerable intelligence, but they were generally from other States.

The true Arkansan knows nothing, and learns nothing. He regards education in every form as a Yankee invention that has a tendency to interfere with the institution of slavery, which many of the poor whites adore, because they own no negroes.

With several of the most intelligent people in Benton County, and with some of the prisoners, I conversed on the subject of the Union sentiment in Arkansas; and they said the people, strange as it may seem, would never have gone with the "Confederacy," if they had been allowed to determine the question for themselves.

Throughout the entire State men went as emissaries of Secession, and told the people they must go out of the Union if they did not wish to be deprived of their slaves and ruled by the "Yankees," who would compel them to perform all menial offices.

Their property, their wives, their children would be taken from them; they would exchange position with their negroes, and the latter be made their masters.

Those arguments even the Arkansans could comprehend, and, in a few weeks after the diffusion of such nefarious sentiments, the State was thrown into a terrible excitement.

A reaction occurred. A few thinking Union men enlightened the half-crazed community, and told them they were deceived; that Secession would ruin them; that their only safety was in the Union, and that President Lincoln had no disposition and no intention to interfere with any of their constitutional rights.

The advice came too late. The Rebels had by that time gained the power by seizing all the arms and organizing themselves throughout the State; and thereafter they had full and absolute sway.

They pillaged and destroyed wherever they went, and the people found their worst enemies were at home.

Terror-stricken, they yielded, for they knew their lives were in the hands of the oppressors, and after that period hardly a man had dared to lift his voice against the outrageous tyranny imposed upon the State.

Perhaps the oppressed were wise in their reticence, for the means of enforcing eternal silence were not wanting.

Men were often carried off by armed bands who broke into quiet habitations at unseasonable hours of the night; were whipped, tarred and feathered; dragged through horse-ponds, and often hanged or otherwise murdered, because they were charged with disloyalty to the South.

Loyalty to the Union was the unpardonable offense, and the individual suspected of any such sentiment was liable to assassination anywhere.

Hundreds of men escaped from the confines of the State, leaving their families and all their property behind, fearing to remain longer where their lives were not worth a moment's purchase.

Any scoundrel could make an accusation against an honest citizen that would destroy his life, or drive him, an outcast and an exile, from his home and all the associations he held dear.

CHAPTER XVIII.

DOWN THE MISSISSIPPI.

A Weary Siege.—Inaneness of Existence on the Flotilla.—Monotony and Dreariness of the Scenes.—Melancholy Character of the Mighty River.—Out in the Night.—A Celestial Symbol.—A Canine Convert.—A Perplexed Correspondent, and Would-be Bohemian.

During the latter part of the month of March, 1862, we were besieging Island No. 10, and, for several weeks, life on the National Flotilla was dull enough.

There we were anchored in the midst of the mighty river, or tied to the submerged trees, watching the occasional shells from the mortars, the turbid eddying of the swollen stream, or the leaden sky that hung over the dreary scene like a funeral pall.

We could go nowhere except on one of the little tugs that plied ceaselessly from gunboat to gunboat, and transport to transport; and then we could not imagine the direction of our journeying, or anticipate the time of our return.

The Mississippi was shoreless; no land was visible; and so we paced the deck of the vessel and gazed out into the dull, dreary waste of waters, and listened to the rush of the waves, and the whirl of the eddies, until the mind stagnated and the spirit sank.

We had no books to peruse, no papers to read, no letters to expect, no women even to tease or talk to; and indeed we were as wretched a set of mortals as ever committed matrimony, or contemplated suicide.

No resource was left us.

No remedy had we for our innumerable ills.

There was no satisfaction in to-day, and no hope in tomorrow.

All the days staggered gloomily along, and awoke with stumbling feet the weary echoes of the dreary solitude.

The cave of Polyphemus was not more dismal than were our own surroundings. Nature seemed to sorrow everywhere—in the sky, in the forest, on the river.

No Future was apparent there. The Present was born in agony, and sank with pain and without resignation into the arms of the Past.

Was ever river more dreary than the Mississippi? It is tristful as the chant of Ayesha, or the plaint of the Burmese bird.

It is the terrestrial Styx, and the Acheron of America.

Grand it may be; but it is grand as the Sphynx is, and as melancholy.

No change, no relief on either side.

The gray cotton-woods greeted one at every turn, looking like skeletons by day and spectres at night.

The sombre moss covered them like a mantle of mourning, as if Beauty were dead, and Nature were going to her funeral. Deep, dark, dismal, the formless, shoreless stream.

How it whirled and boiled, as if it were seething above unseen furnaces of unseen fire!

The sky appeared to borrow the sombre semblance of the river. No gladness, no promise, no consolation there.

The clouds were murky as the waves.

The horizon touched the tops of the dreary trees, and the dreary trees stood drearily in the dreary waters.

Misfortune, disease, and death were the portents of Nature; and the eye read the fate of Atreus in every external thing.

Often I paced the deck of our sable craft, long after all hands had piped to quarters; when the Night and Morn were passing each other in awful silence, and looked out upon the darkness, and into the despairing face of Nature.

How impressively still, how utterly desolate was all!

No marvel one then believed that Pain is the creative secret of the Universe; that Sorrow is the inheritance of the Sphere.

All ghastly stories, all horrible destinies, all Buddhist doctrines seemed true, as one gazed down the sad murmuring river, and watched the sombre clouds as they stole ghost-like among the vapory graves of the troubled and angry sky.

Dreariness, desolation, despondence, despair!

Individuality and Spirit, how weak when the superstition of Imagination wraps them round!

Still the clouds glided ghost-like, and the river surged; and the Night waned mournfully; and Thought made Hades for the soul.

* * * *

Very much reason to doubt is there if what we call Heaven ever sympathizes with War; but, one morning, as we lay on the Fleet, we had an indication of celestial recognition of our strife.

The Eastern horizon was clouded as the sun rose; and soon the golden beams burst out from half a dozen clear spaces, streaming downward to the rim of the concave, and lying in yellow light along a heavy bank of shadow, giving an exact representation of a Fort with embrasures, parapet, and bastions, behind which the Grecian gods might have been struggling for their ancient realm of Chaos and of Night.

The scene certainly was striking, and by a superstitious mind would have been invested with a meaning, and translated according to the promptings of Desire and of Fear.

To Reason, it was naught but vapors and the sun. To the Poet, it was the correspondence of the Outward with the Interior; to the Philosopher, the conformation of Nature to the thought of Man.

* * * *

To change from the sentimental strain, let me relate an anecdote of a dog—formerly the Rebel General Tighlman's—which remained behind after the capture of Fort Henry, and then divided his company with different officers of the fleet.

"Ponto" seemed to be a strong Unionist in his feelings, and to have deserted the insurgent cause as soon as he had an opportunity.

After his master was taken prisoner, he would not recognize him, but would growl whenever he approached, and take refuge near the Union soldiers or sailors.

That he had cut Tighlman's acquaintance was evident; and his growls were canine rebukes of his traitorous course.

"Ponto" had grown a great favorite, and was invited to various repasts upon the boats. He was exceedingly sensitive, and left no doubt of the political complexion of his mind.

If called Jeff. Davis, "Ponto" would howl most dolefully; and if styled Abe Lincoln, would bark joyously.

We had a Rebel banner on board, and whenever that was shown him, he endeavored to tear it in pieces, and lost his temper for an hour; but the sight of the Stars and Stripes restored his amiability; induced him to walk on his hind legs, and display all possible symptoms of pleasure, and uncompromising allegiance to the Republic.

I do not suppose "Ponto" had more genius than many of his canine brothers, but he had been carefully taught his line of conduct, and, being an apt pupil, frequently amused spectators not a little.

* * * *

We had on the Flotilla at that time a Correspondent, who at different periods had much amused the Bohemians by his unique and old-womanish ideas about every thing, but especially about War. He seemed to have adopted his nomadic pursuits of his own election; and yet he was one of the most miserable of men.

He was always hunting battles, and still had never seen one; but, invariably arriving at the scene after the engagement had become a thing of the past, mourned most bitterly over his untimely absence. The next time there was a fight, he vowed he would witness it; but somehow, before the battle took place, he would be called off in another direction, and reappeared only to curse his ill fortune.

Nothing pleased, nothing satisfied him. He was a perpetual complainer and grumbler; and if he had had a growlery, after the manner of John Jarndyce, he would have been its continuous occupant.

He suffered like a domestic Prometheus; and, though rather amiable by nature, swore like a steamboat-mate on every expedition, and declared the times, the army, the situation, the Administration, every thing, entirely wrong.

His baggage was always lost; he was ever too late; his head ached, or his boots were too small.

The World refused in any instance to go right with him. The Fates were opposed to him; the Furies pursued him as they did Orestes, and not even his maledictions would appease, nor his misfortunes mollify them.

Poor devil of a journalist! he could never learn to be a Bohemian, which generally means an ill-fated fellow, of æsthetic and luxurious tastes, born out of place, and in opposition to his circumstances—who assumes indifference to all things, and scoffs because he cannot smile.

It was not strange the Correspondent mentioned should be disgusted with the life he sought to lead, and its thousand annoyances; but he certainly ought to have retired from his profession, or played the devil-may-care part that belonged to his rôle.

The Bohemians talked of "buying him off;"—he soon after abandoned the tribe, poor fellow, and in sheer desperation became a Benedict—for his perpetual maunderings had so moved their compassion as to ruffle the self-composure necessary to the self-poise of a true disciple of Zingara.

CHAPTER XIX.

INAUGURATION OF BATTERY-RUNNING.

The Carondelet and Pittsburg Defying the Guns of Island No. 10.—Preparations for the Hazardous Enterprise.—Scenes on the Flag-ship.—Departure of the Pittsburg.—An Anxious Period.—The Artillery of the Rebels and of Heaven —Thunder, Lightning, and Gunpowder.—Safe Passage of the Union Vessels.

THE first time the Rebel batteries were defied, was in April, 1862, at Island No. 10. The experiment was then regarded as desperate; and they who made the attempt were considered members of a forlorn hope.

The gunboat Carondelet took the lead in the enterprise, and the Pittsburg followed. I was quartered on the flag-ship Benton at the time, and witnessed the novel and exciting scene with no little interest.

Early on the morning of April 6, it was believed on the Benton, from certain outward signs, that the dangerous experiment of running the blockade would be tried again on the first dark night; and before evening it was whispered that the Pittsburg was the gunboat selected.

Commodore Foote sent for Captain Thompson, and the two were closeted together for some time, while the active movements, and the air of unusual bustle on board the Pittsburg, corroborated the opinion already entertained.

At eight o'clock, or four bells, as they say on shipboard, the sky, which had been clear and bright all day, began to cloud; and as the evening advanced, the indications of a storm increased. Many were the meteorological prognostications; and it was noticed that the Commodore and Captains Phelps and Thompson anxiously watched the sky, as if the nature of the night would shape certain important events.

All the officers and crew gathered on deck after dark, and debated about the weather until ten or eleven o'clock.

Some thought it would be squally, and others clear; and many under the former impression "turned in," to use a nautical phrase, contending that the blockade would not be run during the night.

The correspondent of *The Tribune* concluded to remain up, for the night was very warm, and the atmosphere so close below that sleep to him was a matter certainly not to be dreamed of.

I felt an interest in the coming tempest, if there was to be one; and so I paced the deck and smoked. until long after midnight.

Between one and two o'clock it was evident we would be favored with a storm, from the augmented darkness, thunder, and lightning.

About that time, Captain Phelps and Commodore Foote appeared on deck, and directed their attention especially to the Pittsburg, lying to the right of us against the Missouri shore. The Pittsburg looked ready for action, and I then knew the blockade was to be run before dawn.

Ten minutes after two, the Pittsburg moved out into

the stream so quietly that no one who had not been on the watch would have noticed her.

On the side she would expose to the Tennessee shore, on her downward passage, was a barge loaded with bales of hay, entirely covering her casemates, and designed, of course, to protect her from the Rebel batteries.

She had not moved a hundred yards before it appeared the crew of the Benton had been apprised of what was on the tapis.

Some thirty or forty sleepy-looking fellows came on deck, and turned their optics—from which all drowsiness was soon dispelled by the interest felt in the occasion—towards the gunboat, leisurely moving down the stream.

"There she goes!" "That's the Pittsburg!" "Good luck to the craft!" were heard, in low tones of voice; and all eyes were strained through the darkness, which was dispelled every few seconds by the lurid lightning.

Much fear was entertained for the Pittsburg's success—far more than had been for the Carondelet—because it was believed the Rebels had profited by their first experience, were more on the alert, and had probably depressed their guns, which they had shot over the latter, as she passed within musket's reach of their roaring mouths.

Hundreds of hearts beat anxiously as the Pittsburg moved placidly down-stream; no light and no living thing visible on board, even when the lightning danced, and played, and blazed, over all the sky.

It was an impressive spectacle, to witness the solitary

and gallant gunboat gliding down the broad river, amid the tempestuous and howling night.

"What would be the fate of the brave souls on board?" occurred to many minds; but no one could answer the question.

The Pittsburg passed the first battery, which had been spiked a few nights before, and was consequently hushed, and was opposite the second, when a volley of musketry and a roar of cannon greeted her.

The artificial thunder made numerous hearts leap and pulses throb; but the sable craft seemed to regard it not, keeping on as before, mysteriously and silently.

The third, fourth, fifth, sixth, seventh, and eighth batteries were passed, and all the shore guns, and those from the island opened on her with terrible din. But we saw by the glare of the skies that she was neither crippled nor sunk. Many thanks were offered, and devout wishes shaped themselves into prayers for the success of the gallant vessel.

In twenty minutes after starting, she was hidden from view by the bend in the river; but the firing continued, and her signal-guns, anxiously listened for, were not heard.

Not a few feared she was lost; but the majority declared she must be safe, and the sailors offered large bets of rum on the successful issue of the enterprise.

About three o'clock we thought we heard the Pittsburg's signal-guns; but no one could be sure, for the thunder and the enemy's batteries, and the echoes so mingled that no one could distinguish any of the sounds with accuracy.

Captain Phelps and a number of the officers remained

on deck until four o'clock, when the enemy still fired at intervals, and the night had grown darker, and the tempest was falling with greater fury. They could see and learn nothing new; but, hoping for the best, they went below, and I with them, in dripping garments, though not to sleep, into the oven of a cabin.

The anxiety continued until after breakfast, when we learned the Pittsburg had gotten through safely; that four transports and two barges had reached New Madrid by means of the canal, and would probably be enabled to convey General Pope's forces across the river whenever he desired.

CHAPTER XX.

SURRENDER OF ISLAND NO. X.

A Mysterious Vessel astern.—Preparations for Battle on the Benton.—Proposition for the Enemy to Surrender.—Unconditional Terms asked.—The Rebel Prisoners and their Opinions.—Curious Scene.—Feminine Accompaniments to a Siege.

AFTER the running of the Rebel batteries of Island No. 10, and the passage through the canal to New Madrid, Mo., of the transports and barges mentioned in the last chapter, great interest was felt, especially on the afternoon of Monday, April 7, to hear from General Pope, and to learn the progress of affairs in and about the latter place.

Every one was waiting with anxiety for the next turn in events; and while the officers and men were on the deck of the Benton, a little before nine o'clock they discovered a strange vessel turning the point in the river below, and coming up astern of the flagship.

No one could imagine what she was or her purpose, and all the ship's glasses could not solve the question.

Probably it was a Rebel gunboat that had run Pope's blockade, or perhaps the Floating Battery, of which we had heard so much, under tow of a Secession transport.

That there was an opportunity for a fight, every one believed. The gunners were called; the fifty-pound rifled Dahlgrens at the stern were run out, and every preparation made for action.

All on board the Benton were on the *qui vive*, and orders were given to reserve fire until the supposed enemy had come within a mile's distance.

In less than a quarter of an hour after the boat had been discovered, she was heard to give four sharp, shrill whistles; and then the prospect of an engagement was materially decreased.

It was probably a friendly steamer, or it might be a Rebel fraud to deceive the Benton.

The gunners still held their position, while the flagship answered the signal, and along the shore and among the woods the echoes responded to the scream of the escaping steam.

The Commodore's tug was ordered to drop down, and determine, if possible, the mission of the stranger; and Lieutenant Bishop stepped into the Dauntless, and steamed away into the shadows of the night.

In less than half an hour the tug returned, and with her two young Rebel Lieutenants under a flag of truce, with the information that they wished to confer with the Commodore.

They were at once escorted to the cabin, and proved to be Lieutenants George S. Martin and E. S. McDowell, empowered to propose the surrender of the Island on certain conditions.

The Commodore replied mildly, but firmly, that it was unnecessary to name the conditions, as he could listen to no proposition based upon conditions; that an absolutely unconditional surrender was the sole thing possible.

The young Lieutenants seemed in excellent spirits, and augmented them at the request of Lieutenant Bishop, after leaving the Commodore's presence, by imbibing an artificial quantity. They said they were unable to make reply to the Commodore's demand without consulting their principal, Captain W. Y. C. Humes, the commander of the Island.

They departed, therefore, in company with Captain Phelps of the Benton, for the De Soto, which had brought them up, and still lay half a mile astern, and returned a little after midnight to give us the almost unnecessary intelligence that they had accepted the flag officer's terms—an unconditional surrender.

In regard to the shore batteries, they stated they could say nothing, as they had no command over that part of the fortifications, and were ignorant of the officer in charge of the forces there.

From the fact of the proposition of surrender coming through two Lieutenants, it was believed that the greater part of the Rebel forces, with the chief officers, had already made their exodus—a surmise that subsequent circumstances proved entirely correct.

At daylight a number of white flags were seen flying from the Island, and no person could be discovered along the Kentucky and Tennessee shore.

The gunboats St. Louis and Mound City, and one or two of the transports, went down about seven in the morning; and, soon after, a tug from the Benton steamed over to the shore batteries with Captain Phelps of the flagship, one or two other officers, and myself.

On the Island there were about three hundred prisoners, mostly Tennesseeans—the command of Captain Humes, who had surrendered to Commodore Foote.

They were all artillerists, and their officers generally quite young men.

I had several hours' conversation with the captives, and from them learned the sentiments they held in regard to the War. They were all bitterly opposed to their principal commanders; said they had had different leaders every day or two; and that they had been most unexpectedly deserted by the forces on the main land.

The privates universally expressed themselves weary and disgusted with the War; and gave it as their opinion that the Rebellion was well-nigh crushed; that the South could not carry it on but a month or two longer, and that it must sink beneath its own weight.

How much they were mistaken!

They said if they were released, they would not serve in the ranks again; that they had been cruelly deceived by their leaders, and that the Rebellion had been undertaken by a few demagogues and unprincipled parties for the purpose of self-aggrandizement.

They appeared extremely well satisfied with their new position, and were the most cheerful prisoners I remember to have seen.

The privates were healthful and good-looking men, for the most part, and possessed of more than the average degree of intelligence found among the common people of the South. They were comfortably though poorly clad, and said they had an abundance of food, but had not received a dollar in payment for their services during the time—a period of some six months—that had expired since their enlistment.

The officers generally held—at least expressed—very

different opinions; and, though cautious, manifested an earnest attachment to the cause of the Rebellion, and declared they were determined to adhere to it while there was the least hope of success.

They acknowledged they did not believe the stories, so extensively circulated by the Southern newspapers—that the North designed to abolitionize the Slave States (the North had no such intentions then), or plunder their homes; or ravish their wives and sisters; or that the Yankees were a horde of barbarians and blood-thirsty ruffians; or any of the absurd twaddle the editors published, but knew to be utterly false.

All such statements, the officers confessed, were designed to influence the common people, and render them devoted to the cause they had espoused.

The officers furthermore remarked that the South had long been jealous of the steadily augmenting power of the North, and believed that the latter was encroaching upon the Slave States, and was likely to extinguish the peculiar institution by restricting it to certain limits, which must insure its ultimate destruction.

The election of a sectional candidate to the Presidency had rendered the South universally restless; for they regarded it as the inception of an open contest against Slavery, and that they could not remain in the Union without danger to their servile property.

They had grown up with and among slaves, and while they did not ask the North to admire Slavery, they claimed for themselves certain rights under the Constitution, which they thought they could not retain if they waited until the expiration of Lincoln's term of office.

They were attached to Slavery on account of the benefits they believed it conferred, both on the black and white race; and they were convinced the great agricultural interests of their section could not be served without compulsory labor.

They held the opinion that there was an irrepressible conflict between the Free and Slave States, as had been first announced by William H. Seward, and that the disposition of the North to interfere with the local institutions of the South, would necessarily result in war; and that for this reason they desired a separation.

They greatly desired peace; but the present struggle had destroyed all hope of it, and had rendered the restoration of the Union an absolute impossibility.

Of course, such arguments, if they deserved the name, are old and threadbare, and have been refuted again and again; and I only give them as specimens of the sentiments and conversation of the Rebel officers at that time.

* * * *

At one of the encampments on the Tennessee River, about twenty well-dressed and quite comely women were discovered as sole occupants of the place.

They said they were friends of the officers, who had left their baggage in their charge until they met again.

The women were from Memphis, and it required no very penetrating optics to determine their position and calling. They belonged, of course, to the Lorette school, and had endeavored, doubtless, to assuage the severity of the campaign by the tenderness of their devotion and the warmth of their attachment.

Some of them were quite pretty and very young, and

appeared to regard the surrender of the Island and the flight of their lovers as a pleasant jest; and seemed to enjoy it vastly.

Quite cosmopolitan in character, they were unquestionably as willing to extend their gentle favors to the National officers as to their late Rebel protectors; knowing that Love makes friends of enemies, and by the alkahest of its subtile chemistry melts all distinctions in a common crucible.

* * * *

A day or two after the surrender of the Island proper, General Pope followed and captured about twenty-six hundred of the retreating Rebels that had been doing duty at the shore batteries, which furnished the main strength of the position.

Pope had crossed the river, and, by a skillful disposition of the two gunboats and his forces, so completely cut off the insurgents, with the assistance of the high waters on the shore opposite New Madrid, that they surrendered at discretion, without the loss of a single life on our side by the casualties of battle.

CHAPTER XXI.

SHILOH.

Desperate Determination of the South.—Confidence of the Enemy.—Cause of the Early Action.—The First Day's Fighting.—Fearful Struggle.—Intensity of the Excitement.—Recklessness of Life.—Panic-stricken Regiments.—Arrival of General Buell.—The Second Day's Fighting.—Defeat of the Foe.

THE Union forces, on the clear, pleasant, balmy Saturday night of April 5, 1862, when they sought their tents to rest, had little thought the quiet of the beautiful Sabbath would be marred by the roar of cannon, the rattle of musketry, the hoarse battle-cry, the clash of resounding arms.

They were taken at disadvantage; but they soon rallied, and waged the fierce battle as if they had been looking for its coming at the very hour.

It was notorious among the enemy, that General Buell was marching rapidly to join his force with that of General Grant. He had been anxiously expected for several days; and to drive back and inflict a heavy and fatal blow upon Grant, before his allies could come to his assistance, was the best of policy, if not a military necessity.

The Rebels numbered over one hundred and twenty thousand of their choicest troops. Kentucky, Tennessee, Arkansas, Mississippi, Alabama, Louisiana, and Texas had sent their best soldiers to fight the decisive battle; and one hundred and sixty-two regiments had gone forth from the South to annihilate the "barbarous Yankees," and establish for Secession a prestige and glory that future time should not destroy or dim.

No one who had not traveled, during 1862, in the Slave States, could have any idea of how the South moved Heaven and Earth to render a great victory on the Tennessee absolutely certain. The South contributed her strongest weapons and her best men to the purpose.

Every disloyal community had been drafted. No person capable of bearing arms was permitted to remain at home.

Old and young alike shouldered their musket, or rifle, or shot-gun, and departed for the scene of action.

The most inflammatory appeals were made. When appeals failed, threats were used; and when threats were insufficient, violence was employed.

Every Southern woman exercised her influence in the cause of the Rebellion; bade her husband, brother, father, lover, friend, make another struggle for his fireside and country, and victory would reward his efforts.

The power of the North would be broken; the foreign hirelings of the tyrant Lincoln would be expelled forever from the "sacred soil," and future generations would rise and call him blessed who flew to his country's succor in the hour of her extremest need.

The best of Southern Generals were summoned from every quarter to conduct the great battles, to lend their counsels, and employ their strong arms in the service of Secessia, and make a last and desperate effort for the independence of the "Confederacy."

Manassas was evacuated that the best soldiers on the

Potomac might contribute to the army on the Tennessee.

Pensacola was abandoned that the experienced artillerists of the South might depart for Corinth.

Island No. 10 was weakened that the regiments there assembled might give their combined strength to the forlorn hope.

A mighty army had taken its stand on the shores of a river which was to be made immortal by the overthrow of the North and the triumphant success of the South.

Beauregard, and Johnston, and Polk, and Bragg, and Jackson, and Breckinridge, had united in their counsels, and taken great oaths to do or die in the cause of Slavery, and for the extinction of Freedom in the model Republic.

When the battle was forced upon us, on Sunday, April 6, 1862, the enemy very far outnumbered us, and was confident of success. He had been assured he could not be defeated. He had confidence in his leaders, and he had sworn, as Hannibal had sworn in his early youth, to conquer or to die—a rhetorical phrase very popular in the South, and most frequently employed when death seems at the greatest distance.

The engagement was brought on by a body of the Union infantry who were ordered to capture a troop of some three hundred Rebel cavalry, who had for several days greatly harassed our army.

The cavalry was supposed to be at a certain point beyond our lines, and the infantry marched on expecting to surprise them, but were surprised, as was General

Grant's entire command, who had no idea of a general engagement.

Beauregard had had for two weeks, it is said, a number of spies in our camp, and was as fully informed of our plans, opinions, and expectations as if he had been the confidential friend and adviser of the Commander-in-Chief. He had employed the cavalry as a decoy, and was aware our army was entirely unprepared for an engagement.

In that condition, at that most critical and unfortunate hour, the great body of the Confederate army had advanced within range, and suddenly opened a terrible fire of musketry upon General Prentiss's Division, throwing the left wing into great confusion; at the same time pouring into our encampment a perfect storm of canister, grape, and shell, causing terrible destruction.

For some minutes much disorder prevailed, and the officers feared at first that a panic would seize the soldiers; but the coolness and bravery of the principal commanders prevented such a disaster.

A line of battle was speedily formed, amid the shower of shot and the deafening roar of Rebel artillery, and a stout resistance made.

At that juncture, the fire of the Rebels for a few moments diminished, but was soon reopened as fiercely as ever upon the left and center of General Sherman's division, which was driven back with great loss, exposing our extreme left, under General McClernand, to its destructive sweep.

After ten minutes, our whole army was formed in line, and our brave soldiers, extending three miles, began to return the fire of the foe with steady and continuous volleys of musketry, sending many a Rebel, who had expected another Manassas, to his eternal rest.

During a period of four hours the deadly strife continued; the enemy displaying a degree of obstinate courage he had never before shown; and fighting with a desperate determination that compelled our forces to recede gradually before him.

The generalship on the part of the "Confederates" was consummate—far exceeding ours, and deserving, from a military point of view, of the highest admiration.

When we attacked a certain point, we met with resistance from a new quarter; when we went to the right, we were attacked from the left; when we advanced to the center, a deadly fire was opened on us from the right; and so we were perpetually deceived by the skill and strategy of our foes.

Constant efforts were made to flank our regiments, and in many instances the Rebels narrowly escaped success; so much so was this the case, that we were again and again put upon the defensive, when the offensive was the need of the hour.

By that time the enemy had occupied a large portion of the ground on which we had been encamped when the action began; and we were still falling back before the "Confederates," who seemed to be fighting with more and more determination, and who were doubtless cheered and encouraged by their early success.

The Union center evinced unmistakable symptoms of giving way, for it was sorely pressed, and the fortunes of the day appeared to be against us, when General Hurlbut's division was ordered to its support. The division moved in good time, and did good service.

Hotter and hotter grew the contest; fiercer and fiercer the struggle.

Each man fought as if success or defeat depended on his own right arm; and charge after charge was made on the Rebels to regain the ground we had lost.

They stood firm as a rock; and though our artillery often swept down their ranks, and left fearful gaps in their columns, they manifested no trepidation, nor did they waver for a moment.

The living supplied the place of the dead. The musket that had fallen from a lifeless hand was seized at once, and the horrid strife swept on as before. The force of the enemy appeared increasing, and where the greatest havoc was made, there the strongest opposition was shown.

Hand-to-hand contests were innumerable. Every struggle was for life.

Quarter was asked on neither side, and the ground drank up the blood of hundreds of brave fellows every hour.

Men lost their semblance of humanity, and the spirit of the demon shone in their faces.

There was but one desire, and that was to destroy.

There was little shouting. The warriors were too much in earnest. They set their teeth firm, and strained their every nerve to its utmost tension.

Death lost all its terrors, and men seemed to feast upon the sight of blood.

The light of the sun was obscured by the clouds of sulphurous smoke, and the ground became moist and slippery with human gore.

The atmosphere trembled with the shock of the armies, and the earth shook with the tramp of the thousands and tens of thousands of warring foes.

The balance of victory ever varied. It now inclined to this side, and now to that. Here the Unionists gained an advantage; there the "Confederates."

Advance was followed by retreat; success by repulse.

At this point we drove the enemy back, but were driven back in return. Success was always shifting, but never settled.

Hope and fear, joy and sorrow, seized the soul by turns, and every hour held a month of emotions.

All consciousness of time ceased; all thought of the Future, all recollection of the Past. Every thing was absorbed in the sanguinary Present, and external Nature assumed the hue of blood.

Men glared at each other as at wild beasts; and, when a shell burst with fatal effect among a crowd of the advancing foe, and arms, legs, and heads were torn off, a grim smile of pleasure lighted up the smoke-begrimed faces of the transformed beings who witnessed the catastrophe.

Soldiers were wounded and knew it not, so intense was their excitement, and often a mortal hurt was announced to the victim only by the cessation of vitality.

Men with knitted brows and flushed cheeks fought madly over ridges, along ravines, and up steep ascents, with blood and perspiration streaming down their faces.

Men with shattered fingers changed their muskets to

their left hands, and still fired their pieces as best they could.

Everywhere was mad excitement; everywhere was horror. Commanders galloped wildly to the front of their regiments, and cheered them on, using their sabers on each and every foe, and urging their spirited steeds where ever the troops were falling back, careless of their own life, as if they had a million souls to spare.

Captains, majors, colonels, and generals fought like private soldiers, and it was not uncommon to see a field-officer firing a musket or charging with his revolver upon the advancing foe.

There was no pause in the battle. The roar of the strife was ever heard. The artillery bellowed and thundered, and the dreadful echoes went sweeping down the river, and the paths were filled with the dying and the dead.

The sound was deafening, the tumult indescribable.

No life was worth a farthing; for he who lifted his musket this moment fell the next, a stiffened corpse.

Yonder a fresh regiment rushed bravely forward, and ere they had gone twenty yards, a charge of grape sent the foremost men bleeding to the earth.

Whole heaps of corpses lay upon the murmuring ground, and fixed eyes stared at the surrounding strife, with the awful stare of death.

Wild mockery! dreadful vision! But who cared?

Death was not to be thought of, but to be met with indifference, come when it might.

Death was in the air, and bloomed like a poison-plant on every foot of soil.

During Sunday afternoon, eleven or twelve of the Union regiments, after fighting bravely for two hours, were thrown into disorder by a number of shells which burst above and around them; and at the same moment a Rebel battery opened upon them, at a distance of half a mile, with terrible devastation.

They could not endure the murderous fire. They turned and fled, and several of their officers endeavored in vain to rally them. They were utterly panic-stricken at first, and they would have run if the Infernal Pit had opened before their hurrying feet.

No appeal, no censure, affected them. Many threw away their arms, and sped as a country school-boy, who thinks he has seen a ghost in the village church-yard.

A number of flying soldiers, having recovered from their alarm and regained their pride, returned to their posts, fighting more bravely than before, to wipe out the stain; but the greater part ran beyond the reach of the human voice, even crossing the river and going to Savannah.

As the sun was sinking towards the west, General Buell's column, so anxiously expected, so needful in the great emergency, appeared on the opposite side of the river, and the enemy redoubled his efforts to insure our defeat; knowing that on the morrow our numbers would nearly equal his own; and that he must put the last remnant of strength into the contest.

The Rebels did so. They summoned a large portion of their reserve, and fell with unexampled fury upon our ranks, shouting like madmen, and striving in every possible way to extend the panic with which the unfortunate twelve regiments had been seized.

Every one of their cannons seemed at play; every musket performing its natural office. The resources of their generals were exhausted. They told their troops the condition of affairs; that that was the golden opportunity; that all depended upon winning a victory before the darkness should compel a suspension of hostilities.

The Rebels swept like an avalanche upon the loyal troops, and the shock had its effect.

Our soldiers wavered, for they were nearly exhausted with the long, hard fight, and the enemy's fresh forces gave them the advantage.

Here was a crisis, and General Grant rode along the whole line, amid a storm of balls, and encouraged the men, and assured them that if they held out until the next morning, Buell, with his thousands, would have crossed the river.

His brief remarks added courage to many a faint heart, and strength to many a tired arm; and our ranks fought with a desperate and invincible spirit.

Still they could hardly cope with the overpowering force of the Rebels, until Colonel Webster, chief of General Grant's staff, planted several batteries, and brought them to bear directly upon the enemy's right; and about the same time, the gunboats Lexington and Taylor, so near were the contending armies to the bank, opened a heavy fire upon the advancing Rebels.

The foe endeavored heroically to endure that terrible double fire; but his columns had not the fortitude to stand and be mowed down by hundreds. They began to waver and to break.

Beauregard and Johnston attempted to hold their troops in position, and they exposed themselves most recklessly to prevent them from falling back, but to no purpose. Every discharge of the batteries, every roar of death from the gunboats, sent the Rebel regiments reeling to the grave; and in less than half an hour they moved backward, leaving us in possession of all the ground we had occupied in the morning.

In this part of the action, General Albert Sydney Johnston fell, and Beauregard was very slightly wounded in the left arm.

* * * *

During the night, General Nelson's division of Buell's army reached the battle-field, and early in the morning the engagement was renewed, Nelson occupying the left, and General Wallace the right.

Nelson and Wallace opened upon the enemy with a heavy fire, and caused him to fall back. For several hours the victory seemed to be ours; but about half-past ten o'clock the Rebels, who must have been re-enforced, made a series of gallant charges, and caused our troops to retire for a quarter of a mile, pouring most fearful volleys of musketry into our ranks.

Again the prospect looked dark, and thousands of hearts felt alarmed, not for themselves, but for the fortunes of the great battle on which so much depended—perhaps the salvation of the Republic, and the happiness of unborn generations.

General Buell had crossed the river below the point

where Nelson had, and at this juncture came up with fresh troops, and flanked the enemy, and captured a number of pieces of artillery.

The Rebels here made a terrible charge to recover their loss, but they were unsuccessful.

They wavered and were driven back—rallied, and made a final attempt, but were repulsed; Buell's forces meeting and engaging them in a splendid manner.

Our army saw their advantage, and followed it up in magnificent style; and from that hour the Rebels seemed to have lost faith in themselves.

They could not be rallied, though their commanders hallooed themselves hoarse. They could not keep their ground, and they slowly retired, with their faces still to the Unionists, and fighting, though somewhat languidly.

Their hope and energy appeared to diminish steadily, and they soon gave evidence of demoralization, and, before six o'clock in the evening, retreated with celerity, pursued towards Corinth by six thousand of our cavalry.

CHAPTER XXII.

OFF FORT PILLOW.

Ravages of the Musquitos.—Their Secession Proclivities.—Battles between the Insects and Correspondents.—Anecdote of General Pope.—Discovery of an unexpected Official.

THE countless musquitos in the vicinity of Fort Pillow, during the month of April, 1862, must have had strong Secession sympathies; they certainly were bitter enemies of the Nationalists, and phlebotomized them without mercy. They never were so numerous and venomous before at that season of the year, in that latitude, and they bled our soldiers and sailors as perseveringly as did ever Dr. Sangrado his system-murdered patients.

Those annoying insects were always vigilant, and had the honor of extracting the earliest sanguinary fluid during the bombardment.

They had no fear of gunboats or mortars, artillery or bayonets. They recognized no distinction in rank, attacking Commodores and Captains, Bohemians and Brigadiers alike.

One hundred did I slay, even while writing half a dozen lines; and yet there were thousands to supply their places. They seemed as anxious to die as the Rebels pretend to be.

The difference between them was, they did die, and

the Rebels did not—when they could help it. Mortifying reflection to vain-glorious Man! Musquitos are braver than the three hundred devoted Lacedæmonians who fought and fell beneath the shade of Xerxes' arrows.

Sleep was often an impossibility, on the Fleet or in camp; and a number of the Bohemians rose one morning with their optics so nearly closed, from the attack of the musquitos, that the poor fellows would have been entirely excusable if they had taken what, in bar-room parlance, is classically called, an eye-opener.

Confound the musquitos! I used to exclaim every minute. They were the pests of the South, and of summer, and, like the Thane of Cawdor, did murder sleep!

Every thing was very dull about Pillow the first two or three weeks, with the exception of the constant battles between the Bohemians and the musquitos; the latter having declared unrelenting and ceaseless war against the knights of the pen.

The strife went on without intermission, day and night; the musquitos relieving each other punctually, and mounting guard every five seconds.

We had no bars on the fleet (and none in the Mississippi, for the matter of that), and we were therefore victims to the remorseless cruelty of the venomous insects at all times and in all places.

The Correspondents, as I have said, often arose in the morning with their visuals so swelled, from the bites of the winged pests, that they looked as if they had been taking a few first lessons in the "noble and manly art of self-defense," from the Tipton Slasher or the Benicia Boy.

I pitied the poor fellows, but the fact that my own sufferings were even greater than theirs, prevented that complete exercise of commiseration which an intact epidermis would have insured.

The musquitos in that vicinity must have been of the true Secession order, being opposed—as the Richmond papers used to be—to reading and writing; believing it conducive to error and disobedience.

We never took up a book or commenced any manuscript but the musquitos attacked us in force, and showed the most desperate determination to drive us from our labor or our lore.

The reason of this was, I conjecture, that the musquitos hated writing because they themselves could not write, and they therefore made their mark—most effectually, too, as my crimson-spotted hands and face fully and convincingly and painfully attested.

* * * *

I heard, while at Pillow, an anecdote of General Pope—an officer of ability, but sometimes a very unpleasant man, with a pompous and hectoring manner—which will bear repetition. While at his head-quarters, the General was approached by a rather small, plain-looking, and entirely unassuming man, in citizen's attire, with the question: "Are you General Pope, sir?"

"That is my name," was the answer, in rather a repelling tone.

"I would like to see you, then, on a matter of business."

"Call on my Adjutant, sir. He will arrange any business you may have."

"But I wish to have a personal conversation with you."

"See my Adjutant," in an authoritative voice.

"But—"

"Did I not tell you to see my Adjutant? Trouble me no more, sir;" and Pope was about walking away.

"My name is Scott, General," quietly remarked the small, plain man.

"Confound you! What do I care," thundered Pope, in a rising passion, "if your name is Scott, or Jones, or Jenkins, or Snooks, for the matter of that? See my Adjutant, I tell you, fellow! Leave my presence!"

"I am," continued the quiet man, in his quiet way, "the Assistant Secretary of War, and—"

What a revolution those simple words made in the General's appearance and manner!

His angry, haughty, domineering air was dispelled in a moment, and a flush of confusion passed over his altered face.

"I beg your pardon, Mr. Scott, I had no idea whom I was addressing. Pray be seated; I shall be happy to grant you an interview at any time."

Possibly a very close observer might have seen a faint, half-contemptuous smile on the Secretary's lips; though he said nothing, but began to unfold his business without comment.

After that unique interview, Pope and the Assistant Secretary were very frequently together, and I venture to say the latter had no reason subsequently to complain of the General's rudeness.

CHAPTER XXIII.

LIFE ON THE FLOTILLA.

A Profane Captain.—Piety of Commodore Foote.—Interruption of Religious Service.—Easter Sunday on the Flag-ship.—Horrible Persecutions of Unionists in Tennessee and Arkansas.—A Loyal Man Crucified.—Cold-Blooded Murders in the South.

DIVINE Service was held upon the Flotilla, off Fort Pillow, every Sabbath, and even some of the transports observed the day, though after a rather secular fashion.

An old steamboat Captain, for many years engaged in the Cincinnati and Southern trade, was in the habit of going about the vessel every morning, and saying to his men: "D—— your sinful souls, I want you to come to prayers to-day, by ——;" and, after services, adding to delinquents: "Why the —— and —— weren't you on hand to-day to hear the Bible read? You'll go to —— surely, and, —— you, you ought to, too, by ——."

It is deeply to be regretted that that man's external piety did not improve his mode of exhortation; but this was one of the countless instances in which a time-honored custom was observed after the spirit that might have made it sacred had departed.

Quite different from the profane steamboat Captain was Commodore Foote, who seemed to regard the observation of Sunday, when it was at all possible, as quite essential to the discipline of his officers and men.

He read the Scriptures regularly and punctually on the first day of every week, and summoned the entire crew of the Benton to his religious lectures.

Most of the sailors were addicted to falling asleep, and frequently snored so loud as to disturb the solemnity of the occasion. The Commodore took no notice of their drowsiness, believing, perhaps, with some of the theological metaphysicians, that when rapt in slumber they could commit no sin.

It certainly is a virtue of many religious exercises, that, if they do not convince, they cause sleep, and thus give rest to the body, though they furnish no consolation to the soul. Goldsmith's familiar line might, I am sorry to say, often be so travestied as to read with truth :

> And those who went to pray remained to sleep.

The Commodore was not so painfully pious as to allow Sunday to interfere with the obligations of his secular position.

While reading, at Island No. 10, this extract from the Epistle of Paul to the Ephesians :

"Blessed be the God and Father of our Lord Jesus Christ, who hath blessed us with all spiritual blessings in heavenly places in Christ. According as He hath chosen us in Him before the foundation of the world, that we should be holy, and without blame before Him in love ; having predestinated us unto the adoption of children by Jesus Christ."

At this moment the officer of the deck reported a suspicious craft coming round the head of the Island, whereupon the Commodore ordered the stern guns to be run out, and closed the Sacred Volume and the service at once, remarking that the reading would be continued on a more auspicious occasion.

* * * *

Each Sunday the Commodore read from the sixty-fourth Psalm, in a deeply impressive manner:

"They encourage themselves in an evil matter: they commune of laying snares privily; they say, Who shall see them?

"They search out iniquities; they accomplish a diligent search: both the inward thought of every one of them, and the heart, is deep.

"But God shall shoot at them with an arrow; suddenly shall they be wounded."

Doubtless the Commodore referred to the Rebels; but, as if not satisfied with that apt quotation, he read these even more appropriate lines:

"They are all gone out of the way, they are together become unprofitable; there is none that doeth good, no, not one.

"Their throat is an open sepulchre; with their tongues they have used deceit; the poison of asps is under their lips: whose mouth is full of cursing and bitterness:

"Their feet are swift to shed blood:

"Destruction and misery are in their ways: And the way of peace have they not known: there is no fear of God before their eyes."

So pertinent were these quotations that the sailors did not sleep, or even nod, during the reading, which was impressive and eloquent, from the earnest voice, the serene face, and the sincere manner of the gallant Commodore, who was, in the best sense, a gentleman and a true Christian.

* * * *

Several of us went up the river, toward the latter part of April, in a skiff, a short distance, to the half-submerged house of a Union family named Armstrong, residing on the Tennessee shore. They were from Ohio, but had lived in Lauderdale County for four or five years, and were far more intelligent and civilized than the class that usually vegetates along the banks of the Mississippi from Cairo to Vicksburg.

We had a long conversation with the family, who had had an excellent opportunity to witness the progress of the Rebellion in Tennessee, and they gave a fearful account of the outrages that had been practiced in the name of the Rebel Government.

Immediately after the State was declared, in spite of the expressed opposition of the people, out of the Union, armed bands of marauders and outlaws, generally from Shelby County, began to abuse and rob the citizens of Western Tennessee.

They impressed all the men they could find into the Rebel service, upon pain of death; and the family assured me a number of loyal citizens were hanged for no other reason than for their attachment to the Union.

Mrs. Armstrong says she knew six men who were executed; and that in one instance a poor fellow who had been coerced into the Secession army, and had twice deserted, was captured, carried off in the night, and actually crucified; spikes being driven through his hands and feet; thus fastening him to a tree, and leaving him to a lingering and horrible death.

The unfortunate victim was gagged, that his cries might not call any one to his assistance or relief; and nearly a week had elapsed before he was discovered. He was still alive, but hunger, exposure, and pain had so exhausted him, that, though removed to the house of a neighbor, and carefully nursed, he died the second day after his release.

In addition to that, men suspected of disaffection were assassinated by outlaws so disguised as to be irrecognizable; and it was quite common for Unionists to be called up at the dead hour of night, and shot when they went to the window or door to determine the nature of the summons.

In Arkansas, too, in Mississippi, Crittenden, and other river counties, robbery, tarring and feathering, assassinations, and hanging were among the favorite amusements of the inhabitants of that highly enlightened State.

* * * *

The extent of the outrages perpetrated in Secessia against Union men will never be known, and hundreds of persons have mysteriously disappeared whose fate will never be explained, but who were doubtlessly removed through violent means by the advocates of the Rebellion.

CHAPTER XXIV.

FEATURES OF SECESSIA.

Melancholy Suicide of a Slave.—Triumph of the American Eagle.—Reminiscence of John A. Murrell—His Decease a Loss to the Secession Cause.

WHILE lying off Fort Pillow, a Union man, who had been driven from Memphis some months before, told me of a sad tragedy that had occurred in the city while he was there. A finely formed and rather intelligent mulatto had been taken to Memphis from Hardaman County, having been torn, against his most urgent entreaties and earnest prayers, from his family, to be sold to some Louisiana or Texas planter. The poor fellow, who seemed so overcome with grief as to be unconscious of externals, was placed upon the block, and knocked down to a cotton planter residing near Galveston.

After the sale had been made, and the papers signed, the mulatto seemed, for the first time, to fully realize his situation. Having been ordered to follow his new master, he walked quietly along until he was separated from the crowd, when he suddenly drew a pistol, concealed about his person, and blew out his brains.

The slave could not endure the idea of separation from his family, and preferred death to eternal divorce. No one was shocked; no one pitied him, or cared for the cause of the suicide. He was only a "nigger;" but to the new owner he had represented so much money, and therefore the planter was very mad, and swore excessively over the mutilated corpse of the slave.

*   *   *   *

An incident occurred on the transport John H. Dickey, while I was on the Fleet, which would indicate that the American Eagle—at least one of the family—understands the importance of the position assigned him in this country as the symbol of Liberty and Independence.

The clerk of the boat had been presented with an eagle, and kept him in the engine-room below, tied to a stanchion with a strong cord.

Soon after the bird was placed there, a coop full of chickens, among them three game-cocks, was captured on a deserted farm on the Arkansas shore, and removed to the locality, and the roosters given the freedom of the deck.

The Secession cocks immediately began to strut about in much the same style as the vulgar Gascons assuming to represent the chivalry of the South, and crowed loudly and frequently, greatly to the disgust of the eagle, which eyed them very closely, and was evidently attempting to exercise his patience to the fullest possible extent.

The cocks crowed louder and louder, and walked by the bird as if they regarded him as an inferior.

The eagle began to lose his temper, and, eying the feathery blusterers more and more keenly, commenced to peck at his hempen fetters in an excited manner.

The roosters still crowed and strutted, and strutted and crowed; and while they were at the hight of their pomposity, the eagle, which had released himself, flew at them, and in less than a minute three headless roosters lay bleeding amid a quantity of feathers.

The eagle had resented the indignity to himself, and the insult offered him as a representative of the Nation, and had taught the insolent Rebel cocks the lesson the grand army of the North is daily teaching to Secessia.

The turn of the Gallic cock may come next. Let him beware!

* * * *

During my sojourn near Fort Pillow, I went several times over to Arkansas, in the vicinity of Osceola, noted as the place where the first Rebel flag was raised in the State.

When we remember that Mississippi County, of which Osceola is the capital, was part of the theater of John A. Murrell's operations, we cannot but acknowledge a singular aptness in the elevation there of the symbol of treason.

No doubt the people of the State missed him greatly, and believed he died before his time. He should have lived to the days of the Jeff. Davis conspiracy, to receive the honors of Secessia for his past deeds, and encouragement for the continuation of his career. He was fitted by nature, education, habits, and association for a Secessionist, and had he not been one of the prominent Rebel generals, he would have been at least a member of the Cabinet at Richmond.

He could steal, burn, and murder as well as the best of them; and in such threefold capacity lie the power and prestige of the cause he would have been proud to advocate, and on which even he might have shed at least a ray of damning glory.

CHAPTER XXV.

MAYING IN ARKANSAS.

A Beautiful Day.—Prodigality of Nature.—Assault of Gnats and Sand-Flies.—Ridiculous Adventures.—An Altered Physiognomy.—Saturnine Reflections.—A New Jeremiad.

THE 1st of May was bright, balmy, and beautiful, but so very dull on the Flotilla, that another Correspondent and myself concluded to make a short excursion into the region of Arkansas lying opposite Fort Pillow, by way of celebrating the occasion.

The very idea of going Maying, as the school-girls style it, in the Patagonia of America, was ludicrously absurd; and for that reason we selected it as the field of our vernal recreation.

The day, as I have said, was beautiful, and the violets of the heavens bloomed in their softest blueness, while the gentle zephyrs crossed the Mississippi on wings of balm. The birds sang more sweetly than was their wont to the morning sunbeams; and the sunbeams bathed their leafy homes in glory.

Delicious dreams were in the fragrant atmosphere, and a spiritual voluptuousness sighed through the love-whispering trees.

All that was very generous in Nature; but so much æsthetic wealth was entirely lost on Arkansas, where Art is regarded as an Abolition innovation, and the Ideal supposed to mean an unfair game of draw-poker.

What a sad waste, thought we, of Beauty, when we saw the blue arch bending in charmfulness over the swamps of the benighted State, and heard the choristers of the groves chanting to the scattered woods and the unsightly shore!

We crossed the river in a skiff, exhausting ourselves and blistering our unhardened hands, and were soon a short distance below Osceola, looking round for a spot of dry land whereon to recline, and wondering what Nature designed when she created Arkansas, which I have always regarded as a mistake.

We found, after a long and diligent search, and no little wading, a spot of green large enough for two graves, and looking as if they were such.

A few sickly violets grew among the tufts of grass, and the poor little flowers looked up to us timidly and shrinkingly, as if they were trying to apologize, but could find no excuse, for blooming in such a place.

Tiny blue-eyed tremblers! We plucked them from their stems, and knew it would be happiness for them to die somewhere else. They exhaled their gratitude in sweetness, and we said: "As flowers were found on Nero's tomb, so are there violets even in Arkansas."

Not a minute had we reclined our fatigued forms before the sand-flies and gnats assailed us in force; and before we could effect our escape, we looked as if we had just recovered from an attack of the small-pox.

One of my optics was closed, and my companion's lips had assumed the proportions of a full-blooded African's.

The winged pests covered us in swarms, and for five minutes our motions resembled the wild movements of dancing Dervises. Indeed, I doubt if the Dervises ever danced as we did.

With our swinging limbs and ceaseless gyrations, we must have seemed like human windmills, turning to every point of the compass at the same time.

We leaped ourselves out of our boots and hats and coats; and, in the midst of his bewilderment, I found my associate endeavoring to put on a cotton-wood tree, and myself trying to draw a large swamp over my burning feet, and cover my head with a mud-bank.

After a while, we began to grow used to it; but, at the same time, seriously arrived at the conclusion, that, however interesting such excursions might be to the natives, they were not altogether fascinating to civilized beings.

So we went off precipitately through marshes and morasses, breathing gnats and sand-flies as if they had all our lives composed our natural atmosphere; trying to wipe off the blood that had started from our faces with our boots, and to cover our pedal extremities with our handkerchiefs.

While we were struggling along like men under the pressure of forty cocktails, we heard a sharp rattle, and looking before us with what eyes the gnats had left us, we saw two huge snakes coiled, and ready to spring.

Rattlesnakes had no terrors for us then. We were desperate.

At that moment I believe I would have walked into the roaring mouths of a battery, or even up to the matrimonial altar, without shrinking.

We regarded rattlesnakes as symbols of Secession, and we knew the sandflies and gnats were of the Rebel tribe. So we attacked the venomous serpents with our boots; beating to the right and left, quite indifferent whether we struck them, or they struck us.

We had leather pyrotechnics, boot Catherine wheels, for a short time, when the hateful rattling ceased, and we saw the snakes were dead.

We thought we had killed them; but I know now the flies and gnats had swarmed down their throats and strangled them.

Little inclination had we to investigate the matter, but rushed on through the swamps, and at last reached a skiff—whether ours or not was a question of indifference—and, leaping into it, rowed over the river again.

After we had reached the Tennessee shore, we fell into the back water, and ultimately got on board the Flotilla, with one boot between us, no hats, physiognomies that would have set Lavater mad to contemplate, and bearing a close resemblance to the horribly tattooed faces so greatly in favor with the New Zealanders.

I looked into the glass—a thing I rarely do, for I hate repulsive spectacles—and, as far as my defective eyesight could determine, I thought I discovered a striking resemblance between myself and the Egyptian Sphynx, and that I appeared as if I might be a brother of the grotesque figure with four heads, by which the Brahmins sometimes represent their chief deity.

However hideous, I looked no worse than I felt, and I immediately celebrated my Maying in Arkansas by going into full mourning of wet towels and bread-and-milk poultices, and was afterwards mistaken by some intimate acquaintances for an Ojibeway Indian, or the Calvinistic

Devil, escaped from the diseased mind of a believer in the moral effect of eternal brimstone.

I have seen Arkansas since that occasion; but I cannot say I regard it as fondly as Leander did the shores of Abydos, or Manfred the vision of Astarte.

I marvel much whether Job would not have blasphemed had he ever gone to Mississippi county on a May excursion. To be afflicted with boils is bad enough; but to be besieged by Arkansas gnats is absolutely beyond endurance; and I know the man of Uz could not and would not have borne it stoically.

Talk of straining at gnats. Who would not strain at them in my case? Rather than not do so, I would take a contract to swallow all the camels—including the concomitants of caravans—that ever crossed the Arabian Desert.

In the midst of my pain and poultices, I cried out, after the manner of the son of Hilkiah:

O that I had a deadly enemy, and I were a million of gnats, such as are found in Arkansas!

O that Arkansas hung by one silken strand over the abyss of Tophet, and I stood near with a glistening cheese-knife!

O that I were a Rebel, that I might hang myself for the good of my country, and the benefit of my example to my fellow-traitors!

O that I were a Confederate note! Then no one would touch me—not even a gnat.

O that I were Jeff. Davis or Wigfall! Then I would be deader than the Ptolemies. O that I were the Rebellion! Then I'd be a thing of the past.

CHAPTER XXVI.

COMMODORE FOOTE'S FAREWELL.

Impressive Scene on the Flag-Ship.—Address of the Commodore.—Emotion of the Sailors.—Exciting Tug-Chase.

During the siege of Fort Pillow, the condition of Commodore A. H. Foote's health became such that he was compelled to ask to be relieved, and toward the latter part of April, 1862, he was superseded by Captain Davis, of the Navy. The Commodore had for several months been very feeble, and was often unable to go on deck for weeks at a time.

When the day was appointed for the Commodore's departure there was quite a stir in the Fleet, and, as he was greatly beloved, his fellow-officers and the sailors generally deeply regretted the loss of their gallant commander.

When the hour came for his going up the river, the deck of the Benton was crowded ; and as the Flag-officer appeared, supported by Captain Phelps, he was greeted with tremendous huzzas. Old tars swung their hats, and not a few of their eyes moistened when they looked, as they supposed, upon the brave old Commodore for the last time, as indeed they did.

The Flag-officer paused for a few moments, and, removing his cap, gave those near him to understand he would address them.

The Commodore said he had asked to be relieved because he knew he could not fill his office in his existing condition of health. He was willing to sacrifice himself for his country, but he knew he would be injuring the cause by retaining his position any longer.

He had been growing feebler and feebler every day, and his physician had often told him he could not improve while exposed to the excitements of the service and confined to the Flag-ship. He complimented the officers and crew of the Benton in the highest manner. He had always found them faithful, brave, and true, and had fondly hoped to remain with them until the War was over. That he could not was a cause of great regret; but wherever he went, he would bear with him the memory of the Benton and her gallant crew, and, if his life were spared, he would often revert to the scenes he had passed among them with mingled feelings of sorrow and of pride. The interview was impressive and affecting, and at the close the Commodore could hardly speak for emotion, and the tears, answered by many who were present, stole down his thin and pallid cheeks.

An hour after this, the De Soto dropped down to the Flagship to convey the Flag-officer to Cairo, and he soon made his way, with the assistance of Captains Davis and Phelps, to the transport, where he was placed in a chair on the guards, looking toward the crew of the Benton, who stood, an anxious crowd, upon the deck.

The Commodore was moved deeply, and was extremely nervous, laboring greatly to conceal his agitation; but he could not succeed; and he placed a palm-leaf, which he carried, before his face, to hide the gushing tears.

As the De Soto moved away, the crew pulled off their caps and gave three loud and hearty cheers, at which the Flag-officer rose from his chair and said, in an excited manner and in broken accents: "God bless you all, my brave companions! I know you will succeed in all you undertake, for such a cause, in such hands, can not fail. I had hoped to stay with you. I had rather died with you than go away; but I go for your good and the good of my country; and I can never forget you,—never, never. You are as gallant and noble men as ever fought in a glorious cause, and I shall remember your merits to my dying day."

I thought I had seen the Commodore for the last time; but after the De Soto was out of sight, it was discovered the mail had been left behind; and Captain Phelps ordered the Captain of a tug lying alongside to take the mail, and catch the transport by all means.

A fellow-journalist and myself leaped on board the little marine Mercury, and were immediately steaming rapidly up the river.

Faster and faster darted the tug through and against the strong currents of the Mississippi.

Sixty pounds of steam was all the boats were allowed under ordinary circumstances to carry; but in ten minutes the steam-gauge marked ninety.

The firemen worked nobly, and the boilers glowed anew. The little boat fairly leaped out of the water; throwing the white spray above the speeding bow.

One hundred and ten, twenty, thirty, declared the steam-gauge; but still we seemed to be gaining little on the De Soto.

"Fire up, boys!" shouted the Captain. "We have orders to catch that boat; and I'll do it if I blow the tug to h—l."

Open flew the doors of the furnace, and the coal crackled in the blazing fire; and the boilers rang shrilly and ominously, while the steam-gauge went up to one hundred and sixty. The tug trembled in every joint, and radiated heat on every side, as we darted through the sweeping tide of the mighty river.

One hundred and seventy—and eighty and ninety proclaimed the steam-gauge; and as we went flying through the water, the engineer hallooed: "She won't bear much more. Something will break soon."

"Let it break," shouted the Captain, who had overheard the remark. "Our orders are to catch the De Soto, and we must do it. Never mind the tug. We'll do our part. If she don't do hers, that's her business."

We were gaining rapidly on the boat. We saw her smoke rising around a bend; and as we sped after her, I observed we were carrying exactly two hundred pounds of steam.

There was something exciting in the race against time. and the spice of danger made it interesting.

Gods, how hot the tiny craft was! how swift we went! She threw out heat as a house on fire. Every joint shook; every seam cracked; every square inch throbbed under the high pressure of the chained vapors that seemed burning to discharge their painful deaths upon the slender crew.

The tug ran like an aqueous greyhound; and while we were speculating upon the chances of being blown into fragments, we darted through a narrow shute, and in less than five minutes we passed out, and were by the side of the De Soto.

The race was over. The orders had been executed.

Perhaps more than one person on the tug breathed freer as we ran alongside and delivered the mail. But the excitement was gone. The interest was at an end; and the tug became an ordinary tug, as the steam-gauge fell to seventy again, and danger dwindled away, with the blue vapor, into the invisible air.

While the Captain of the tug was busy on the De Soto, my companion and myself went into the cabin of the boat, and found the Commodore lying exhausted upon a sofa. I then noticed for the first time how very pale, and worn, and thin he was. Had he remained another month on the Benton, I do not think he would ever have left her alive.

As we approached, the Commodore extended his wasted hand. We expressed the hope that he would soon be better; that our loss would prove his gain.

"It is the cause that will be the gainer," answered the Flag-officer, feebly. "My life is nothing. My country is welcome to so poor an offering at any time; but I can not injure our sacred cause by striving to fill a position for which illness has unfitted me. My country first; myself afterwards."

So we parted from the gallant Flag-officer, and never saw him more.

CHAPTER XXVII.

NAVAL ENGAGEMENT AT FORT PILLOW.

Unexpected Appearance of the Hostile Vessels.—Commencement of the Attack. —Character of the Enemy's Boats.—Warm Work on a Warm Day.—The Rebel Sharpshooters.—A Gallant Captain and Determined Lieutenant.—Explosion of a Rebel Ram.—A Paymaster acting as Gunner.—Incidents of the Fight.—Victory Decided in our Favor.

THE Rebels at Fort Pillow had so often made menaces of attack upon the National Flotilla, that no one on board believed they had any idea of putting their threats into execution. And yet for once they made their words good, not allowing their gasconade to end altogether in inanity, as it has so often done in the flatulent regions of Secessia.

It had generally been supposed, if the enemy designed to engage us, they would take advantage of the night, and endeavor to surprise us amid the darkness. No one imagined the Rebels would come up in the face of open day and offer us battle; nor do I believe they would have done so, had they not learned our position the day before.

When five or six of the enemy's gunboats and two or three of his rams appeared, about seven o'clock, on the morning of May 10, 1862, above Craighead Point, they created some little astonishment, but no alarm, notwithstanding we were taken at great disadvantage. Not one of our boats had any thing like a full head of steam, and some of them barely a fire in their boilers.

As the Cincinnati, Captain Roger A. Stembel, was about half a mile above the Point, guarding two of the mortars, and the other gunboats were at least a mile and a half still above him, the Rebel gunboat McRea, and three rams, the Van Dorn, Webb, and Sumter, immediately steamed toward the solitary guardian, while the remainder of the hostile fleet stopped in the bend near the Tennessee shore, after firing half a dozen guns.

It was evident, from the beginning, that the foe designed to make his fight with the McRea and the rams, not caring to expose his other gunboats to ours.

The enemy's gunboats, excepting the McRea, were, as they had been represented, tow-boats, cut down to the boiler deck; their machinery inclosed with iron, with bow and stern guns very slenderly, if at all, protected, save by bales of cotton, piled several feet high both fore and aft.

The McRea, formerly a schooner, and very fast, was about one hundred and twenty-five feet long, and a fine model. Her engines and boilers were protected by railway iron; and though it was supposed that she had six, seven, or eight guns, only two were perceptible.

Her bow and stern were covered with bales of cotton, which were also piled up some distance on her deck, acting as breastworks; and behind those was a large body of infantry and sharpshooters, whose duty it was to pick off whomsoever they could on our gunboats.

The three rams, the Van Dorn, Sumter, and Webb, were protected and ironed like the McRea, but were smaller and lower, being constructed out of tow-boats. The Van Dorn was formidable, having a sharp, strong

GUNBOAT FIGHT AT FORT PILLOW.

iron prow, partially under water, as the McRea and Sumter had, that must have proved very effective against the strongest vessel.

The two rams had stern and bow guns, and musketeers and riflemen, protected by bales of cotton.

But two sailors were on the deck of the Cincinnati, engaged in washing it, when the McRea, considerably in advance, went steaming rapidly toward her. The alarm was given, and the officers and crew, who were at breakfast, were soon at their posts.

They had no time to get out of the way, but they fired their stern guns first, and then a double broadside at her without changing her course. The McRea struck her with great force on the port quarter, knocking a great hole in her, and immediately filling the shell-room with water.

The gunboats were all built with different compartments designed to be water-tight, so that if one of them sprang aleak, the others would remain dry. The timber used, however, was green instead of seasoned; and, having shrunk greatly, the filling of one compartment with water was equivalent to filling them all—a fault of the builders to which the disaster to the Cincinnati was owing.

The McRea now backed off and prepared herself for another blow; but before she had started on her return, our gunboat had fired her bow guns and another broadside into her, at a distance of not less than one hundred and fifty yards. Of course, every shot struck her, and some of the cotton-bales were displaced; but she did not seem at all disabled.

By that time the Van Dorn had arrived, and, though she was received with several guns, she struck the Cincinnati in the stern, and in less than a minute the McRea had come a second time into collision with our craft, near the wheel-house, on the starboard side.

The Cincinnati was rapidly taking water, and in a very unpleasant predicament; and some of the officers feared she would be sunk before the Mound City, Captain A. H. Kilty, which was hastening to her aid, and the Benton, Captain S. L. Phelps, which was dropping down without steam, could come to her assistance.

Very soon, however, the Mound City arrived at the immediate scene of action, having been firing very accurately at the three Rebel vessels while she was making her mile of distance.

Her shot struck the McRea and Van Dorn again and again; and as she moved up, the former leveled her long guns at the bow, and was on the eve of giving her a raking fire, when the gallant Union craft sent a thirty-six pound shell against the cannon, and completely dismounted it.

The Van Dorn now turned her attention to the Mound City, leaving the McRea to take care of the Cincinnati, which would have been the recipient of a fourth thrust, had not the broadside of the Benton caused the enemy to veer round and miss her victim.

On the altered schooner the sharpshooters were active, trying to kill the officers at the same time that they insured security for themselves. Their rifles were visibly protruding between the cotton-bales, and thrust over their tops, and numerous bullets whizzed by the ears of our gallant sailors. No human figure, however, could be seen, except the man at the wheel; and Captain Stembel, knowing how much depended on removing him, called for a gun, and shot the pilot, who fell apparently dead.

A few seconds after, the pilot of the Cincinnati hallooed out, "There is a d——d scoundrel getting ready to shoot you, Captain."

Stembel, who looked up and saw a man pointing a gun at his head, discharged his own piece and a pair of revolvers, and stepped forward to screen himself behind the pilot-house.

He was too late. Before he had half covered his body with the intervening object, the Rebel sent into his left shoulder a ball that passed out of his throat, about two inches under his chin.

The brave officer, whose principal fault was that he exposed himself too recklessly, fell to the deck, and it was supposed, at first, he was killed. He was picked up and carried below, where he retained his consciousness, and every few seconds opened his eyes and anxiously inquired as to the progress of the battle. His wounds were so serious, however, that he was not able to resume his duties for a number of months.

The Cincinnati seemed settling; and as Lieutenant William Hoel had then succeeded to the command, he, under the impression that the boat would soon be at the bottom of the river, addressed the crew for a few seconds, telling them never to remove the American ensign, but to go down with it, if they must go down, and giving three cheers for the Stars and Stripes.

That little speech, so full of genuine patriotism and

courage, made the sailors shout lustily ; and then they turned away to their duties.

The Cincinnati was rolling from side to side, and the inexorable McRea was, for the fifth time, running toward her. That blow might have been attended with disastrous consequences ; but, as she was speeding to the crippled craft, the Benton fired two of her rifled Dahlgrens, and one of them passed through the boilers of the McRea, which exploded with a tremendous noise, that was but faintly heard, however, above the roar of battle.

Her deck was observed to rise, while piercing shrieks rent the air, and a number of persons were seen to leap on the cotton-bales, and fall back wounded, dying, and dead.

At that moment she hauled down her soiled Rebel flag, and Captain Phelps, of the Benton, ordered his men to fire on her no more. The McRea still floated down, and as she was turning the point she again hoisted her tattered ensign, and disappeared behind the intervening land.

After the McRea had passed out of sight, and while the Van Dorn and another ram called the Sumter were engaged with the Mound City, the tug Dauntless ran out to the Cincinnati, and towed her to the Tennessee shore.

Though disabled, the officers of the Cincinnati were still disposed to fight, and more desperately than ever, and would have sunk in the middle of the Mississippi with their brave spirits unconquered.

Just before the McRea exploded her boiler, Captain Stembel's crew had been prepared for resisting boarders, as it was thought some of the enemy's gunboats or rams would make an attempt of the kind. The sailors were ready with revolvers, cutlasses, boarding-pikes, and hand-grenades, and unfortunate and summary would have been the fate of the Rebels if they had made the rash effort. The Union crew were very anxious to give the foe a warm reception, and a howl of disappointment arose as they beheld their last hope of engaging the McRea fade away.

The Mound City, Captain A. H. Kilty, fought the Van Dorn and Sumter bravely; the Captain being on deck all the while, and firing at the pilots with a musket. Every man on the boat was active and watchful, and it was very strange no one was hit by the enemy, as a steady fire of rifles was kept up from behind the cotton-bales.

The Mound City bore many marks of musket-balls on her pilot-house and paddle-boxes, and the officers heard the music of the small leaden vocalists more than once in close proximity to their imperiled ears.

Paymaster Gunn—afterwards killed in action up the White River—although he knew nothing whatever of artillery or projectiles, and had no duties to perform in the gun-room, seeing two pieces lying idle, induced a couple of men to load them, and pointing the cannon at the Van Dorn, only a hundred yards distant, had the satisfaction of planting two shells in the very center of the ram, which appeared to do excellent execution.

The Sumter had struck the Mound City twice with her iron prow, but had done her little damage; while the gunboat had riddled the ram, and so alarmed the sharpshooters that they remained silent, cowering behind their defenses. The Van Dorn finally had a favorable chance, and struck the Mound City with great force on the bow, causing a large leak, which there was no time to attempt to stop.

The Benton was now near the rams, which were so afraid of the flagship, knowing her superior strength, that they steamed away from her as soon as possible. The Benton placed herself between the Van Dorn and Sumter, and fired four or five guns at a third ram, which was running toward the Carondelet, and, striking her wheels and machinery, disabled her.

That ram, said to be the Webb, began floating off with the current, and, as she neared the point, the Benton fired two of her fifty-pound Dahlgrens, and the next minute steam was pouring out of every part of her.

Soon after one of her boilers exploded, and she was half a wreck as the last glimpse was caught of her, passing the first fortifications of Pillow.

The Van Dorn appeared to bear a particular hatred to the mortar rafts, which must have annoyed the enemy not a little with their perpetual firing over the irremovable Craighead. She even paused from her attack on the Mound City, and fired two thirty-two pounders at the crew of one of the mortars, perforating the thin coat of iron as if it had been glass.

The Rebel marines fired a number of shots at the mortar-men, and two of the Secession officers climbed on the cotton-bales with muskets, and discharged their pieces, but with no effect.

The mortar-men were not to be bullied; so the crew

loaded one of the monsters, and sent a thirteen-inch shell in the direction of the Van Dorn. The enemy was not materially injured, for the bomb coursed off at an angle of forty-five degrees.

For four or five minutes the Benton, under the control of the cool and skillful pilot, Horace Bigsby, turned several times completely round as on an axis, firing in succession her bow, stern, and broadside guns. The Rebels knew her strength—indeed, they had long been acquainted with the particularities of the Flotilla as well as we ourselves—and did not dare to attack her; and as she riddled their rams with her guns, they felt they had no prospect of success, and at last made an effort to get out of harm's way.

That they had much difficulty in doing, in consequence of the condition of their machinery; and the rams were often struck by the Mound City and Benton before they could escape. The former gunboat fairly touched the stern of the Van Dorn once, and fired a Dahlgren, whose ball passed entirely through her, and must have proved very destructive to human life.

The Rebel gunboats in the lead, near the Tennessee shore, perceived the danger of their allies, but lacked the nerve to go to their assistance, and at last steamed down the river, leaving the rams to their fate.

The Van Dorn, Sumter, and Webb, at last happened to strike a favorable current, and passed away from the Benton, which was very unwieldy, and floated toward the Point.

Had our gunboats at the time had more power—by that I mean a higher pressure of steam—they would have experienced no trouble in conveying the hostile rams to Plum Point as prizes.

The rebel gunboats having fled, and the rams escaped, the battle was of course over ; no enemy remaining to be engaged.

Cheer after cheer went up from our Flotilla as the enemy, one after another, dropped away, and three times three arose from the flagship while the last of the Rebel rams was passing by Craighead Point.

Only three of our gunboats were engaged ; but the Carondelet, Captain Henry Walke, and the St. Louis, Captain H. Erben, Jr., fired a number of shots from their original positions off the Arkansas shore ; though it was not probable, at the long range, that they did any material damage to the foe.

The action did not occupy more than half an hour, and much of it was concealed by the heavy smoke that rested like a vast fog upon the river, on the close, hot, blazing morning of the engagement. Our skiffs, yawls, and tugs were plying here and there, occupied by persons anxious to witness the fight, which surprised every one by its brevity. Our sailors had counted on a long battle, and were therefore disappointed, but the engagement was warm while it lasted.

Our success, under the circumstances, was very flattering, for it cannot be denied that the attack was well planned and matured by the foe, and was at least a partial surprise to us. No one on the Flotilla had any idea of the Rebels coming up to engage us. And the Cincinnati did not see the McRea or the rams before they had gotten some distance above the Point.

CHAPTER XXVIII.

FALL OF MEMPHIS.

A Gasconading Rebel.—The Brilliant Gunboat Fight.—The Vessels Engaged.—The Nautical Situation.—Commencement of the Action.—Union Rams Taking Part.—Increased Warmth of the Contest.—Sinking of the General Lovell.—Magnanimity of our Seamen.—Flight of the Southern Commodore.—Explosion of the Jeff. Thompson.—Harmony of Northerners and Southerners after the City's Occupation.

BETWEEN five and six o'clock on the morning of June 6, 1862, the most spirited and decisive battle that had occurred on the Mississippi was fought, for the possession of Memphis, opposite that city, between five of our gunboats, assisted by two of our rams, and eight of the enemy's gunboats. The engagement was witnessed by thousands of the citizens, who expected, no doubt, to see the Unionists driven from the river, as they had been frequently told by Commodore Edward Montgomery, that he would, when the proper time came, annihilate the whole Yankee fleet.

The fight was a glorious one. Out of eight of the hostile vessels, seven were destroyed, sunk, or captured, and but one escaped; while only one of our rams was injured, and but two persons were slightly wounded.

The Union gunboats, five in number, Benton, Cairo, Carondelet, Louisville, and St. Louis, and the two rams,

Queen of the West and the Monarch, left their moorings below Paddy's Hen and Chickens—as the group of islands five miles above Memphis is called by steamboat men—about half-past four in the morning, and slowly steamed toward the city.

The morning was clear and calm, balmy and beautiful; and, after passing a bend in the river, we saw the city in the distance, reposing very quietly upon the border of the broad stream that had poured whatever Memphis had of wealth into her ungrateful lap.

The river was clear of all craft. Not even a skiff skimmed its surface, and the officers of the fleet thought we should meet with no opposition to our possession of the city. The seamen were very fearful lest that would prove true, and prayed, after their peculiar nautical fashion, that the Rebel vessels would come out and give us fight.

After the engagement of the 10th of May, the gunboat crews felt as if that action required continuation, and they were longing for another battle most anxiously.

The sailors' orisons seemed to be answered.

The Flotilla was just opposite the upper part of the city, when the boats of the Rebel Fleet were seen in a slight bend of the river, about a mile and a quarter below.

Our crews cheered lustily at the grateful vision, for they knew there was a prospect for a fight. The Flotilla still steamed leisurely along, and the enemy soon advanced towards us.

Commodore Davis did not wish to bring on an engagement at so early an hour, preferring that the men should eat their breakfast, and thus be qualified to fight better than when suffering from physical depletion. He therefore ordered the five vessels under his command to retreat; and the foe, perceiving that, grew evidently emboldened, believing we were anxious to avoid a battle.

As we retraced our course the enemy followed, and, in a few minutes, the flagship Little Rebel, on which was Commodore Montgomery, fired a shot at the Benton, which was in the van, without injuring her, and then a second and third, with the same effect.

This braggadocio became intolerable. Commodore Davis must have so regarded it, for he at once ordered an advance, and the Benton, Captain W. L. Phelps, and the Louisville, Captain B. M. Dove, assumed the front position, with the Cairo, Captain Bryant, the Carondelet, Captain Henry Walke, and the St. Louis, Captain Wilson McGunnigle, in the rear.

The hostile fleet, in addition to the flagship, was composed of General Beauregard, General Bragg, Jeff. Thompson, General Lovell, General Price, Sumter, and General Van Dorn.

The Cairo was the first of our boats to discharge a gun at the enemy, and followed it up by two more that fell very near the Little Rebel, without striking her.

The Carondelet and Louisville imitated the worthy example, and the Lovell and Thompson, Bragg and Price, on the other side, took part in the nautical entertainment, and lent the deep bass of their guns to the warlike concert.

In less than three minutes both fleets were engaged in a most animated action, and every vessel was thundering away to the best of its capacity. The river and sky seemed to shake beneath the roar.

The boats were gradually approaching nearer each other, and were enveloped in such a volume of smoke that one could hardly be distinguished from the other, except when a fresh, stiff breeze lifted the curtain of heavy vapor.

The engagement continued thus for more than twenty minutes, and at the end of that time the combatants were more than half a mile apart, and were still firing heavily.

We had frequently hit their boats, but they had not touched ours; their gunners being in a state of excitement or unskillfulness that caused them to entirely waste their ammunition.

At this juncture, two Cincinnati rams, the Queen of the West and Monarch, appeared about half a mile behind the Flotilla; and the enemy, as soon as he perceived them, began to retreat, conscious if he could not sustain the attack before, he would be still less able to do it after the rams had entered upon the action.

The Queen of the West darted out at rapid speed ahead of its companion toward the Beauregard, which fired at her opponent four times without striking her once, though in one or two instances no more than two hundred yards distant.

The ram, nothing disconcerted, ran in boldly, designing to butt the Rebel near the bow, and would have done so, had not the gunboat been so adroitly managed by her pilot. The Beauregard moved suddenly to the right as the ram passed—the movement was very skillful and very opportune for the enemy—causing the latter to miss her aim altogether.

The ram, finding herself thus foiled, determined to test her capacity upon another vessel, and so turned her attention to the General Price, and hit her heavily on the wheel-house before she could get out of the way, tearing off a good portion of her side.

The Beauregard immediately went to the rescue, and was steaming towards the ram, when the latter reversed her engines and receded a few yards, causing the gunboat to collide with the injured Price, and knock a large hole in her bow.

Such peculiar attention from an ally was unexpected, and more than the Price could endure, for she had been leaking from her first injury, and now the water poured into her in streams.

The Beauregard seemed inclined to avenge her own mistake upon the Queen ; and, before the latter was well aware, struck her a heavy blow upon the side that made her timbers crack, and take water freely.

The water was quite deep at that point, and there was a probability the ram and gunboat would both sink ; but, to remove doubt on the subject for one of the pair, the Beauregard was on the point of hitting the ram a second time, when the close proximity of the Monarch induced her to look out for her own safety.

The Beauregard fired several times at the Monarch, and struck her once upon the wooden bulwarks, without producing any particular effect. The Monarch then took charge of the Queen and the Price, and towed them ashore to prevent them from sinking ; though not before she had made a large hole in the stern of the Beauregard, and rendered her prospect of keeping above water, for any length of time, extremely problematical.

The Beauregard was crippled, but as she was still able to run fairly, and to render obedience to the helmsman, she continued to participate in the fight with great obstinacy.

During the scenes of the action in which the rams had taken part, the gunboats had continued firing steadily and heavily; the Unionists often hitting the Rebels, while the latter missed their objects almost invariably.

The gunboats on both sides, having been separated somewhat by the rams, came up nearer, again to pay their respects to each other, and the cannonading grew heavier than it had been at any previous time. The distant report of the single guns was lost—they all blended together in one loud, deafening roar.

The Benton was still in the van, and within range of the Lovell, when Captain Phelps thought he would try one of the fifty-pound rifled Parrotts on the foe.

The conical shell went whizzing out of the long and formidable piece into the Lovell, just above her waterline, cutting a deep hole in her, and increasing the rate of her insurance fearfully.

The Lovell, it was immediately discovered, was leaking like a sieve, and indeed she was already beginning to sink rapidly, and, from appearance, must go down very soon.

Her crew appeared aware of this, for they were seen on the side of the vessel, forgetful of every thing but their own safety. Self-preservation was their only law at that juncture.

The Lovell was descending lower and lower, and the Benton, anxious to save any of the poor fellows that might be launched into the rapid river, prepared her cutter, which, in the haste, was twice swamped.

The seamen were soon in the cutter, however, and approaching the doomed gunboat, which had just run up a flag of truce, and which, thirty seconds after, went down in fourteen fathoms of water.

At least twenty-five or thirty of the Rebels leaped overboard after the accident, with the intention of swimming ashore. Some of them succeeded; but the greater part perished miserably in the stream.

The Union flag-ship reached the spot in time to pick up ten or twelve poor fellows struggling in the river, and save them at least from the death which Friar John, in Rabelais, predicted would not fall to the lot of Panurge, and would never occur to them for the same reason.

The efforts of the loyal seamen to preserve the lives of those who had been but a few minutes before their avowed and bitter enemies, was a beautiful spectacle, and proved conclusively the falseness of the charges of inhumanity and blood-thirstiness which the Secessionists have brought against the brave and loyal people of the North.

From the first inception of the fight, the wharf and bluffs of Memphis had been crowded with interested and anxious spectators; and as the boats moved down the river the throng followed, as if fearful they would lose the smallest part of the highly exciting battle. The people were thus made witnesses of our actions and those of the Rebels, and were not to be deceived with Munchausen-like stories, when they had the facts immediately before their eyes.

The magnanimity of the crew of the Benton must have had a salutary influence upon them, for it proved that loyal hearts were as generous as they were brave.

The Little Rebel was leaking more and more rapidly, and, having been struck several additional times with heavy shot, Commodore Edward Montgomery doubtless began to feel uneasy, and therefore ran the flagship over to the Arkansas shore, where she was followed by the Carondelet so closely that her officers had no time to burn her—as was doubtless their intention—but had ample leisure to leap on the bank and escape through the woods.

The Carondelet threw a dozen shells among the trees after the alarmed fugitives, but did them, in all probability, not the least harm. It is said that Commodore Montgomery was the first man ashore—he, the truculent boaster and presumptuous braggart, who had ever been threatening to devour the Yankees, and completely depopulate the d—d Abolition North.

Perhaps he thought, as John B. Floyd said at Donelson, he could not afford to be taken.

Queer—is it not?—that the fellows who prate so unceasingly of their determination to die upon the smallest provocation, and affect such magnificent indifference to death, should, when the test comes, reveal more love of existence than the most ordinary and least obtrusive natures, that never defied a respectable shadow.

The Jeff. Thompson was struck a number of times, and was so severely injured that she also was run to the Arkansas shore, about a mile below the city, and deserted by her officers and crew, after the manner of the Little Rebel.

A shell had set the vessel on fire; but the flames were extinguished—or it was thought they were—by some of the Union sailors in gigs, and the five uninjured ships of the National Fleet continued their pursuit of the Sumter, General Bragg, and Van Dorn.

After the gunboats had followed the retreating enemy a mile further, firing steadily, and the Rebels replying, though more and more feebly as the chase was extended, the Sumter's pilot put her head to the Arkansas side, and beached her, giving her valiant crew the means of escape through the wilds and swamps of that classic State.

The General Bragg had received a shot through her wheel-house, early in the action, and was unable to move about very readily; but she contrived to get over the river, thus furnishing the frightened Rebels an opportunity to emigrate further South.

The General Van Dorn, the only boat now remaining of the Rebel Fleet, was still steaming toward President's Island, three miles below the city. The Cairo and Carondelet followed her for two miles, hoping to cripple her with a shot, but neither of them succeeded, and they at last gave up the pursuit.

Surely our gallant sailors ought to have been satisfied with the brilliant successes of that day. They had placed *hors de combat* seven out of eight of the insurgent vessels, and had gained one of the most brilliant naval victories on record, without any loss to themselves worthy of mention.

While the Union gunboats were on their way to the city, they perceived that the Jeff Thompson, lying off the Arkansas shore, was on fire again, and the flames were pouring out all over her deck.

The cause of the new conflagration was not positively known. Some persons declared that the old flames burst out anew; and others, that the gunboat was set on fire by a party of Rebels who returned to the vessel, applying the torch after the Flotilla had passed down the river.

The latter opinion was probably correct. The Jeff. Thompson was blazing higher and higher, and the flames attracted a crowd of persons to the Tennessee shore, because it was supposed she would blow up as soon as the fire reached her magazine.

The gunboat appeared to burn for hours, so much did expectation burden time, and the flames were creeping down to the water's edge, apparently; and yet no indication had been given of an explosion. It was supposed that the powder had been removed from the Thompson, and a number of persons were turning away disappointed, when a tremendous explosion rent the air, and an immense flame shot up into the radiant morning, while hundreds of heavy reports were heard in rapid succession half a mile above our heads.

Those were the shells of the gunboat, which had been thrown upward with ignited fuses from the vessel, and burst with the tremendous crackling sound that vast buildings sometimes give before they fall to the earth in ruins.

Looking over to the spot where the Jeff. Thompson was, we saw nothing but a few black and charred fragments on the water. She had been literally blown to atoms—a worthy fate for a Rebel vessel, and typical of the termination of the Rebel cause.

* * * *

The most pleasant relations seemed to exist between the Union parties that captured Memphis on the 6th and the resident citizens; and it was amusing to observe how amiable, and almost fraternal, were the associations between the Bohemians from New York, Cincinnati, Chicago, and St. Louis, and the journalists of Memphis, recently so ferociously malignant and bitterly vindictive against the Abolition Press.

The Bluff City journalists called upon us daily at the Flotilla, or at our head-quarters in the city, and we talked and laughed over the gasconade of the South, its mighty promises and small performances, in a most pleasant manner. One could have seen the *New York Tribune* and the *Memphis Appeal* sitting in pleasing converse over a bottle of champagne, at the dinner-table of the Gayoso; the *Chicago Tribune* and *Memphis Argus* strolling through Court Square, arm-in-arm; and the *Cincinnati Times* and the *Memphis Avalanche*, forgetful of the present, discussing the relative merits of Grisi and Gazzaniga on the lyric stage. Who, after that, could say the journalists were not an amiable and a forgiving race, and that the people of the North and South were not a band of brothers?

If the day of our occupation was not a gala-day in Memphis, it appeared strangely otherwise. It reminded me of a Fourth of July I had passed there a few years before, except that it was far more quiet and orderly. The people stood in knots and groups in the streets, at the corners, before the hotels and restaurants, but were not uneasy or annoyed.

The negroes lounged listlessly about, and seemed to regard the whole thing as a pleasant joke, or a glorious event—it was difficult from the expression of their countenances to determine which.

The women were not in force, but most of them were of that class of which Memphis had ever had far more than her just proportion. Still, there were not a few of the sex abroad; and a number I saw sitting in their parlors, or on their door-steps, were eminently correct in conduct and respectable in appearance.

No dark looks, no rude gestures, no studied insult from them. They conducted themselves in a most lady-like manner; and even the lorette class were subdued and reserved.

The Cyprians were often young and comely, and expensively attired, though frequently with sober and excellent taste. They were too broad to be bound by political creeds or formulas. They were universal.

Hundreds of them had witnessed the naval engagement from the bluff, and one of the city papers had assumed that they were Southern ladies, who could not restrain their tears of mortification and rage when they beheld the discomfiture and almost total destruction of the hostile fleet.

The idea of their weeping! The source of their tears had long been dried. They mourned not for Adonais dead, or living either. What cared they which side was victorious? What was Hecuba to them, or they to Hecuba?

Curiosity and personal interest called them forth on that day; and many of them, no doubt, speculated from the first hour of the Union occupation upon the same subject—though from a different motive—that so perplexed the mind of the antique female at the siege of Saragossa.

Memphis bore all the appearance of a subjugated city; and yet it had been as violent in its treason as Charleston.

The people accepted their altered condition without a murmur; and they were wise in so doing.

When I saw our gunboats with their ports triced up, and the long, black guns bearing on the town, I must confess I rather liked the new order of things.

I was glad Memphis had learned the lesson so many other nests of treason have since learned to their severest cost.

CHAPTER XXIX.

THE EXPEDITION UP WHITE RIVER.

Its Object and Strength.—Cautious Progress.—Character of the Stream.—Desperation of the Arkansans.—Progress of the Fleet.—The Engagement near St. Charles.—Position of the Hostile Fortifications.—Explosion of the Mound City.—Terrible Destruction by Steam.—Horrible Scenes of Suffering.—Inhumanity and Barbarity of the Rebels.—Their Defeat and Punishment.

THE White River expedition left Memphis, Tennessee, in June, 1862, for the purpose of ascending that stream as far as Jacksonport, three hundred and fifty miles from the mouth, supplying General Curtis's force with provisions, and capturing the transports the Rebels were supposed to have stolen and concealed there.

The expedition, which was only partially successful, consisted of the iron-clad gunboats Mound City (flag-ship), the St. Louis, the two wooden gunboats, Lexington and Conestoga; with the tug Spitfire, armed with a twenty-pound howitzer, and the transports New National, White Cloud, and D. Musselman, carrying part of Colonel G. N. Fitch's Forty-sixth Indiana regiment, and a large amount of supplies.

The expedition tarried at the confluence of the Mississippi from Saturday afternoon until Monday morning, and then proceeded cautiously and slowly up the river, having heard obstructions had been placed in the water, and batteries erected to resist the progress of the fleet.

The gunboats steamed along—the flagship in advance, the St. Louis in her wake, and the wooden boats about half a mile behind—all of Monday, without meeting any thing of consequence, or the least exciting occurrence.

Monday night they anchored in the stream, which, though quite deep, is very narrow; being in some places no more than two hundred yards from bank to bank.

There are bluffs, or more properly ridges, along the river at intervals; and these ridges rise to hights of thirty, forty, and fifty feet, rendering the stream very favorable for defense.

Almost anywhere on the White, a skilled marksman could shoot an enemy in the middle of the river, and in many places on the opposite bank.

Captain Kilty, of the Mound City, had been informed that Rebel batteries had been planted near St. Charles, Arkansas, about seventy miles from the mouth; but, when he had made that distance, he saw no signs of them.

However, to obtain as early intelligence of them as possible, he began to shell the woods along the banks, which, in various localities, offered fine opportunities for ambuscade. The St. Louis and Conestoga also threw shells, while the Lexington lingered in the rear to guard the transports, and to preserve a sharp look-out for the enemy.

The Arkansans had for some time been growing desperate, and more than usually menacing, on account of the overrunning of their State by the "Yankee hordes of barbarians," and the peculiar tantrums of Governor Rector. They were fearful, no doubt, if thoroughly invaded by the Northern people, that they might grow civilized; and if such an unnatural thing should happen, they would lose their identity completely, and cease to be regarded in this country as the Patagonians are by the nations of Europe.

The brilliant prestige of Arkansas would be gone. Its classic communities would turn their attention from the high-toned and chivalrous amusements of imbibing Minié rifle whisky, and assassinating unarmed men, to the vile Yankee habits of healthful employment and general culture.

The Union Fleet had proceeded something over eighty miles up White River, when the vessels were fired upon from a battery on the south side, but so hidden among the trees that the officers could hardly determine the spot whence the pieces were discharged.

The guns of the enemy were not very heavy, sounding like twelve and twenty-four pounders; and subsequent examination proved they were such.

Two of the shots struck the casemates of the St. Louis, but glanced off harmless, while most of them passed over the deck.

The Mound City and St. Louis both fired at the Rebel batteries, and frequently perceived that their shells fell very near, if not inside of, the works.

After seven or eight minutes, the enemy appeared fatigued with his efforts and fired only at intervals, whereupon the Mound City pushed on, leaving the first battery to the St. Louis and Conestoga, which were throwing a few shells at the Rebel fortifications at a mile's distance.

At that place there was a bend in the river, and further up a more decided turn toward the South, the general course of the stream being East and West.

The first battery was opposite the former bend, on the top of a ridge, about fifty feet high; and the opinion that it had a companion was soon established by a heavy report from a point half a mile above, the howl of a round shot across the bow of the Mound City, and the burial of the iron missile in the bank on the opposite side.

A second shot came, but it went wide of the mark, and cut off the branches of a tree two hundred yards in the rear of the vessel. The new ordnance was heavier than that in the lower battery; and the flagship promptly proceeded to pay her compliments to the loud-voiced stranger.

The Mound City fired her bow guns twice, and then her port guns, as she steamed up the river a little further—making the distance between her and the upper battery less than half a mile.

The second fortification was on the same bluff or ridge as its fellow, but a little further from the shore, and in a southwesterly direction from the flagship, preventing its guns from bearing directly on the Mound City.

The effect of the flagship's shots could not not be well determined; but they appeared to be falling where the gunners desired, and the cannonade on her part, as well as on that of the St. Louis, was warmly kept up for eight or ten minutes; less than twenty having elapsed since the first gun had been fired from the lower battery.

In the mean time, Colonel Fitch had landed his five or six hundred men on the southern bank, below the first battery, with the intention of attacking the upper works in the rear, and surprising the enemy at his guns, which he had no doubt of accomplishing.

The Colonel was already on the march, and had signaled the Mound City to cease firing, that his own men might not be injured, when an unanticipated accident, of the most horrible character, almost entirely destroyed the officers and crew of the flagship.

A large cylindrical shot, with iron flanges on each side, known among the Rebels as the pigeon-shot, struck the casemates on the port side, in the upper port, near the first gun, at an angle of about ninety degrees, passing through the casemate and connecting-pipe of the boilers, killing a gunner on the starboard side, and alighting in the steward's pantry.

The effect of severing the connecting-pipe may be imagined.

All the steam of the boilers at once rushed, with a shrill, hissing sound, into every part of the gunboat, which presented no means for its escape except through the port-holes and skylights.

It was like injecting steam into an air-tight box; and when we remember that there were nearly one hundred and eighty human beings below the deck, the ineffable horror of their situation may readily be conceived.

The burning steam fairly mowed them down. They shrieked, and leaped, and writhed with pain. But the steam did not pity them: it seemed rather to delight in their sufferings, extending its vaporous torture to new victims.

Horrors upon horrors accumulated in that low, square, seething, boiling, fiery inclosure, where man endured all the fabled agonies of the damned, and yet could not die.

To some, Fate was merciful, for they perished at once. As many as forty-five or fifty, who had stood on the gun-deck a few moments before, with buoyant hopes and elated spirits, lay there in pallid death, unconscious of the pain around them, of the terrible moaning and groaning of the sufferers.

It was easy to die, but it was hard to suffer so. And many a pain-gleaming eye turned to the scalded corpses that strewed the deck, and wondered in agonizing accents why Heaven had not been so kind to all.

Oh, the horror of that scene! Oh, the fearful power of man to suffer!

Who that saw what was visible that day can ever forget it?

Will not that wail of distress fall upon his ear in dreams, and make him start in dread even from the arms of her he loves above his life?

As soon as the first shock had passed, those who had not been slain, from full inhalation of the steam, were prompted, mad with pain, to leap into the river to cool their burning bodies.

The impulse appeared to seize upon all simultaneously, and out of the open ports plunged one wretch after another, until seventy or eighty were struggling in the water.

Some were so badly scalded that they could not swim, and they, most fortunately, were drowned; while others, refreshed and cooled by the river, struck out for the bank, as if they had been uninjured.

At that crisis, when every principle of humanity called for aid and succor, the Rebels proved themselves worthy of the antecedents that had dishonored and disgraced them from the beginning of the War.

Instead of imitating the example of generosity and magnanimity set them by a brave and loyal people, struggling for the preservation of a great and glorious country; forgetting the heroic conduct shown by our seamen, who endeavored, in the gunboat fight off Memphis, to save the lives of the unfortunate crew of the General Lovell when she went down—the Rebels, most merciless and dastardly, made every effort to destroy the poor fellows who, with agonized bodies, were seeking to reach either the land or our vessels.

Perpetual shame and eternal infamy to the people who could forget the common promptings of Nature in the demoniac hatred that strove only to destroy!

The gunners in the upper battery turned their guns upon the suffering officers and seamen of the Mound City; and Captain Fry, the Commander of the works, ordered his sharpshooters to kill every Yankee before he could reach the shore, or succor could be brought.

The devilish enemy needed no second bidding. He ran with alacrity down to the boat, and there, under cover of the trees, fired muskets and rifles at the wounded swimmers with a cool diabolism that a South Sea Islander would have blushed to witness.

Many a brave fellow was killed and sank in the river, and others were wounded several times before they obtained the needful assistance from their loyal friends.

The Mound City was powerless, and drifting with the

current. She could not aid them; and the St. Louis was then opposite the lower fortifications.

The Conestoga, which was just below the Mound City, promptly lowered two of her boats, and sent them to save the survivors of the horrible accident.

No sooner had her gigs been manned, and no sooner were the seamen pulling at their oars, on the divine errand of mercy, than the upper work opened its heavy guns upon the succorers of distress.

The Union gigs were struck—one in the bow, the other in the stern; but, strange to say, they were not swamped, nor were they prevented from rescuing from the river some of the ill-fated crew.

A third boat from the St. Louis was struck with Rebel shot, and shattered; but none of the inmates were hurt or drowned.

The enemy was still bent on his demonaic work, and would have fired his last cartridge at the defenseless sailors, had not the brave Indianians, under Colonel Fitch, succeeded by that time in reaching the rear of the fortifications that Captain Fry commanded, and arrested the fearful progress of deliberate murder.

The Forty-sixth Indiana rushed with a shout and a volley of musketry into the hostile works, and then charged with bayonets the inhuman foe.

The Rebels were completely taken by surprise. Before they had time to throw down their arms, or cry for quarter, they were lying in their intrenchments and their life-blood ebbing away.

Some of the Secessionists fought with dogged obstinacy against superior numbers, and fell covered with ghastly wounds. Their bravery commands respect, but their cruelty must forever dishonor their memory.

Those of the Rebels along the shore who had been firing at the Unionists in the water, were soon charged upon by the Indianians, for whom they did not wait, but took to flight along the bank toward the village of St. Charles.

A portion of the insurgents ran to a place above where the river had been obstructed, and, jumping into a few small boats they had moored there, crossed the stream and disappeared in the woods.

The rout was complete. The victory was ours! but, alas, at what a price!

The White River by that time began to fall rapidly, and on that account the expedition returned; the officers commanding it having serious apprehensions, if they continued up the stream, that their vessels would get aground and be lost.

CHAPTER XXX.

THE BRAGG-BUELL CAMPAIGN.

Trip from Louisville to Frankfort.—The Occupation of the Kentucky Capital by the Enemy.—Sudden Conversion of Romantic Women to Loyalty.—The Inauguration of the Pseudo-Governor.—Sudden Exodus of the Usurpers; their Strange Self-Delusion.—Bohemians in the Horse-Market.—The Battle of Perryville.—A Journalistic Rebel Colonel.—Sketch of John H. Morgan.

DURING the Bragg-Buell Campaign in Kentucky, in October, 1862, when the Rebels partially occupied the State, I learned at Louisville, on the evening of the 8th instant, that the Louisville and Frankfort Railway had been repaired, and that a train would leave for the Capital very early the following morning. Consequently, a fellow-Bohemian and myself deemed it journalistically wise to visit the recent scene of the Rebel occupation.

On board the cars we found the morning papers, which announced that John H. Morgan, with three thousand cavalry, had taken the town after General Sill's departure, and still held it in his undisputed possession. Many doubted the statement, while others affirmed its truth. We concluded to solve the question to our own satisfaction, and pay a visit to John Morgan himself if we could do no better.

The people all along the route seemed to be very glad

to see the cars running again, and to know the Rebel reign was over in Kentucky.

We reached the terminus of the running distance—Benson's Creek, where the first bridge was burned down—without accident or interruption. From that point we were compelled to walk, over a very rough road, more than nine miles in the burning sun, which was Summer-like in its heat in that latitude; and at last we came in sight of Frankfort, and beheld our cavalry on the heights about the place, having seen no bands of marauders, or guerrillas, except one fellow across the river, who was skulking behind trees and firing his rifle at those who passed within his range.

Arriving in the city, we learned that it had been reoccupied by the foe the night previous about an hour; but that he had precipitately retreated before General Dumont's advance.

At the "Governor's" inauguration in Frankfort, October 4th, a number of good-looking and well-dressed women from Fayette, Woodford, and Scott counties were present, and caused more enthusiasm than the masculine traitors themselves.

A number of the young and romantic women of Kentucky, present on the day of the pseudo-inauguration, strange to say, saw the Southern soldiers for the first time, and expressed themselves greatly disgusted with them. They were not at all what they had expected. They had been told, and believed, that the Southern troops were composed of the true chivalry of the Cotton States; of young men of birth, education, and fortune. They thought they were handsome fellows, who could talk Poetry and Sentiment to them; who would walk with them tenderly by moonlight alone, and kiss them sweetly and artistically under its rays. How terribly were the imaginative darlings disenchanted!

Were those ragged, soiled, and plebeian breasts the kind they were to lean upon, and to nestle their luxurious tresses in?

Were those thin and pallid, or coarse and bloated lips, the ones they were to kiss

"In ecstasy supreme and rhapsody divine"?

Were those rough, harsh, vulgar voices the dulcet tones that were to tell them of Petrarch's love and Eloisa's passion? Alas! No! Their dream was over.

Secession was stripped of its meretricious tinsel, and the army of the South lost its attraction in the eyes of the romantic girls at a glance. They were cured—they were converted; and many of them who, two weeks before, were the fairest and stanchest of Rebels, became the truest and most devoted of Unionists. They cleansed themselves from Secession in the pure stream of Nationality, and the aroma of Loyalty (to speak after the manner of Kentucky) added a new sweetness to the graceful motions of their fascinating forms.

Strange as it may seem, the Rebels, when in Frankfort, declared and believed they could not be driven from Kentucky; that they would remain in the State as long as they desired, let the Yankees do what they could to dislodge them. "Governor" Hawes had made his arrangements to occupy the gubernatorial mansion, and the family of Governor Magoffin were preparing to leave the premises on his account.

"Governor" Hawes's speech, read from manuscript, was a most lame and impotent effort. He is very old, has a cracked and unpleasant voice, and this, with his stammering, and hesitation, and nervousness, rendered his address painful to hear and ridiculous to remember.

When the courier entered the Capital during the inaugural ceremonies, and informed General Buckner of the approach of Dumont's forces, and the intelligence was whispered around to the chief conspirators, the august assembly suddenly dispersed in great confusion. Richard Hawes is said to have displayed the locomotive capacity of youth in his departure. No one supposed a man in the vicinity of seventy could have manifested so much physical energy and vigor as he did on that memorable occasion.

If the old gentleman could have run as well for, as he did from, the Governorship, he would have been Chief Executive of Kentucky many years ago.

While the Rebels were in Frankfort, the people were cut off from all intelligence, and had no idea of what was going on around them. They saw no papers, not even those from Louisville, though the "Confederate" officers received them daily. They circulated and insisted upon the truth of the most absurd stories. McClellan was dead; Washington and Baltimore had been captured; Lincoln had fled to Philadelphia; Louisville and Cincinnati had been surrendered; Union Commissioners had gone to Richmond under a flag of truce, to sue for peace, with kindred and equally improbable statements.

So far did the Secessionists carry their system of deception and falsehood, that they caused a fictitious Louisville *Journal* to be printed at Lexington, and circulated among their troops and the citizens of that vicinity. This sham sheet was full of telegrams, letters, and editorials of the most startling character, all of which went to prove that the cause of the Union was utterly hopeless.

Persons who saw the Lexington publication say it bore a striking resemblance to the *Journal;* that its type was similar; many of the advertisements were the same; and on the whole it was very well calculated to deceive casual readers.

* * * * * * *

During the Bragg-Buell campaign in Kentucky, several of us Bohemians endeavored to procure horses in Louisville, and encountered many difficulties in so doing. Hiring a horse was impossible; and buying any one that I had seen for sale in the city seemed a hazardous speculation, as none of them conveyed the impression that they would last till they got out of the lines.

Their owners said they were not exactly "first-class animals;" that they had a few slight ailments, such as spavin, stringhalt, botts, blind-staggers, scratches, ringbone, and that, in some cases, they appeared addicted to stumbling over their own shadow; and, indeed, to all manner of equine eccentricities—save the foible of running away; but that, with those exceptions, they were as good horses as could be found in Kentucky.

One morning I chanced to discover a very good-looking horse of the gentler sex; plump, round, and well conditioned, and had agreed to purchase her. Going to close the bargain in the afternoon, I learned, to my chagrin, that the poor creature had duplicated herself—a probability I had before suspected, and suggested to the jockey, who stoutly denied any such reflection on the animal's character.

Then, however, facts visible to the naked eye spoke for themselves. But the jockey insisted on his honesty, and vowed the case to be one of immaculate conception.

Buying a horse at that time and place was a ponderous business—something approximating the superhuman.

If Hercules had then attempted the purchase of a steed in Louisville, he would have failed.

He could cleanse the Augean Stables, and slay the Lernæan Hydra; but he would have found an equine expedition quite another affair. For four full days several of us Correspondents were engaged in the horse business, and we succeeded at last in purchasing them; but that was not half the labor.

We needed saddles, bridles, and other equipments. We obtained them, and were on the eve of starting, when we discovered that our animals wanted shoeing. For fifteen hours the shoeing process went on, and then was not finished. During that period, the horses had broken their halters, gone lame, and become out of order generally.

Still, we did not despair. We hoped to get off during the Autumn—horses, saddles, shoes, blankets, Bohemians, and all.

Several of our party had grown sick from delay, vexation, and annoyance, and were unable to take the ride after the Rebels.

Our steeds, I fancy, had all the ills that horse-flesh has been heir to since the primeval steed was christened by Father Adam. They were cheap animals—that is, we had not paid more than six times their value (and they were warranted sound for the price)—which guarantee meant that, if very tenderly treated, they would go a mile a day and recover from the exertion.

I was assured my horse was less than a hundred years old, and that he gave fair warning before he fell down. Who says he was not a good steed?

From his peculiar gait and idiosyncrasy of manner, I am led to believe he had served a long and faithful apprenticeship in a tread-mill, for he had a delightful habit of going round and round, in a manner exceedingly suggestive of that or some other kindred avocation. If my suspicions were baseless, and the Pythagorean doctrine true, the soul of my horse must formerly have inhabited the body of a servant-girl addicted to wooden shoes and waltzing.

All our horses were atrocious. Each one had his specific peculiarity; but they all had one common generic peculiarity—that of not being worth a d—n.

No danger of those nags being seized by guerrillas, who would not have captured them if they had been paid for it.

* * * * * * *

The battle-field of Perryville I visited a few days after the fight. It extends over a distance of ten miles, and its appearance at that time did not indicate a very fierce contest. The principal part of the fighting, however, was confined to an area of less than a mile square, and was marked by numerous graves of men who died the death of heroes, but have left no heroes' fame.

The ground is rolling, somewhat similar to that of Wilson's Creek, though more favorable for a general engagement. Every few hundred yards there is rising ground; and upon those swells different batteries were placed, giving free scope for mowing down the advancing columns of infantry. The severest struggle occurred in the open country, where there was little timber, though the small hills immediately adjacent were covered with soldiers, who, at so short a range, did much execution with the musket. There could have been little advantage of ground, except that the Rebels had a creek and much broken land in their rear.

The dead had all been buried; and beyond the fresh heaps of earth, the fragments of clothing, and the carcasses of horses, there was nothing to tell the visitor of a general engagement. The appearance of the place indicated little more than a brisk skirmish. I have seen battle-fields which gave more evidence of a fierce contest, months subsequent to the event, than Perryville did only a few days after the fight.

The trees were rarely scarred, though here and there one saw a tall hickory from which the bark was ripped, or an oak whose branches had been cut off by the shells and cannon-balls. The houses in the immediate neighborhood were struck frequently by the projectiles; and even those in town were pierced by the artillery.

When myself and companions visited the field, it looked as peaceful and pleasant as though no warrior's foot had ever pressed the undulating soil. The country surrounding is picturesque, and the landscape lay bathed and beautiful in the warm October sunshine. Silence reigned on the hill and in the valley, and the shrunken creek looked like one of those "rural scenes" artists represent contiguous to an idle and deserted mill, with cattle on the brink, lowing, with partially slaked thirst, to the sultry Summer.

The battle of Perryville is one of the most inexplicable military events of the War, so far as our army is concerned. I have no disposition at this late day to find fault with any one; but the conduct of General Buell in permitting nearly, if not the whole, of Bragg's forces to engage a portion of ours, and refusing to give our regiments, when they stood there burning to rush into the contest, permission to re-enforce their overpowered companions in arms, is to my mind, and to that of nearly every Union officer who was on that field, beyond the power of satisfactory explanation.

Bragg's army ought to, and could, have been almost annihilated on that very spot. The opportunity was golden, and could not be regained. If ever there was a place where a skillful General would have desired to meet an opposing force—if ever there were circumstances that seemed to promise a crushing victory, that place was Perryville, and those circumstances the surroundings and situation and *matériel* and *morale* of our army.

Buell and his friends have endeavored to give a solution of the mystery of Perryville; but they have only made the darkness deeper. I have never known so universal an expression of disapprobation—to use a very mild term—of any General as there was of Buell on the part of his army after that battle. I should not like to repeat the terms of opprobrium that were employed toward him; but I must say that every one of his officers, from Generals to Second Lieutenants, and even the non-commissioned officers and privates, were so entirely dissatisfied with him, after they had been compelled to give up the pursuit of the enemy, that it was deemed absolutely necessary, for the sake of subordination, to supersede their commander-in-chief.

* * * * * * *

Lieutenant-Colonel James O. Nixon, formerly editor and proprietor of the New Orleans *Crescent*, was acting Colonel of Scott's Louisiana Cavalry during the campaign in Kentucky. Nixon has had some queer experiences, and not of the most agreeable character either. Eighteen months before, he was supposed to be worth five hundred thousand dollars; was the principal proprietor of the *Crescent*, then a very valuable journal, and an owner of a great deal of real estate; but when with Bragg, as he himself stated, he was not worth enough to buy a beggar's coat.

Nixon I very well remember in New Orleans, some years ago, as a very pleasant, good-looking fellow, exceedingly well dressed, and affecting the elegant and luxurious to a very large degree—a *bon vivant* and fashionable man of the world.

The "Revolution" revolutionized him, certainly, and converted him into a ragged, desperate Rebel, with a dead Past behind, and a dark Future before him. Still, when such men can endure what he endured for a bad cause,—and endure it too with patience and cheerfulness as he did,—it speaks well for their earnestness and their inverted heroism.

* * * * * * *

If there was one man more detested and admired than another in Fayette County, Kentucky, in 1862, it was John H. Morgan, a former resident of Lexington. The Unionists hated him as they did his Satanic Majesty; and the Secessionists were disposed to apotheosize him for what the Loyalists regarded as his villany. Morgan made his name a terror in Kentucky, and gained a widespread fame for daring, energy, and skill as a military leader, though he did very little to merit such a reputation.

Beyond the commission of outrages on defenseless persons, and wholesale plunderings in unguarded neighborhoods, he performed few acts that should have entitled him to the consideration even of the "Confederates." He and his men knew how to steal good horses, and to procure fresh ones when the old ones were exhausted; and by that means he was enabled to move rapidly from point to point to some undisturbed field of plunder. Deprived of that peculiar forte, he became nothing save John Morgan the sporting-man, an unprincipled and a common swaggerer.

Morgan had some notoriety as a libertine, and is said to have cruelly wronged several poor and unbefriended girls in that vicinity; which, perhaps, accounts for the worship rendered him by the feminine Rebels in Lexington during the hey-day of Secessionism in that State.

It has been said that women love best the men who wrong them most, and Morgan appears to have been a shining verification of the aphorism.

When the War broke out, no woman who had any self-respect would have suffered him to approach her—and yet, two years after, those who assumed to be fine ladies crowned him with garlands, and vied with each other for the honor of the attentions of a somewhat romantic ruffian and a common black-leg.

Secession makes wonderful revolutions in petticoats. Feminine voices, modulated to sweetness by culture and refinement, proclaimed him hero, whom—a little while before—to have recognized would have been degradation.

So much for Success! It is the world's fascinater, and the bender of unwilling knees.

CHAPTER XXXI.

THE RAM ARKANSAS DEFYING OUR FLEET.

The Expedition up the Yazoo.—Unexpected Meeting of the Rebel Monster.—Her Engagement with the Union Vessels.—Their Discomfiture and Retreat.—Her Passage of the Union Flotilla.—Her Exposure to a Terrible Fire.—Explosion on Board the Lancaster.—Casualties on both Sides.—Bohemian Reflections on Running Batteries.

At the commencement of the siege of Vicksburg, in July, 1862, the famous Rebel ram and gunboat Arkansas ran down the Yazoo into the Mississippi, and by the entire Union Flotilla. Her intention was to descend the river by night, but she was unavoidably delayed. Her officers had, of course, been fully informed by spies and scouts of the situation of Farragut's and Davis's vessels, and of the fact that they did not have up steam, on account of the sickness on the Fleet and the excessive heat of the weather.

The famous and formidable gunboat Arkansas, of which the enemy had been boasting for months, which was run off from Memphis in an unfinished state and towed up the Yazoo, was discovered by us on the 15th of July—if not to our sorrow, at least to our intense mortification.

The Arkansas was no myth, as many had begun to believe: her strength and power of resistance were no idle boast. She did the things of which the foe affirmed her capable. She surely bearded the lion in his den—the Douglas in his hall.

Think of her—with twelve guns, running the blockade of fourteen or fifteen vessels of war and several armed rams, with more than twice an hundred guns! Was it not delightfully, refreshingly daring?

The powder gunboat Tyler, Captain William Gwin, and the steam ram Queen of the West, Captain Joseph Ford, started at five o'clock in the morning on a reconnoissance up the Yazoo, designing to go as far as Liverpool Landing, sixty-five miles from the mouth, to determine the character of the Rebel defenses there, and learn, if possible, something of the condition of the far-famed Arkansas, claimed by many to be equal in impenetrability to the world-renowned Merrimac. Another Correspondent and myself had made arrangements to go on the expedition, but were a few seconds too late; the vessels having started half an hour before the appointed time.

From the best information we had been able to gather on the Fleet, it was believed that the Rebel gunboat was still unfinished, and lying aground in the Yazoo above the blockade, with no probability of making her appearance during the War.

The Carondelet, Captain Henry Walke, accompanied the gunboat and ram as far as the mouth of Yazoo River, and then took her position, while her two companions ascended the stream. The latter had not gone more than six miles before they discovered a strange-looking craft descending, which they could not make out. It was thought she must be a tug; but surely there never was such a queer tug before. Her appearance was anomalous, and glasses were directed toward her with little advantage. She was moving rapidly down, and the conclusion was reached that she must be the Arkansas—she could be nothing else.

After that little speculation, the stranger was within a hundred and fifty yards of the Tyler, and that there might be no doubt of her intentions and character, she fired a large gun at the gunboat, but did not strike her. The Tyler fired in return, and was rounding to, to give a broadside to the enemy, but could not do so for lack of time. The foe was almost at her stern, and discharged two of her guns with their muzzles almost resting against the Union vessel's side. The Tyler backed for a little distance and fired several times, giving herself full leisure and opportunity to perceive her antagonist was a powerful iron-clad ship that could every way overmatch her.

There was no hope of success in such an unequal struggle, and Captain Gwin, a most gallant officer, whose valor and patriotism had been proved by the severest tests, concluded to save his men, if possible, by out-running the Arkansas.

The Tyler's bow was soon down stream, and the Arkansas very little behind her, firing rapidly, and the pursued replying with her stern-guns coolly and regularly. The Tyler's shot seemed to have little, if any, effect upon the Rebel, while the latter's fire was often destructive, entering the Unionist's sides, and piercing her timbers, and sending showers of splinters over her deck.

Before the Tyler had reached the mouth of Yazoo River, eight of her men were killed, and seventeen wounded. Five of the sailors' heads were shot entirely off by a single ball from the enemy, and the unfortunate fellows fell together—a bloody, deformed, and hideous mass of quivering death.

The Queen of the West, seeing the Tyler turn from her enemy, and observing that the Rebel was a powerful ram as well as gunboat, knew it would be useless to attempt to butt her adversary. Besides, as she was under the command of the gunboat, and saw her consort avoiding the action, she thought it proper to imitate her example.

The Arkansas had an immense wrought-iron prow or beak, weighing several tons—before which the little wooden ram could have offered no more resistance than a paper boat.

The Tyler and Queen passed rapidly out of the Yazoo River, to give the fleet in the Mississippi warning of the approach of the Arkansas; but as soon as they appeared above the bend the cause of their early return was suspected. The heavy firing had been heard for an hour, and as it grew louder and louder, it was evident that our vessels must have met a formidable and powerful foe.

The Carondelet, Captain Henry Walke, saw and knew her antagonist at once, but determined to give her battle, and she did so in the most gallant style.

The Union vessel sent several shots against the mailed sides of her foe as she advanced, but did her no apparent harm. The Arkansas answered with heavy and metallic voice, and her responses told fearfully on the valiant craft, whose officers, however, were nothing daunted by their powerful antagonist.

Before the third Rebel shot, a number of the crew were killed and wounded on the Carondelet, which, during a spirited engagement of ten minutes, lost nine men in killed, and twenty-two wounded, and three missing. One of the hostile shots severed some part of her machinery, and, causing the steam to escape, so alarmed a portion of the crew, that they jumped overboard, to avoid, as they supposed, being scalded to death.

As soon as Captain Walke perceived he could not injure the Arkansas with his guns, he resolved to board her, and gave the order, which hardly passed his lips, when the Unionist ran along aside, and a brave band leaped on the narrow deck of the enemy.

But every thing was iron-proof, and tightly closed. Only the ports and loop-holes were open for the sharpshooters. After endeavoring in vain to get inside the Arkansas, for some minutes, the seamen were forced to return, dispirited and chagrined, to their own boat.

A few more shots were exchanged ; when the Arkansas made off, and hastened so rapidly down the river, that the Carondelet, in her crippled condition, could not follow her.

Very soon after, the dangerous enemy was seen coming with diminished speed towards the Fleet ; very few of the vessels having steam up, and the rams themselves carrying little more than enough to make head against the current. Every officer on the Flotilla was anxious to see if the Arkansas would have the temerity to attempt running by the entire cordon of Union ships. She left them little time to doubt. She moved on in a measured and deliberate manner, and in a direct line.

As she passed the rams, the Lancaster, with only sixty pounds of steam, attempted to butt her; but, before she could place herself in position to do so, the Arkansas fired several times into her side, wounding several of the ram's crew, and exploded her mud-receiver.

The steam poured out all over the Lancaster, and it was thought her boiler had exploded, especially as she began drifting down the river. Several tugs and transports went to her assistance, and towed her up stream, when it was discovered that two of her negro deck hands had been killed, six of the men scalded, and two or three were missing; the last having been drowned by leaping overboard.

The Arkansas continued her course by the Hartford and Richmond, neither of which gave her a broadside, though they fired at her repeatedly; passed the Oneida, Iroquois, Wissahickon, Cincinnati, Sumter, Bragg, Essex, Benton, and all the rest. They all fired at her when she was above, as she went down, and when she was below; but, though heavy shot often struck her, they did not seem to injure her. Now she had run the gantlet, and was seen turning the bend; and soon after she passed under the guns of the water-batteries at Vicksburg, reposing under the shade of the laurels she had so nobly won, and welcomed by every true Rebel heart in the Rebel stronghold.

The Cincinnati and the Benton in fifteen minutes got up more steam, and ran down the river, again opening their guns upon the batteries and the Arkansas, both of which replied vigorously. The Benton steamed immediately under the enemy's guns, and was struck a number of times, three of the shots passing into and through her. One of her crew had his head and a part of his body shot off while holding the end of a lanyard, and two others were so dangerously wounded, that the surgeon had little hope of their rècovery.

The Benton was damaged, but not materially. A number of the rooms on her gun-deck were completely riddled, and a one hundred and twenty-eight pound shot passed into her port quarter through the Third Master's room, and then through the culinary department, and finally into the Commodore's cabin, where, after destroying a good deal of furniture, it very pacifically went to bed, and lay upon the pillow on which, two hours before, the Flag-officer had been peacefully reposing.

Whether the Arkansas was injured or not during the fight was then a matter of conjecture ; but, since then, I have seen the report of Lieutenant Isaac N. Brown, commanding the vessel, which states that she was badly cut up, her smoke-stack and pilot-house destroyed, and her armor frequently perforated. Ten of her crew were killed outright, and eighteen men, including three of her officers, were wounded. Those who ran the gantlet suffered fearfully from heat and want of air. Lieutenant Brown, who has the reputation of a very daring, and even reckless man, is reported to have said that no consideration under Heaven would have induced him to try the terrible experiment again.

* * * * * * *

Speaking of defying guns and fleets prompts me to

give here, though somewhat out of place, the sensations one experiences in scenes of peril such as running batteries, in which interesting experiments I have had my share of experience on the Mississippi, and by which, some months before my capture, I had the honor, through a very genteel wound, to lose exactly fourteen drops of my sanguineous fluid.

That the sensation is pleasurable in itself, I do not believe; but that it is somewhat exciting and rather peculiar, those who have tried it will generally admit. The fact that it is dangerous usually attracts, and the chance of its resulting in your quietus, removes it from the class of vulgar sensations.

Most men feel their greatest uneasiness before the batteries they expect to pass have opened fire, because uncertainty and anxious expectation are severer tests of the nerves than any tangible reality, however horrible.

Few cultivated mortals, possessed of sensibility and imagination, but are capable of fear, though they may not reveal it. They have a natural horror of pain and peril, and yet they possess, in most cases, pride and will enough to overcome the weaknesses of instinct.

They are not brave, but they may be courageous, and are so usually, when experience has enabled them to calculate probabilities, and taught them a half indifference to what they have often escaped without harm.

When a man is under the fire of batteries in an unarmed vessel, and hears the crash of timber, or the explosion of a shell overhead, or the roar of a round shot as it passes not far from him, he begins to think he has been in more agreeable places, and contrast suggests quiet and pacific scenes, where gunpowder is not burned, and the trade of the undertaker is not coerced into unnatural animation.

If he sees a poor fellow stricken down or disemboweled at his side, or the groan of a dying unfortunate reaches his keenly sensitive ear, he can hardly resist a shudder, and wonders when his own turn will come.

But it does not come, and as the long minutes pass, he begins to believe it will not, though the shot plunge about the boat as before. At first he was alarmed; then he grew desperate.

Now he is rising into coolness, and becomes capable of reasoning upon his situation, which seems far less perilous than it did.

Perhaps at no time did the apprehension of death disturb him so much as that of a dreadful wound which would cause intense suffering.

If a man in the midst of battle could be certain that the shot which would reach him would prove instantaneously fatal, he would be calmer than he is; for the idea of pain, to a sensitive nature, is more cruel than death.

To a philosophic mind, and one capable of making its philosophy practical, death must not only be, but must seem, unavoidable—something which, if escaped to-day, will come to-morrow.

No human power can avoid the dread necessity. Nothing is certain on this Planet save death; and who can say it is better to perish this year or the next, in youth or old age?

Most mortals are as well prepared, to use an orthodox phrase, of very unsatisfactory significance, to quit the world at one time as another. In fact, they are never ready to go. There is always something left undone—a little delay is ever desirable.

The business of existence is rarely closed up so that a balance-sheet may be struck between the known and the unknown.

Once life is snuffed out like a candle, there is no more dying, according to the popular belief (though we have no more reason to think this than that we never lived before we entered the World), and that ought to be a species of melancholy satisfaction.

No one can unravel the future, whether it be for good or evil, happiness or misery. What is to be will be; albeit the trouble is to determine how much we are the subjects of free will and how much of fate.

This sounds very speculative for a brain passing batteries; but the active mind will so think, though it were far better not to reason at all under such circumstances.

With the beginning of action, all thought, except that conducive to action, should subside. Then there is no introspection, no anticipation of unseen things, no hightening of peril, no illusion of pain.

But every thing terminates, and you get out of the batteries' range, and a new sensation fills you.

You feel more comfortable, and you marvel you were not more uneasy than you were, and at the same moment wonder your pulse was quicker than when sipping Château Margaux at an elaborate dinner.

How much more peril you saw than there was! How many more wounds and deaths were in your mind than in the assignment of Fortune!

You do not know whether you are more like a timid child or a hero after your experience, and you conclude, subsequently, that you little resemble either; that men are very uncertain animals, touching Heaven and Earth at the same time, and vibrating ever between Achilles and Thersites—the angel and the clay.

It is difficult to calculate upon a man's courage, as it is called.

The boldest may be frightened at a shadow.

We cease to love ourselves when we comprehend ourselves; and yet we may perceive good enough within to engender contempt for others.

The philosophic life is but a series of experiments upon ourselves, and though we learn much therefrom, the last analysis brings nothing positive, nothing absolute; and we are still but an atom in the sunbeam, a sand-grain on the sea-shore.

Whether we run batteries or stop bullets, make poems or statues, lead armies or live in solitude, obtain fame or dwell unknown in the by-paths, all experience is unsatisfactory, all possessions are poor, all honor worthless.

We are ever drawn by the Ideal, and deceived by the Possible.

The blossom withers while we hold it: Love dies in our first embrace: the Future, to which we all stretch out our longing arms, has no existence. And yet what is to be will be!

But where is the subtle magician of the mind who can reveal to us the purposes of Fate, or illumine for a moment the darkness that must ever surround the Sphere?

CHAPTER XXXII.

PLANTATION LIFE IN THE SOUTH.

Expedition in Search of Cotton, Cattle, and Guerrillas.—Plantations along the Mississippi.—Anxiety of the Negroes for Freedom.—Sad Scenes on Shore.—An African Andromache.—A Miscegenated Southern Family.

DURING the latter part of the siege of Vicksburg, under General Grant, in March, 1863, two or three of the Bohemians, seeing no prospect of any immediate activity in that vicinity, joined a foraging expedition up the river in quest of any adventures that might result from the trip. Consequently, we steamed up and down the Father of Waters, and wandered through Louisiana, Mississippi, and Arkansas, looking out for cotton, cattle, and guerrillas.

Among other places, we touched at the American Bend, in Washington County, Mississippi.

The principal plantations there were owned by Dr. Wm. W. Worthington and his brother Samuel, both advanced in years, and having four sons in the insurgent army. They were very wealthy before the Rebellion, owning three plantations each, and some two or three hundred negroes, many of whom had been taken back into the swamps and to Texas.

The private residences and grounds of the brothers Worthington were far superior to those one usually sees in the South. They made some assumption to comeliness as well as comfort, and were on the whole rather pleasant, which must be attributed to the fact of their owners coming from Kentucky, which has been largely influenced by the spirit and enterprise of the North.

While at the Bend I had frequent talks with the contrabands, and found them without exception most anxious for freedom. They were willing to run any risks almost, provided they could have any assurance of escaping bondage. They manifested the utmost aversion to slavery, and declared they would rather be free, if they had to toil harder and live upon the merest pittance in the North, than be idle and live in comfort in the South.

An elderly negress, Harriet Garratt, told me a sad story, which, though by no means novel, will, I think, bear repetition, and which I know to be true, from the names of persons, and from circumstances she mentioned in Kentucky, where I was quite well acquainted. She belonged to a young woman residing in Mason county, Kentucky, and after her mistress's marriage, was taken to Cincinnati, and there manumitted. Harriet, hearing soon after that her husband was to be sent to Mississippi, determined to follow him, and accordingly accompanied him, with her free papers on her person.

Arrived there, a slave-dealer, one Hines, in whose keeping she and her husband, with other negroes, were, discovered and destroyed her papers, and sold her to Dr. Worthington, from which time she worked in the cotton-fields.

Harriet was very desirous of going North, and her eyes moistened at the mere idea, though she had long ceased, she said, to hope for the freedom of which she had been so basely defrauded. Her tale interested my Bohemian companion and myself, and we made an arrangement with the captain of one of the transports to take her and her youngest daughter—she had three—as washerwomen.

The next morning we visited the sable auntie, and communicated the intelligence to her. She received it with delight, but with conflicting emotions. Her eyes filled with tears ; her bosom heaved ; she spoke with difficulty. Had her nerves been more delicate she would have fainted ; but swooning is a pretty trick the unenlightened daughters of Africa have not yet learned. At first she poured out her heart in gratitude. She would go at once ; asked us a hundred questions in as many seconds ; told her daughter, who stood near, to make preparations for their departure, and was tremulous with excitement, laughing and weeping hysterically by turns.

In a few minutes, however, a new idea seemed to enter the old woman's mind, and a shadow fell upon her face that was visible even through her sable skin. Her husband and her other two daughters, whom she had forgotten in the first ebullition of her feelings, had occurred to her. "I cannot leab de ole man and dem ere childern, my good massas. Dey would grieb demselves to deff, suah. I couldn't hab any joy in de dear old Norf when I knowed my ole man and de gals was down heah in Dixie workin' in de cotton wid de hard lashes on deir back. O no! Gawd bress you bofe for your kindness to ole auntie ; but I couldn't do it. I nevah feel right in my heart if I did." And the old slave was silent, for her voice was choked with tears, and her frame trembled with emotion.

Many other negroes of both sexes stood near, as we were at the slave quarters, and though they did not hear what was said, they felt what was passing, and looked on in silence and in sympathy.

It was a touching scene—that struggle between love and the desire for freedom, both so natural, and yet so opposed—the yielding to one destroying the hope of the other.

Most gladly would we have furnished to auntie and her whole family the means of going North ; but we could not. We had no power. We had done all we could ; and so we told her. "I knows dat, my young massas," she sobbed out. "You's bery good. I'se bery tankful. God bress you !"

I lay no claim to religion, as it is usually understood, and see little meaning in theological terminology ; but there was an earnestness in the woman's benediction that was not without its impressiveness.

Many a time I have heard "God bless you !" which

> "By daily use hath almost lost its sense,"

and from lips that were fresh with youth and rosy with beauty ; but the celestial invocation, I am sure, never came from a more grateful heart, or fell from a tongue, albeit uneducated, more sincere in its impassioned utterance.

When the devotion of this poor ignorant negress to her husband and children was made so pathetically manifest, I could not help but contrast it with the connubial and maternal feeling of many of the fair daughters of Fortune, the darling favorites of Society, who lounge on satin sofas, or tread with dainty feet the luxurious boudoirs of Fifth Avenue or Madison Square.

* * * * * *

Finding it very difficult to obtain cattle at the American Bend, we returned below to Sunny-side Landing, Arkansas, hoping to have our quest there rewarded. At that place, very near the Northern Louisiana line, was the plantation of a third brother of the Worthingtons I have mentioned. His name was Elisha, and he had never been married, though he had availed himself of the recognized succedaneum of the South, having, many years before, taken as his mistress the daughter of a Choctaw Indian and a negress, and admitted her to all the privileges and advantages supposed to belong to the uxorial state.

That gentleman of rare taste and choice morals had two children—a son and daughter—probably eighteen and seventeen years old, whom he educated in Ohio, and sent to Europe, but who still bore the appearance and something of the manners of the native African. They lived in their father's mansion, one of the most comfortable I have seen in Arkansas, keeping house for him during his absence in Texas, whither he went last June, after the fall of Memphis. He was a notorious Rebel, and fled from what he believed to be the Yankee wrath, knowing, no doubt, far better than we, how well he deserved hanging.

CHAPTER XXXIII.

CAPTURE OF THE TRIBUNE CORRESPONDENTS.

Reflections on our Return to Freedom.—The Effect of Imprisonment.—Rapidity of Restoration to One's Normal Condition.—Running the Batteries of Vicksburg.—Incidents of the Undertaking.—Terrible Fire from the Rebel Stronghold.—Complete Wreck of our Expedition.—Brilliant Prospects for Dying.—Adventures of the Bohemians.—Grotesque Appearance of the Prisoners.

Not many weeks ago, when the author dwelt in the midst of Filth and Misery, Despair and Death; when those had been his constant companions for long and wearisome months, and dreary seasons that knew no change; it seemed as if no other than a prison-life had been his—that Freedom, Beauty, Abundance, Pleasure, were mere ideals of an aspiring soul, and had only shone upon the soft landscape of his dearest dreams.

Even so does the Past now shrink before the Present. The by-gone horrors appear phantasms of the brain amid the comforts and the luxuries of metropolitan life.

As I peer out of the window at the vast and varied human tides of Broadway, and hear the hum and roar of its mighty throng, and the heavy peals of the passing hours from the City-Hall clock, the intermediate space between two periods of liberty is stricken out.

The years before and since the War come together like the shifted scenes of the theater, shutting from view a dark dungeon and its darker recollections.

As freedom and civilization were once too good, so rebel prisons and their painful associations are now too hideous, to be believed. The existing sensation is the measure of the mind, which realizes with difficulty a past consciousness of opposite impressions.

"How happy you must be!" has often been my greeting since my arrival within our lines; and the expression is very natural.

If a man who has been a prisoner in the hands of the enemy for a long while could only preserve the remembrance of his surroundings as a criterion for the future, his restoration to freedom would be a return to paradise.

But the truth is, the man changes with his situation.

He glides so easily and readily into his normal status that the abnormal seems at once insupportable.

Therefore, the Fifth Avenue, the Central Park, the Academy of Music, Beauty, Banquets, Diamonds, have no special charm. They are the things of course, the every-day garniture of civilized existence.

But the retrospect of not many weeks makes us shudder, and wonder at what now appears an impossible philosophy.

Walked I ever amid those pestilential scenes unmoved? Stood I ever, calm and steady-voiced, beside all those suffering forms? Bore I ever those heavy burdens, physical and spiritual, so long, without fainting or perishing on the weary way?

We know not what we can endure, is as true as truth, and is no oftener considered than by the poor wretch whom the fortunes of war have consigned to a Southern prison. He finds, after months have passed, that he is still alive and sane, in spite of starvation, freezing, tyranny, and isolation, and believes himself of iron mold.

The scene changes, and liberty and kind fortune dawn upon him. Then he looks behind, as the traveler who has passed the brink of a precipice in the darkness, and shudders while he thinks how narrow has been his escape; how horrible would have been his death.

A few months since I would have relished the coarsest food, and deemed it delightful to dwell in the meanest hut. Now—so soon does man grow pampered in places of purple—the choicest viands tempt me all in vain, and I toss with restlessness upon the softest couch.

An age ago it seems, and yet the almanac tells me it was on the night of May 3d, 1863, since my confrère, Mr. Albert D. Richardson, and Mr. Richard T. Colburn of the *World* newspaper, with some thirty-two others, left the head-quarters of General Grant at Milliken's Bend, Louisiana, to run the batteries of Vicksburg, Warrenton, and Grand Gulf, where hostilities had already begun.

I had tried to run the batteries of Vicksburg before; but circumstances interfered; and, as the Calvinists would say, I was pre-ordained.

The expedition,—consisting of a steam-tug, the Sturges, and two barges loaded with provisions and bales of hay,—was very badly fitted out; the hay lying loosely about, where any bursting shell might ignite it, and neither buckets, in the very probable event of a conflagration, nor small boats as a means of escape, having been provided.

In addition to this, the moon was at its full, whereas the other battery-running expeditions had gone down on dark nights; and, about the time we reached the point of danger, was in the zenith of the heavens. The night was as light as day.

As we sat smoking our cigars on the barges, we could see every tree on the banks of the mighty river; and as we neared the peninsula opposite Vicksburg, we could observe the different streets and buildings of the city that had so long defied the combined power of our army and navy.

An officer with us had a bottle of Catawba, and as there was some probability that, in the storm of shot and shell which awaited us, its flavor might be damaged, we quaffed its contents to the speedy downfall of the hostile stronghold, and the early suppression of the Rebellion; to the women we loved—dwellers in the region of the Infinite—and to the consolation of the unfortunately married—surely a generous sentiment in favor of an ample class.

Ours was indeed a merry party; and long shall I remember the agreeableness of the occasion before Rebel gunpowder interfered with its harmony.

We smoked, and laughed, and jested, and chatted, saying if that was to be our last appearance on any (earthly) stage, that we would remember it with pleasure when we obtained a new engagement—on some celestial newspaper.

There seemed no anxiety among our little band.

They had all volunteered, and were desirous of an adventure, which they had in extenso.

As we neared the hostile stronghold, we lighted fresh cigars; destroyed our private correspondence; settled our affairs, in the event of accident, after the Bohemian fashion; and would have commended our souls to our creditors, if we had known we had any—*i. e.*, either the one or the other—and our bodies to the classic process of incremation.

The incremation process was a flight of romance. We knew, if lost in the Mississippi, we would furnish cold collations for catfish.

About midnight, or a little after, we were within a mile and a half of Vicksburg by the bend of the river, but not more than a quarter of that distance in a direct line, and directly in range of the heavy batteries planted for several miles above, below, and in front of the town.

We were moving very little faster than the current of the stream; and as we began to round the peninsula, the trees on which had all been cut down, to give the enemy an open space for the operation of his guns against approaching vessels, the Rebel pickets, who had most needlessly and very unwisely been permitted to cross the river and take position on the Louisiana shore, gave the alarm by discharging their muskets at us—without detriment, however—followed by a signal-rocket from the city, and the opening of the fiery entertainment to which we had invited ourselves on that bright, soft, delicious night of May.

Now the heavy guns opened with their thunderous roar, and the first struck one of the barges, as we knew from the jar of the boat. "Well done for the Rebels," said we, admiring accuracy of aim even in our foes.

The truth was, the insurgents had, from various causes, never had a fair opportunity on the previous expeditions. The night had been dark; the artillerymen had not been on the alert; the guns had not been well trained; the fuses had been defective.

That time, as we subsequently learned, the Rebels were well prepared. They had, from past experience, obtained the exact range, and felt confident of blowing any craft that made the venture out of the water. Certainly they made a good beginning, and we a bad end of it.

The round-shot howled, and the shells shrieked over our heads, and sometimes cut the straw of the hay-bales in a manner calculated to give any one not entirely *blasé* something of a sensation.

We tried to count the shots, but they were so rapid as to defy our power of enumeration. I had witnessed a number of heavy bombardments during the War, but had hardly known more gunpowder to be burnt in the same space of time.

All along the shore we saw the flashes of the guns.

The fire seemed to leap out of the strong earthworks for at least a mile, and the bright and quiet stars appeared to tremble before the bellowing of the scores of batteries.

Clouds of smoke rose along the river like a dense fog, and the water and the atmosphere shook with reverberations.

Opposite Vicksburg the Mississippi is narrow and deep, and at the same time was rather low, so that at times we were not more than three or four hundred yards from the ten-inch guns.

It did seem strange our frail vessels, which were struck again and again, were not blown to pieces. But the little tug—semi-occasionally we heard its quick, sharp puff—passed on and we were yet unharmed.

We had now passed the bend of the river just above the city, where a sand-bar, on which we had been told we would probably strike and ground, was plainly visible, and the greatest danger was over.

Still we moved on, and the Rebels, as if disappointed and enraged, seemed to augment their efforts.

Faster and heavier the batteries thundered, and louder howled the shot and shrieked the shell above, below, around.

Again and again the shells burst over head, and the iron fragments fell about the little crew; but no groans nor cries were heard. We seemed fated to run the gantlet in safety,—to go beyond the power of harm.

For three-quarters of an hour we were under the terrible fire, and were near the lower end of the city.

Another quarter would put us out of danger, for we had passed the heaviest batteries.

Still the guns opposite, from above and below, belched forth their iron messengers of death; and the stars blinked, and the waters shook, and the sulphurous mist crept like a troop of phantoms along the turbid river.

Every moment we thought a shot might wreck our expedition; but in the occasional pause of the artillery, as I have said before, we could detect the rapid puff, puff, puff of the little tug, which was the sure sign that we still floated.

Suddenly a huge crash by our side, of wood and iron. A deep and heavy and peculiar report. A rush of steam, and a descending shower of cinders and ashes that covered our persons.

We heard the puff of the tug no more; but in its place went up a wild yell which we had often heard in the front of battle—shrill, exultant, savage; so different from the deep, manly, generous shout of the Union soldiers, that we knew at once it was the triumphant acclamation of our cruel foe.

The boiler of the tug had been exploded by a plunging shot from one of the upper batteries. The shot was accidental, but extremely effective. It wrecked our expedition at once. After passing through the boiler, the shell exploded in the furnaces, throwing the fires upon the barges and igniting the loose hay immediately.

"The play is over," said Richardson; "Hand in your checks, boys," exclaimed Colburn; "A change of base for the Bohemians," remarked the undersigned; and we glanced around, and heard the groans and sharp cries of the wounded and the scalded.

We rushed forward to try and trample out the flames, but they rose behind us like fiery serpents, and paled the full-orbed moon, and lit up the dark waters of the Stygian river far and near.

The Rebels, who had ceased firing for a moment, now bent themselves to their guns once more, and the iron missiles swept over and around us, and several of the soldiers on board were wounded by fragments of bursting shells.

Every one was now bent on saving himself. A few of the privates and some of the tug's crew plunged madly overboard, with fragments of the wreck in their hands, and in three minutes none but the wounded and the journalistic trio remained on the burning barges.

We threw the bales of hay into the river for the benefit of the wounded and those who could not swim—for we had early learned Leander's art—and then arranged our own programme.

Richardson went off first on a bale of hay, from which a large round-shot, passing near, and dashing a column of spray into the air just beyond him, soon displaced his corporeality.

Colburn followed ; and I, seeing my field of operations hemmed in by rapidly advancing fire, answered his summons, and dived, after divesting myself of all superfluous clothing, into the aqueous embrace of the Father of Waters.

Several bales of hay were floating below, but I swam to the one nearest Colburn, and there we concluded to get beyond the town and pickets, and then, striking out for the Louisiana shore, make our way as best we could back to the army.

The Rebels had then ceased firing—certainly not for humanity's sake, we thought—and the reason was patent when we heard the sound of row-locks across the water.

The chivalrous whippers of women were evidently coming to capture us.

My companion and myself believed if we kept very quiet, and floated with our faces only out of the water, we would not be discovered.

A yawl full of armed men passed near us, and we fancied we would escape. Like the so-called "Confederacy," we wanted to be let alone.

Just as we were internally congratulating ourselves, a small boat darted round the corner of the burning barge, and we were hauled in by a couple of stalwart fellows, after the manner of colossal catfish, without even the asking of our leave.

In fifteen minutes we were under guard on shore, where we found our collaborateur Richardson safe and sound.

About half our small crew had been killed and wounded, and the rest were prisoners.

More unlucky than the defenders of Thermopylæ—one of them reached Sparta to bear the tidings—not one of us returned to tell the story.

We were all reported lost, we learned afterward; though General Sherman's humorous comment, when apprised that three of the Bohemians had been killed—"That's good! We'll have dispatches now from hell before breakfast"—did not prove a veracious prediction.

The gifted General's mistake arose from his confused topography.

The army correspondents do not usually date their dispatches at his head-quarters.

The Bohemians lost all their baggage; and I, having prepared myself for Byronic exercise, went ashore with nothing on but shirt and pantaloons.

Barefooted was I also, and I appeared most forlorn as I walked in company with the others through the moonlit streets of the town.

A sudden metamorphosis was ours, from freedom to captivity; and we discovered by crossing the river we had reached another phase of civilization.

We prisoners formed a sad and droll procession, as we moved across the bayou towards the town.

A number of the captives were either wounded with fragments of shell or scalded by the steam, and groaned and wailed piteously as we walked along; while others, barefooted, bareheaded, coatless, and begrimed with cinders and ashes, looked like Charon's ferrymen on a strike for higher wages.

The author bore a close resemblance to old Time without his scythe, endeavoring to rejuvenate himself by hydropathic treatment.

All of us, save the poor fellows who had been wounded and scalded, were in the best of spirits; and we marched merrily through the streets, chatting and laughing at our mishap—which proved a farce, so far as we the unhurt were concerned, for it was an escaped tragedy—and gayly speculating upon what would be the next turn of Fortune.

The night was exceedingly lovely; and the moon poured down its tranquil radiance, and the soft May breezes kissed our brow and cheek, while we moved through the Rebel town closely guarded, as if they pitied our condition, and would have consoled us for our ill-starred fate.

CHAPTER XXXIV.

OUR IMPRISONMENT AT VICKSBURG.

Consignment to a Mississippi Jail.—Repulsiveness of the Place.—Character of the Inmates.—Rebel Idea of Comfortable Quarters.—A Fragrant Spot.—Parole of the Captives.—Our Removal to the Court-House—Courteous Treatment.—Kindness of the Citizens.—Peculiarities of Union Men.—Miscomprehension of the Enemy.

One of my journalistic companions, when we were examined by the Provost Marshal, before whom we were taken as soon as we were collected on the shore, remarked, in a rather pompous and exacting tone: "Captain, we have not slept much for two or three nights past, and we would like to have as comfortable quarters as you can give us."

The officer replied, that they were rather short of accommodations just then; but we should have as good as the town afforded.

I can not for the life of me determine how the idea crept into my brain; but I fancied that, at least for that night, we (the officers and War-correspondents) would be given a tolerable lodging-place.

Were my impressions well founded?

We shall see.

After our examination, we were marched out under guard through several streets; and, at last, about dawn, were stopped before a dingy iron gate and a dingier brick wall, which my recollections of the city taught me was the jail.

There a bell was pulled, and we were admitted into the yard by an ill-favored turnkey, who might have been a pirate without doing any dishonor to his physiognomy.

We soon found he was in harmony with his surroundings.

The jail-yard was filled with thieves and malefactors of every kind, Rebel deserters, and the riff-raff of the pseudo "Confederacy." They were filthy, ragged, coarse-featured, vile-spoken, and every way disgusting. They slept on the ground, with very little, if any, covering, and cooked their fat bacon on sticks in the fire.

At least one-quarter of the inclosure was a sink dug about the beginning of the War, and when the May sun arose, hot and sultry in that latitude, the odor that permeated the place was most demoralizing. That huge sink emitted its reeking odors towards the starry heavens in such intensity, that I imagined I saw the glistening sentinels shudder and try to hold their celestial noses above that fragrant spot.

That certainly, we thought, was the place where Shakspeare declared the offense was rank and smelt to Heaven.

If rank, by the by, were as offensive as that Mississippi vale of Cashmere, I am sure no one could hire any of our little street-sweepers, for an ordinary sum, to be Major-Generals.

We trio of Bohemians, who naturally had a love of comfort, and even luxury, could not help but laugh at the delicious locality into which we had been thrust, and the distinguished consideration with which we were received.

We concluded, if a man took excellent care of himself there, he might live five or six days, which was a most undesirable longevity in that fecundity of filth and Paradise of perfumes.

"Good quarters," laughed I to my companions, after I had surveyed the yard: "By Jove, it would be delightful to go hence to Hades a while, for change."

We all laughed—a little sardonically, I suspect; but what could we do else?

The idea of putting gentlemen in such a hole as that, was like inviting Lucullus to a banquet in a sewer.

We were all new to prison-life in Secessia; and many things struck us with abhorrence then, which we afterwards learned to regard with resignation. Still, it was not until some months after my removal to Richmond, that I witnessed any thing equal to the squalid scenes of the Vicksburg Jail.

To complete the delightfulness of the place, I should say the ground seemed covered with vermin, and the prisoners there swarmed with them.

We had not at that time grown practical entomologists, nor had it become a daily duty to examine our garments in quest of insects that tortured us. And hence, what we saw, filled us with excessive uneasiness.

We were afraid to sit down, or even to stand still, lest we should be overrun; and so we continued to walk backwards and forwards, with that aimless prison pace that subsequently became so familiar.

Heroes of novels can not perish until the close of the

last volume ; and even we matter-of-fact gentlemen—two of us at least—were spared the very opposite of dying of a rose in aromatic pain, and reserved by some ill-natured divinity to pursue entomological researches, and eat corn-bread and bacon in six other Southern Prisons.

Before noon of the 4th of May, the three Correspondents, and two officers of the Forty-Seventh Ohio, captured with us, were transferred to the Court-House, whose dome we had so often seen from our camps across the river, and were there paroled by Major Watts, the regular agent of exchange at Vicksburg, then the point of exchange for the West.

He assured us we would be sent to Richmond, and thence North by the first flag of truce; that the sole reason he did not return us to the Army from Vicksburg was, that General Grant had refused to receive paroled prisoners from that city. We believed the Major's story, and understood our parole as a solemn covenant which the Rebels and we were mutually bound to observe.

At the Court-House we had fresh air, and a fine view of the Mississippi and much of the surrounding country from the altitude of our position. We could see our transports across the Louisiana peninsula, and our camps up the river from the Court-Room; and we felt not a little annoyed that we were captives almost within musket-range of our friends.

The Rebel officers treated us with courtesy, when they learned who we were. Strange to say, not even the name of The New York *Tribune* excited their anger, although we had been assured by Southern Majors and Colonels that if any of the Correspondents of that journal were taken, they would be executed by the infuriated soldiers.

The officers at Vicksburg did not offer to search our persons, or even ask what we had upon them.

That was not their rule, however, as we learned from a party of men captured after us. Those persons were badly treated, and their money and other valuables stolen —or, in other words, taken, with fair promises, but never returned.

The three days we remained in Vicksburgh we were visited by a great many officers and citizens, who showed us all the courtesy we could have expected.

We were even taken out at night to the head-quarters of General Officers, to be catechised about the opinions of the people of the North respecting the duration of the War; what the North intended to do with the Rebels after they had been whipped; and, especially, what disposition the Yankees proposed to make of the negroes.

As we were New York journalists, and had been with the Army from the breaking out of the War, the officers attached some weight to our opinions; but if they obtained any consolation from our responses, their consolation must certainly have appeared to them as a "blessing in disguise."

Some of the citizens who called on us offered to give us clothes and lend us money, for which we thanked them, but which we did not accept.

They were of course loyal at heart; and here let me say that almost without an exception, during my captivity, I found that the Southerners who revealed any humanity or generosity of disposition were Union men; that their kindness was in proportion to their fealty to the Republic.

Secessionism, by some means that I will not attempt to explain, extinguishes, or at least represses, the better qualities of our nature, and develops the worst elements of human character.

It is quite possible, of course, for an honorable and upright man to be a Rebel ; but it is very difficult to find one among the enemies of his country.

The few there are of the honorable-exception kind do not gravitate to Prisons, I will be sworn ; for Prison attachés in the South are generally men who have been very little if at all in the field, with tyrannical, brutal, and cruel dispositions, and so cowardly withal that they will ever use their power harshly when they know they can do so with impunity.

On the whole, we were as politely treated at Vicksburg as we had any reason to expect ; and we departed thence with the idea that the "Confederates" were not so bad as they had been represented—a gross error, which we had ample time to correct during the twenty months we enjoyed their compulsory hospitality.

During our brief sojourn in the Southern stronghold, we were rather lionized than otherwise. The papers there spoke favorably of us, and complimented us upon what they were pleased to term our singular fearlessness in volunteering without any particular motive to go upon so perilous an expedition. The editors paid us several visits, and indeed we were the recipients of calls every hour in the day.

At our quarters, in the upper part of the Court House,

we might have been said to be holding informal levees. We were certainly regarded with no little curiosity and some degree of admiration, for what the Rebel officers insisted upon considering our devil-may-care spirit, and thorough contempt for their powerful batteries.

One morning, having been invited to visit a General up town, I was compelled to appear in the streets without shoes or hose. My feet, which at least were white, and looked delicate, attracted the attention of some ladies in front of the Court House, as I limped painfully over the rough stones; and when I returned, I found they had been kind enough to send me a pair of socks and shoes, though I was compelled to buy the latter of the Provost-Marshal, who did not inform me they had been given me by the generous-hearted women.

The Provost pretended, as all the Southerners who have the least education do, to be a high-toned gentleman; and yet he could stoop to the petty meanness and dishonesty of taking money from a prisoner of war for a pair of shoes of which a lady had made him a present.

In Vicksburg I made some additions to my wardrobe, having been "presented" with a dead soldier's cap by the jailer, who afterward sent in his bill for the article; and having borrowed a common military overcoat from the assistant surgeon captured with us.

So attired, I traveled to Richmond in the uniform of a private soldier—the first time I had ever donned a uniform—and on such an occasion I must say I was very proud to wear the attire that our brave boys had made so hateful to Rebel eyes, and so honorable in the eyes of the Nation and the World.

CHAPTER XXXV.

AT JACKSON AND ATLANTA.

The Marble-Yard Prison.—Visit to the *Appeal* Office.—Kindness of the Editors.—Tremendous Excitement and Panic at the Mississippi Capital.—A Terrified and Fugacious Mayor.—The *Mississippian* Office Preparing for an Exodus.—Curiosity Excited by the Yankees.—Southern Fondness for Discussion and Rodomontade.—Our Continuous Inflictions along the Route.—Incidents of the Journey.—The Whitehall Street Prison.—A Pertinacious Hibernian.—Abusive Editorial in a Newspaper, and its Effects, etc.

On the evening of the 5th of May, the two Ohio officers and the Bohemians, with a number of privates, were sent to Jackson, Mississippi, and for two days were treated politely in the Marble-Yard Prison.

We were permitted to visit the *Appeal* Office—at last accounts the Memphis-Grenada-Jackson-Atlanta-Montgomery Appeal, very justly styled a moving Appeal, with whose editors we were personally acquainted before the war—and to write notes to our friends in the North that we were still among the living, instead of waltzing obliviously with the catfish in the turbid eddies at the bottom of the Mississippi.

We had no blankets, and had made no additions to our wardrobe, and found it difficult to sleep in the rude quarters assigned us, without even a stick of wood for a pillow.

Still we were journeying toward Freedom, we fondly

imagined, and could afford to put up with a few inconveniences.

The editors of the *Appeal* and one or two others treated us very kindly, lent us money, and gave us such articles as we most needed, for which we are still very grateful, because friends under such circumstances are friends indeed.

Great excitement prevailed in the Mississippi Capital at the time of our arrival, on account of the report that General Grant, at the head of his victorious army—he had then captured Grand Gulf—was marching on the town.

At the street corners were knots of excited men, discussing the prospects of the future with more feeling than logic. To us, who had long been careful observers, it was evident they were at a loss what to do ; and you can imagine we rather enjoyed the trepidation of the Rebels.

We saw a number of vehicles of various kinds loaded with household furniture, and men, women, children, and black servants, all greatly excited, moving rapidly out of town.

A panic of the most decided kind existed among all classes of society ; but we had no difficulty in perceiving that the negroes of both sexes, young and old, enjoyed the quandary of their masters and mistresses.

Whenever we passed, they recognized us as Yankee prisoners, and glanced at us with a meaning smile that to us was perfectly intelligible.

The Mayor had put forth a gasconading hand-bill, designed as a placebo, which was posted in prominent parts of the capital, informing the citizens that there was not the least cause for alarm ; calling the people of Mississippi to arms, to repel the barbarous invader from the soil he polluted with his footsteps, and all that sort of stereotyped rant and braggadocio for which the South has ever been famous.

The bellicose poster, so far as our observation extended, did not seem to have the desired effect.

If the citizens were flying to arms, they must have concealed them somewhere in the country, and have been making haste in that direction to recover them. They were certainly leaving town by all possible routes, and by every obtainable means of conveyance.

The Mayor, I subsequently learned through loyal citizens of Jackson, was himself a fugitive before the paste on his defiant pronunciamiento was fairly dry. The office of the *Mississippian*, one of the most virulent Secession sheets in the whole South, was manifestly disturbed and distressed, and not only contemplating, but indulging in, an hegira to a safer quarter.

When we went by the office, there were cases of type on the sidewalk ready for instant removal, and the entire concern was in a palpable state of chaos and confusion. Under the existing condition of affairs we were anxious to tarry in Jackson, hoping we might very soon be greeted with the music of Grant's guns.

We had no doubt then our parole would be observed; but we preferred recapture to any regular release, and we would much rather have rejoined the Union army at once than be sent three or four thousand miles a roundabout way to accomplish the same purpose.

The Rebel officer, a Lieutenant of a Louisiana regiment, no doubt feared our wishes might be realized, and hurried us away on the cars after we had passed two days in the town. We had not been placed under guard, the officer accompanying us merely as escort, nor were we until we reached Atlanta.

Along the route we had a great many privileges, and could have escaped at any time, but having been paroled, we considered ourselves bound by our parole, and thought our best interest would be served by remaining with our escort, and getting to Richmond as speedily as possible.

When the cars stopped at the station for meals, we repaired to them as if we had been traveling in the North, without the least surveillance.

On the boat, at Selma, we wandered about wherever we chose, as we had done at the village of West-Point, Georgia, and other places.

In Montgomery, we put up at the Exchange Hotel, the Rebel Lieutenant sleeping in a different part of the house from where we lay; and in the evening, having stated that we would like to bathe in the Alabama, he ordered a corporal, without arms, to accompany us to the river, and show us the best place in the vicinity for our balneation.

On the route we attracted a good deal of attention, especially at the small way-stations; and whenever the cars stopped any time, we were surrounded by persons who plied us with questions, the chief of which were those put to us at Vicksburgh, respecting the disposition we would make of the Rebels after they were whipped, and of the negroes after we had given them their freedom.

Our responses might not have been able; but they were

certainly ultra, and more calculated, on the whole, to fire than to freeze that much talked of portion of sectional anatomy, the Southern heart.

The pragmatical fellows who gathered about us were very anxious to discuss the main question, the causes of the War, the wrongs of the South, the encroachments and injustice of the North, and all the subjects that had been argued to death before the secession of South Carolina.

We told them it was useless to employ logic then; that bayonets and batteries had supplied the place of argument; that the period for reasoning had passed; and that the cause of the Republic had been submitted to the arbitrament of arms.

They could hardly comprehend that very well; but finding we would not revive and refute old and exploded arguments, they assured us we never could conquer the South; that we would have to kill every man, woman, and child before we could subjugate the "Confederacy," and all that quintessence of bosh to which they seem so indissolubly wedded.

Not being feminine, we grew weary of talking at last, and were very desirous of some kind of privacy, and of enjoying for a little while the luxury of silence. That we discovered very difficult of obtaining.

We could not sit down under the trees as we did at Montgomery, where we lay over on Sunday, without gathering a crowd; and the officer with us was at last forced to order peremptorily those resolved on our loquacious martyrdom to let us alone.

Gods! those were serious inflictions; and we concluded we had rather run the batteries half a dozen times than undergo the boredom of talking to the countless fools we met all the way between Vicksburgh and Richmond.

Speaking of the Sunday we remained in Montgomery reminds me of an incident that occurred while we were strolling up the avenue toward the State House, in the afternoon, which represents a peculiar phase of Southern inconsistency.

As we passed a dwelling, a coarse, brutal-looking fellow thrust his head over a porch, and addressing a mulatto girl standing on the sidewalk, used the following extraordinary language:

"Mary, G— d— your soul; have you said your prayers to-day?"

"No, master," in a tone quite free from the African accent.

"Well, by G—, if you don't do it before to-morrow, I'll lash the skin off your back, G— d— you!"

So extraordinary was the language—so singular the connection between the man's anxiety about Mary's prayers and his excessive profanity, that we all looked up in surprise, each one supposing he must have misunderstood the fellow.

On asking each other what the brute had said, we all repeated the same language; and there can be no doubt we interpreted his orthodox solicitude and his vulgar swearing aright.

It is not at all unusual in the South, such intermixture of professed Christianity with the violation of all practical morality and decency. Men who transgress all the Commandments, will prate of God and the Bible very flippantly, and denounce a gentle and generous skeptic, whose life is entirely blameless, as violently as if he were a poisoner or a parricide.

On the 9th of May we reached Atlanta, Georgia. The Union soldiers were marched off under guard, the Rebel Lieutenant accompanying them, and leaving us in a sitting posture under a tree near the dépôt.

We sauntered about the city for a while, answering a few questions asked by persons at the doors of the houses we passed, and then repaired to the Whitehall-street Prison, to which the privates had been consigned, to inquire of our escort where we should stop, whether at the Trout House or some other hotel.

Arrived at the Prison, the Lieutenant, somewhat to our surprise, introduced us to Colonel somebody, the commandant, who invited us very politely to walk in.

We did so; the door closed behind us; the key turned in the lock with a harsh and grating sound, and we were in close confinement.

No one visited us during the days we passed there, except a most pertinaciously offensive Hibernian, an attaché of the Prison, who entered every fifteen minutes to inquire if we did not want some liquor, or other contraband article, which he was very willing to get if we would only be kind enough to pay him a "thrifle" for his trouble.

Learning we did not wish any stimulant, he was very anxious to exchange some Treasury Notes for Rebel currency, declaring he knew an ancient Israelite round the corner who would give more for them than anybody in the city.

We gave the Celtic individual some money to get

exchanged, and after trying to cheat us out of it by at least a dozen ingenious manœuvres and flagrant falsehoods, he at last succeeded, with the greatest difficulty, and after the most untiring exertion, he said, in obtaining one dollar and three quarters of the scrip for one dollar of our currency.

My associate of *The Tribune*, while we were standing on the platform of the cars, going from Jackson to Meridian, had had his hat stolen from his head by a South-Carolina Major moving rapidly by on a train passing in an opposite direction.

That generous and chivalrous act, depriving my companion of any article of covering, reduced him to the necessity of tying a handkerchief about his head, and of subsequently employing the son of Erin as an agent to replace his lost hat.

Various were the assumed or actual expeditions made into the city by our Hibernian custodian to procure a head-covering; and the things he brought in were grotesque enough.

Some of them looked like patent hen-coops; some like dilapidated coal-scuttles; others like rat-traps on an improved plan. Mr. Richardson tried them all on, and suffered from a severe headache, and great demoralization in consequence.

At last a cotton cap, dirt-color, and amorphous in shape, was obtained—it reminded me of the head of the woolly horse, as it would probably appear after it had been struck by lightning—and worn by my friend for many months after.

I always felt convinced that it was fortunate for the

wearer he was in prison while under the influence of that cap. Otherwise I think he must have turned highwayman, horsewhipped his father, murdered his grandmother, or committed some other outrage entirely foreign to his nature.

The following Autumn the cotton anomaly passed into the possession of an old and very honest farmer, confined in Castle Thunder for his loyalty; and such was the moral or rather immoral weight of the cap, that the gray-haired ruralist immediately began to steal.

Poor fellow, he was not to blame! Who could resist so potent a pressure, such a thing of evil as that fleecy abomination?

Up to that time we had traveled, as I have said, with a Lieutenant, merely as escort; but an amiable and a chivalrous article in the *Confederacy*—edited, I am almost ashamed to say, by two Vermonters who had been two years in the South—declaring Correspondents the worst persons in the Army; that they, and we particularly, ought to be hanged; and that they (the editors) would be only too happy to hold one end of the rope for our hempen accommodation, caused us to be treated somewhat rigorously, and marched through town, on our way to the dépôt, under a heavy guard.

The two Lieutenants under whose escort we had traveled from Vicksburgh to Atlanta did not know much, but they were at least respectful and courteous.

The third Lieutenant, who took charge of us from Atlanta, was a coarse, ignorant, brutal fellow, who endeavored to interest us by telling stories, to which the most depraved females of Church-street would have declined to listen, and to compensate himself for his entertainment by begging our knives and rings, or any of the few articles we had that attracted his fancy.

At the dépôt we were not even permitted to purchase a paper; and the Lieutenant pretended, as did the commandant of the Prison, that we were in danger of being mobbed, on account of the odium excited against us by the grossly abusive editorial in the *Confederacy*. Whether there was or was not any ground for apprehension, I am unaware; but certainly we felt none; albeit we deemed it quite in keeping with the generous conduct of the Southerners to mob two or three prisoners of war who were entirely unarmed, and therefore at their mercy.

No one threatened or attempted to harm us at Atlanta, which place we left with no little satisfaction, because we were getting so much nearer, as we fondly thought, to our freedom.

Our journey to Richmond, by way of Knoxville, was without accident or excitement.

We were bored as usual with questions as we stopped at the stations, and greatly fatigued, on reaching what *was* the Rebel capital, from riding in box, platform, hog and cattle cars, night and day, without any opportunity or means of sleeping, and at about as rapid a rate as that of a towboat on the Erie canal.

CHAPTER XXXVI.

THE LIBBY PRISON.

Arrival at Richmond.—Our Reception from the Union Officers.—Mistaken Idea about Human Endurance.—The First Shock in Prison.—Entomological Researches.—Sickness and Sentiment.—Violation of the Tribune Correspondents' Paroles.—Character of the Rebel Commissioner.—Determination of the Enemy to Hold us to the End of the War.

ARRIVED at Richmond, about daylight on the morning of the 16th of May, the journalistic trio were told that they must become inmates of the notorious Libby Prison until the flag-of-truce-boat came up, which would be in a day or two, when we would be sent North.

While we stood in Carey street, near the corner of Twenty-first, the Union officers in the upper part of the building looked out of the windows, and cried "fresh fish! fresh fish!" with a vigor of tone and an unction that I must say disgusted me to a point of indignation.

I thought men who could make stupid jests in such a dismal building as the Libby seemed to be, from an external view, ought to be kept there for life.

They certainly looked distressed enough to be dignified; and I was anxious the dramatic proprieties should be observed.

Ushered into the officers' quarters, we were loudly greeted with "Halloo, Yanks!" and plied with questions concerning the place, mode, and time of our capture.

The Libby, though bad enough, was not so bad as I had anticipated. The floor was clean and the walls were whitewashed; but I thought if I were compelled to remain there a month, I should die outright.

How little we know of ourselves!

I passed sixteen months in places far worse than that—in rat-holes, and damp cellars, and noisome cells; and yet resolved to survive the Rebellion if I were allowed half a chance.

And, thanks to an elastic constitution, which, by the by, required no anti-slavery amendments, and the practice of a daily philosophy of the Xenocratic sort—to use the politician's interpretation of Webster's last words—"I am not dead yet."

What first shocked me in the Libby more than aught else was, that my fellow-prisoners, at least once a day, thoroughly examined their garments, for what purpose I will not be unpoetic enough to state—and accompanied their researches with much profanity and considerable phlebotomy.

A few hours proved the urgent necessity of the custom, and from that time until after my escape I made a quotidian investigation—in which, like a jealous husband, I looked for what I feared to find—that never failed to fill me with aversion and disgust.

I envied the Emperor Julian's indifference on a subject which no man less great than he could possibly feel.

The fact, too, that the prisoners were obliged to cook such little food as they could procure, wash dishes, clean floors, and do the general work of scullions, as I have mentioned in detail elsewhere, and all under the most adverse circumstances, rendered me a very rebellious loyalist; and, in connection with a system not yet fully recovered from an attack of intermittent fever in the Louisiana swamps, prostrated me, before two days were over, on the bare floor, with flaming blood and a burning brain.

Sickness was somewhat new to me, and sickness there was a sensation one would not care to have repeated.

I am not much given to Sentiment; but those dreary walls and hard floors, that rough fare and desolate captivity, suggested their opposites, and brought to mind soft couches and softer hands, sweet voices and cooling draughts, thoughts of the Beautiful and memories of Sympathy, that were a torment and a torture there.

"Sick and in Prison, and you visited me not." I found a meaning in those simple words I had not before discovered, and felt in my inmost soul how dreadful an accusation that would be against a heart that had ever assumed to love.

On the 21st of May, the truce-boat reached City Point, and on the day following all the persons captured on our expedition were sent off, except myself and my confrère of the New York *Tribune*. The enemy kept faith with them, and broke it with us; evidently believing that *Tribune* men had no rights he was bound to respect.

Commissioner Ould, when asked by our journalistic friend if he did not design releasing us also, replied, with as many oaths as Hector McTurk, that we were the very men he wanted and intended to keep; that he would hold us until a certain fabulous number of innocent Confederates in Northern bastiles were set free; and vaguely intimated that we should stay in prison until skating became a popular amusement in the Bottomless Pit.

When my collaborateur and I were informed of that shameful violation of faith, we knew our case was hopeless; that the *Tribune* correspondents were in for the War; that no substitutes could be obtained, and that no self-sacrificing and intelligent contrabands need apply.

Subsequently, desirous of obtaining some official repudiation of our paroles, we put them in the hands of an attorney, and stated our case to him. He declared we were unjustly detained; that no prisoner regularly paroled, as we were, had ever before been held; but that, as we belonged to the *Tribune*, he could do nothing for us.

Nor could he.

Ould, with the unbounded effrontery and superlative falsification that characterize him even above other Rebels, declared Major Watts had no right to parole us, and if he had had the right, he (Ould) would have possessed the authority to revoke the parole.

Eminent descendant of Ananias, like Ferdinand of Arragon, he only values a promise for the pleasure he experiences in breaking it.

Trickster, hypocrite, and liar, he represents each character so well that it is impossible to determine in which he excels; nor has he in any one of them any equal but himself.

He is one of the loudest mouthers about Chivalry and Honor in the American Gascony; and yet the only idea he can have of either of those much-abused terms is by practicing their opposites.

When our case was referred to the Southern Secretary of War, in an unanswerable memorial, the following October—that we might have all the official evidence possible of the perfidy of the Rebels—Mr. Seddon's sole answer was our consignment to the Salisbury (N. C.) Penitentiary, as general hostages for the good conduct of the Government.

Who ever heard of making a pair of individuals hostages for the conduct of a Nation?

Of course the thing was a farce.

The Rebels only used that form that they might retain us to the end of the War.

They might as well have held a box of sardines for the preservation of the morals of Sardinia; and they knew it; but they employed the phrase with all seriousness, and packed us off to Salisbury accordingly.

I mention these circumstances to show the animus of the Richmond authorities toward the *Tribune* men, and, if I must be entirely candid, out of pride at the high, but, I hope, deserved compliment they paid us.

Never during the War have I known of another instance in which prisoners have been held, as we were, who had been paroled regularly by an accredited agent of exchange at a regular point of exchange.

For the most honorable exception made in our favor, I feel thankful to the Rebels, generally and individually.

Their whole history is one of inhumanity, and their name is Perfidy; yet are they prolific of excuses and explanations for their perfidious conduct, as may be seen by a single instance.

When I asked Major Thomas P. Turner, the Commandant, if he was aware we were paroled, and had the paroles in our pockets—"Oh, that makes no difference," he replied; "your paroles do not go into effect until after you are on the truce-boat."

"What in Heaven's name do we want of paroles when we are on the truce-boat?" inquired I. "That is like telling a criminal sentenced to execution that he is pardoned, but that he is not to be benefited by his pardon until after he has been hanged an hour."

When Major Turner is hanged, as I am quite sure he ought to be, I trust he will be pardoned with that special proviso.

CHAPTER XXXVII.

LIBBY PRISON.

Arrival and Release of Union Officers.—Therapeutic Power of the Fall of Vicksburg.—Its Wholesome Effect on the Prisoners.—Gradual Resignation to Confinement.—Means of Killing Time.—Journalistic Desire to Write, and the Impossibility of its Indulgence.—Exhibition of the Loyal Captives.—Summer Costumes.—Cruelty of our Keepers.—Petty Meanness of the Commandant.—The Drawing of Lots.—Horror of the Scene.—Barbarous Treatment of Citizens.—Consideration Shown the Officers.—Removal of *The Tribune* Correspondents.

WHEN we first reached the Libby, not more than seventy or eighty officers were confined there, mostly prisoners taken at Chancellorsville; but on the afternoon of the day of our arrival, Colonel A. B. Streight and his command joined us; and in a day or two more, Captain George Brown, of the gunboat Indianola, and his officers, were added to the number, making about one hundred and seventy-five in all. All of us felt very gloomy, at least; but we kept up a cheerful exterior, and endeavored to make the best of our very obnoxious surroundings.

About the 1st of June, the Chancellorsville and naval captives were released. I remember the latter were quite demonstrative over the prospect of their return to freedom; so much so that I expressed to my confrère my surprise at their lack of self-discipline. "You must remember, Junius, they have been prisoners for three months," was his answer; and, on reflection, I ceased to marvel at their display of excessive joy.

Three months in Prison! What an age it seemed! I did not believe I could endure close confinement so long as that: I supposed I must die perforce before a similar period had elapsed. How little do we know ourselves—least of all, what we can bear of trial and of suffering!

The loss of my freedom and the uncertainty of its restoration, with the close atmosphere and the hateful surroundings of the Prison, were, as I have said, too much for me. My system gave way, and ere a week had passed I was prostrate on the floor with a raging fever. Those who felt any interest in me became alarmed, thinking I would die in that wretched place. I did not share their apprehensions. My opposition was excited, and I determined to live if I could, and part with my soul under better auspices.

Through eight weeks I suffered, and yet took no medicine; trusting to the best of physicians, Nature, for my healing.

I was cured at last in an unexpected, but most agreeable way.

We were all anxious about Vicksburg, hearing, as we did through the Richmond papers, that Johnston was besieging Grant in turn, and would soon have him between two hostile armies.

On the afternoon of July 8th, while I lay tossing with fever on my blankets in the hot, confined, unwholesome atmosphere of the Prison, a negro came up stairs and told us Vicksburg was in our hands. The effect was instantaneous with me.

No cordial of Zanoni's could better have done its therapeutic errand.

I rose at once, and joined in a tremendous chorus of the "Star Spangled Banner," which made the air vibrate, and, pouring out into the street, caused one of the Rebel officers below to say: "Do you hear that? Those d—d Yankees must have got the news."

That news, so glorious, proved more potent than an Arabian philter. I had no fever nor ailment of any kind for many a long month after.

The fall of Vicksburg gave me a new lease of life, and strengthened the hearts of the Union prisoners to endure, like the blast of a defiant bugle in the hour of defeat.

That was a happy evening for us, even in Prison. We all said we could afford to be captives as long as the Rebels were soundly whipped; and not a few declared the fall of Vicksburg worth twelve months of freedom.

We sat up till midnight, and awoke the echoes of that quarter of Richmond with the most vociferous singing of National airs, not forgetting "John Brown's body," which was especially obnoxious to the Rebels, and therefore particularly agreeable to us.

We could hear the insurgent officers swearing beneath our windows in the pauses of silence; but their curses were music to our ears, and we chanted louder and more defiantly than before.

Though the Libby, materially considered, was the least bad Prison of the seven in which I was confined in the South, it seemed often that I must die or grow insane there. We had a few books, but I could not read, and I was afraid to think any more than I could avoid, for thought became brooding, and brooding misery, and despair.

When the fever was not upon me, I tried every way to dissipate the dark and haunting fancies, the desolate and despondent feelings, that crowded upon my brain and heart. I tried tobacco for consolation, and, lighting a common clay pipe, I would pace the floor for hours, to and fro, in company with some of the officers, talking of the Past and speculating on the Future. How weary and monotonous was that walk over that wide Prison floor! How it grew into, and became a part of, my life!

My blood leaped and my soul sickened when I stared into the unborn days, and saw no one through which the light of liberty streamed. Weary, worn, restless, I often pressed my pale face against the window-bars and gazed across the river, to the South, at the green slopes and cool forests, that seemed so sweet and refreshing and delicious in the distance. To walk there appeared like Paradise; for there was no restraint, no compulsion. How I longed for the magic tapestry in the Arabian tale, which could transport me where I willed!

At last I began, by slow degrees, to accustom myself to my unnatural situation. I reflected on all the philosophic theories I had entertained, on all the stoical principles I had tried to cultivate, and determined to steel myself to the necessities of the occasion. The determination brought its fruit. Will bountifully repaid me for its exercise. I found, after a few weeks, I could read, and reading was a great consolation. It aided me to strangle the pangful hours; to prevent constant introspection; to turn back the surging tide that threatened at times to deprive me of reason.

All the day, when I was not compelled to be in the kitchen, I stretched myself on my blankets near the window, and strove to forget myself in the pages before me. I could do that but partially; yet it was a great relief; and I was very thankful I had early formed the habit of seeking society in books. After dark we had no lights, unless a small tallow candle, which we were compelled to extinguish at nine o'clock, could be called so; and then a few of us would get together, and talk far into the night.

Fortunately for me, I slept well at that period, and realized in dreams what Fortune denied me. Every night I was free. The body could be imprisoned, but the Rebels could not fetter the spirit. That returned to the dear old North, and dwelt during the sweet hours of slumber amid the scenes it once had loved. So much did I dream of freedom, that, at last, I lost all faith in my visions of the night; knowing they were delusions even while I was under their influence.

When I fancied myself in converse with my intimates; sitting at a luxurious board; surrounded by objects of beauty; joyous amid the joyful, it was most painful to awake and behold the familiar beams above my head, and the rafters of the roof, and the hateful walls of the Libby. I had suffered in that way so often that my reason would no longer succumb to my imagination; and when pleasant and sympathetic voices seemed to fall upon my ear, I knew they were recollections, not realizations, the reflected desires of my own, not the outpouring of another, heart.

As prisoners gathered to the Libby, as they did from Winchester and Gettysburg, greater efforts were made for passing the time resignedly and profitably. Classes in Latin, French, and German were established; books were procured in quantities in the city; debating societies were formed, and manuscript papers begun. I confess I had not the heart, nor was I in the mental condition, to take advantage of those means to lighten the burdens of confinement; but my *collaborateur*, Mr. Richardson, recreated himself frequently in the debating society, and became the most prominent of its members; drawing the officers largely whenever it was known he would participate in the discussion.

Had I possessed the facilities, I should have liked to write something; but how could I do so when we had no tables, except the rough boards from which we ate, and they were always in use; no chairs, or stools, or boxes even, to sit upon; no space, however small, which was free from invasion and disturbance? The book I would have written would not have been on prison-life, or had aught to do with prisons: it would have been something like a novel of society, and filled, I fancy, with misanthropy and bitterness, combined with soft imaginings and voluptuous coloring—the one produced immediately by the scenes about me; the other, through contrast with them.

Reading, smoking, talking, scrubbing, walking, and cooking, made up my slender existence in the Libby. Many of the officers were gentlemen of intellect, culture, taste, and breeding; but some, unfortunately, were so destitute of dignity and manners that we were compelled to blush for them when prominent Rebels, either in military or civil life, were brought into the Prison, as they frequently were, by Major—then Captain—Thomas P. Turner, commandant—to see the collection of Yankee curiosities. The Rebels would walk about the rooms very much as if they were in a zoological garden, and this General, that Colonel, or that Major, was pointed out as would be a Bengal tiger, an African giraffe, or a Polar bear.

Colonel Streight, while we were in the Libby, was the principal lion. The Richmond papers had abused him so much, though for what reason it was impossible to conjecture, that they had rendered him famous. He had failed on his raid, through lack of fresh animals, to strike the enemy the severe blow he had intended; but he was hated as heartily as if he had been altogether successful. The hatred of the "chivalry" disturbed him very little, however: indeed, I am quite confident he enjoyed it; and hated them back with an intensity that must have left some margin in his favor.

Of course *The Tribune* correspondents had their share of attention, and were occasionally exhibited among the Northern monstrosities. Had we been statues we could, not have been more frozen and formal to the hostile visitors or the *attachés* of the prison. We never spoke to any of them, save in the way of business inquiry, unless we were addressed, and then briefly and pertinently as possible. They generally knew our status, antecedents, and opinions—and if they did not they could easily have discovered them—and therefore questioned us very little respecting our views and expectations. We were freed from the perpetual annoyances to which we had been subjected on the way to Richmond, and we profoundly appreciated the relief.

Various were the methods the officers adopted to pass the time. Those of a lymphatic temperament slept about fifteen or eighteen hours out of the twenty-four. Those of a very nervous and active mental organization played cards—poker, euchre, and whist—checkers, and backgammon ; wrestled, romped, and skylarked—as the sailors term it—read and talked about past campaigns and future prospects ; crushing the Rebellion, and settling the affairs of the Nation, every few hours of the day.

The weather was very warm and sultry, and in the Prison, of course, extremely close, and sometimes stifling. We were accustomed, consequently, to wear as few clothes as possible, but went around in nothing but drawers and shirt, without shoes, and, sometimes, even with less attire. Fortunately, there was a bathing-tub in our quarters, and somebody was in it all the while. At any hour of the night we could hear the water running, and the splashing and plunging of the aqueous enjoyers.

No doubt that had much to do with our health, which, contrary to all expectation, was quite good throughout the Summer. There were few deaths during the four months of my incarceration, and not much serious illness. Very strange it was so, when we remember how impure and vitiated the atmosphere was, and how little care and comfort we could obtain when once sick.

During the mid-Summer some of us profited by a ladder

leading to the roof of the building, by which the subordinates of the Prison ascended for the purpose of raising and taking down the "Confederate" flag that flew every day over the Libby. When we went to the hole cut in the roof for ventilation, and placed our faces over it, the air from below was so corrupt, heated, and steam-like, as to almost suffocate us; and yet in that atmosphere we were forced to live, and breathe, and have our being.

When it was discovered that we were obtaining a little fresh air after sunset upon the roof, our cruel custodians ordered us down, and threatened to punish us severely and close the aperture for ventilation if we persisted in going up there. They even did fasten down the skylight for a fortnight, at the most torrid season of the year, because some unfortunate had disobeyed orders.

That was a fair specimen of the cruelty of our keepers. We did no harm on the roof; no one could even see us there from the town; and yet they would not permit us to enjoy the blueness of the sky and the genial air of the evening, when they knew we were gasping and panting in our mephitic quarters for the very thing they denied us.

Shame, shame, upon such inexcusable barbarity, such motiveless cruelty!

Soon after our arrival in Richmond, a paragraph was copied from *The Tribune* into the papers there, speaking of Major Turner as the "infernal brute that commanded the Libby." At that time Turner had not revealed himself, and I supposed the denunciation unmerited. One day, in conversation with the Major on this subject, he remarked, that if he were caught in New York he would probably be hanged. I told him I thought not; that he had no doubt been misrepresented, as I believed then he had. Subsequently I learned better ; and now I indorse the paragraph in question most fully and cordially.

I think if justice were meted out to Major Turner, he would be executed summarily, and that the Prison Inspector, one Richard Turner—no relative of the commandant's, but formerly a Baltimore blackguard, and aspirant for the honors of Plug-uglyism—and a little puppy named Ross, once a resident of New York, would share his fate. They did every thing in their power to persecute prisoners, and richly deserve death at the hands of those they treated so cruelly. Major Turner did not do harsh things himself, so far as I knew ; he was too politic for that; but he permitted them to be done, and is, of course, responsible for the outrages, and they were many, practiced upon the captives under his charge.

Speaking of him, he was guilty of a very small, but entirely characteristic meanness towards us. When Mr. Colburn of *The World* was released, he very kindly left $50 in Treasury Notes with Major Norris for our use, as we were likely to remain in durance for an indefinite period. Major Norris handed the amount to Major Turner, who informed us there were $50 in "Confederate" currency in his office to our credit. I told him Mr. Colburn had agreed to leave us the sum in our money, which, as he was aware, was worth far more than the issues of the South. The Major replied, somewhat nervously, that the notes handed to him were "Confederate ;" and that was all he knew about it. He simply told a deliberate falsehood for the purpose of cheating us out of a few dollars.

And yet he assumes to be a high-toned, honorable gentleman; and, according to the Southern standard, perhaps he is.

During our confinement at the Libby, Captains Flinn and Sawyer were selected by lot to be executed, in retaliation for two Kentuckians whom General Burnside had caused to be shot for recruiting within our lines.

Well do I remember the morning—it was during the latter part of June, I think—the Captains were called out of their quarters. They hurried down stairs gayly, and even boisterously, supposing they were to be paroled. They were taken into a vacant room on the lower floor of the prison, formed in a hollow square, and there informed solemnly and impressively, by Major Turner—even he seemed moved on the occasion—that he had a very painful duty to perform, at the same time reading an order from General Winder to select two of the officers present for immediate execution.

Imagine the sensations of the Captains—some fifty in number—at that moment! What a terrible reaction must have followed! What an icy chill of horror must that announcement have struck to their hearts, swelling a few minutes before with the hope of early restoration to freedom.

It was not the fear of death that blanched so many war-worn cheeks, and shook so many brave hearts; it was the suddenness, the horror of the idea—the cold, deliberate determination, by lot, of a violent death to two of their innocent companions-in-arms.

One of our chaplains was requested to draw the names that had been written on slips of paper and thrown into a box, and the first two were to be the victims. One might have heard the fall of a rose-leaf at that awful moment. Every breath seemed suspended; every heart bursting with its pulsation. Eyes kindled with burning anxiety, and lips quivered with suppressed emotion. Fearful scene! who can forget it?

The names were drawn and announced; and that hollow square took a long breath that was audible in the painfully silent room. The selected Captains did not change countenance. They were pale before; but they turned no paler. Their mouths closed more firmly, as if they were summoning the resolution of brave men to die bravely, and they walked mournfully, though silently, away.

They were taken before General Winder—I am very glad he is dead—who abused them shamefully when he knew they believed they had only a few days, perhaps hours, to live—and thence removed to the subterranean dungeons of the Libby. Every one knows how General Lee, the son of Robert E. Lee, and Captain Winder were made hostages for Flinn and Sawyer, and how the Rebel authorities finally released the chosen victims, although the Richmond papers clamored for their blood, and bitterly denounced Jefferson Davis because he did not dare to execute them. As I told them they would, the very day of their allotment, they obtained their freedom long before *The Tribune* Correspondents; and yet their position was by no means pleasant. The Rebels were growing desperate even then; and it was not unreasonable to suppose they might attempt the inauguration of a bloody retaliation in the hope of compelling, what they had otherwise failed to secure, the interference of European powers for the sake of humanity.

The day of the drawing was a gloomy one in the Libby. We all felt if the Captains were executed, that no one was safe; that retaliation once begun, no one could say where it would end.

Mr. Richardson and myself knew our prospects would be unusually brilliant for sudden removal from the terrestrial ball, if the execution of prisoners once became the fashion; and we discussed with a grim kind of humor the sensations we would possibly experience when we were led out to be shot or hanged. I expressed a decided partiality for shooting, as more military, genteel, and dramatic; and denounced hanging as an undignified and ungentlemanly mode of exit even out of Rebeldom. I remembered what a strong bias I had always had against the gallows, and began to believe that the early developed feeling was a premonition of my fate. I lost no sleep, however, over the matter. I had as much as I could do to live there, anyhow, and concluded, if I had to stay in Southern prisons for many months, hanging might not be so bad, after all.

On the 2d of September, 1863, we were transferred from the Libby to Castle Thunder—a movement we by no means relished, as the reputation of the Castle was extremely bad even in Richmond—but of which, of course, we would have been too proud to complain, even if complaining had been of any advantage.

To leave the officers with whom we had been for four months, and among whom we had many warm friends, was a sore trial, especially when we were going to a place where the worst class of prisoners was kept; but we bundled up our blankets; shook hands with hundreds of men whose countenances we could not recognize in the crowd; and hurried down stairs into Carey street, to gaze at the pallid faces peering at us through the bars, and wishing us good fortune wherever we might go.

The Libby, as I have said, was the most endurable prison of which we were inmates; and I may here state that our officers were in every way better treated than any other class of prisoners. Indeed, they can have little idea of the sufferings of captives in the South, judging by their own experience. Citizens who were held in another part of the Libby, while we were there, were most inhumanly treated: they were not allowed to purchase any thing, though their rations were so short that they were constantly hungry, and we, in the officers' quarters, supplied them surreptitiously with bread and a few of the common necessities of existence, which they devoured like famishing men.

The Southerners have such love of approbation, and draw the line so markedly between gentlemen and commoners, that they hesitate to show to the officers, supposed by the Army Regulations to be of a different race from the privates, the worst side of their character. Beyond the petty tyranny, superciliousness, and generally offensive bearing of the officials at the Libby, we had, during our stay, little to complain of, at least compared to what we saw and suffered elsewhere in Secessia.

CHAPTER XXXVIII.

THE KITCHEN CABINET AT THE LIBBY.

Disappointment and Disgust in Prison Life.—The Union Officers as Servants and Scullions.—Journalistic Cooking and its Trials.—The First Breakfast.—Horrors of the Culinary Art.—Interior View of the Kitchen.—Grotesque and Mortifying Scenes.—Battles of the Saucepans and Skillets.—Complaint, Clamor, and Confusion.

BEFORE my capture, I had imagined all manner of repulsive surroundings and annoying incidents in Rebel Prison; but I had supposed that War-captives were at least allowed full leisure, as some compensation for the loss of freedom.

When I reached the Libby Prison, I was surprised and exceedingly indignant to learn that it was the duty of the Officers, the Correspondents of the *Tribune* included, to clean their own quarters and prepare their own food.

That seemed an outrage upon propriety, designed to degrade gentlemen by association, education, and profession, to the rank of cooks and scullions, and filled me with a violently insurgent spirit.

When I came to reflect, however, that what we did was for our own good; that we preserved our health and insured our comparative comfort by attending to those really menial offices, I grew reasonably resigned.

Subsequently, when I burst into an expression of anger and disgust to the Commandant of the Libby one day, he informed me he would be glad to cook our rations, but that the Officers generally preferred to prepare them for themselves.

That statement—very remarkable do I regard the fact —I found to be true.

The rations—bread, bacon, and rice at the time—were so vilely cooked by the negroes, that the Officers had requested permission to perform the culinary duties, and obtained it.

They disliked watery soup, with dirt, hemp, pebbles, and roaches as condiments, and muscular beef boiled to superlative dryness. They believed they could support life by the consumption of less dirt, if they took the matter into their own hands; and they deemed the experiment worth trying.

The officers were divided into large and small messes—the former containing twenty to thirty, and the latter four to six members—and every day one or more of the members was appointed to do the cooking and dish-washing, and perform the other poetic et ceteras for the twenty-four hours.

The third day, it came my turn to preside over the destinies of the Kitchen; and most alarming was the announcement.

I would rather have attempted to capture Richmond, or pay off the National Debt, or be happy in the Libby; but, as I could employ no substitute, I was bound to rely on myself.

The cooking was not very extensive, nor were the

means; but I felt as awkward as if I were about to address the Tycoon in Japanese.

Imagine the situation of an unfortunate mortal who not only had never done any thing of the kind, but had never seen it done.

The stewing of "Saddle-Rocks" in a chafing-dish, or the preparation of a lobster salad, was as far as I had ever advanced in the mysteries of the cuisine.

If I could have had another wish beside that for my liberty, I would have asked to be metamorphosed into the humblest of cooks.

There was no use of fretting.

Complaint never cooked a piece of bacon, nor made a fire in a broken stove.

I set to work; my companions, who had had their experience, laughing at my earnest endeavors, and my ill-concealed disgust.

There were very few dishes; the stoves were in a wretched condition; the wood was green; the bacon was tough; and my knife was dull.

After laboring an hour, the perspiration streaming down my face, I succeeded in getting some pieces of bacon over the fire, and spilling the grease upon the only pantaloons I possessed. In another hour I had fried some bread in the pan, and at the close of the third I had boiled a little water impregnated with burnt corn, which the Rebels, with a delightful idealism, termed coffee.

We stood up to breakfast,—memories of the Fifth Avenue and Delmonico's, come not near!—one tin dish, a block of wood, and a piece of brown paper serving as the plates ; a pen-blade, our fingers, and a sharp stick, as knives and forks.

I was very hungry when I undertook the matutinal meal ; but my efforts had destroyed my appetite.

I stood and looked on the rough board that served for a table, and if I had been a woman I presume I should have wept like Niobe, and declared I *would* be a nun.

Again and again I had to cook that day, which seemed as if it would never end ; and though for four months I sacrificed myself on the altar of the Kitchen, I never became reconciled to the ultra-prosaic obligation.

Heavy and desolate as was Prison life, the hours that divided me from my cooking-day appeared like minutes, when I thought of that dire necessity.

From seven o'clock in the morning until quite dark I then passed in the Kitchen ; watching my opportunity to get some vessel on one of the fractured stoves, and seeing that no one took it off when it was once on.

Cooking at the Libby was a perpetual struggle, jarring, tumult, and annoyance ; not infrequently involving a personal encounter.

A man who could have preserved his temper there would have excelled human nature.

The process of operating in the kitchen would have irritated a saint, and made Fénélon blasphemous.

Just picture the place to yourself.

In a room twelve by twenty feet were three broken stoves, in which at least seven or eight hundred men had to cook. The pans, pails, and cups were very few ; not one where twenty were needed.

The stoves smoked like Vesuvius ; the apartment was

always sky-color; the atmosphere hot and pine-impregnated to suffocation.

One was required to wait sometimes an hour before he could get a place on the stove; and, as soon as had, he was likely to lose it by some other person removing his dish, and putting his own in its stead.

One could not lay down a knife or fork without missing it; could not turn his back without being deprived of some portion of his rights.

I would have liked to see the South try to get its rights there.

Astræa herself could not have obtained hers.

Under such circumstances there was constant bickering, wrangling, and contention, with more violations of the Third Commandment than I care to record.

Threats were made, insults offered, and even blows exchanged; all of which appears now very silly and undignified; but then I did not wonder at it.

We were all in a condition of suppressed irritation. Our nerves were morbidly acute. The law of our Being read backwards. Our temperament was revolutionized. We were disposed to visit on each other what under different circumstances would have been visited on the common foe.

The mishaps and contretemps of the Kitchen were too numerous to mention, and, to a man who could keep his temper, exceedingly ludicrous.

It was singular, such was the aggravation and provocation at all times, that there were so few actual pugilistic engagements. We had a hundred incipient affairs of the kind every day, and several personal encounters were usually generated out of that number. Generally, however, the bitterness of feeling wasted itself in words.

All the prisoners felt that it was disgraceful for officers of the United States Army to be engaged in personal quarrels ; but when a man had his vessel, which he had been two hours in getting, stolen almost before his eyes ; had hot soup poured down his back ; scalding coffee turned into his boots ; or his rice-pail filled with potatoes ; was it strange that he was deprived of his amiability, and ventured the assertion that he could whip somebody—it mattered not whom ?

The scenes that occurred there every morning were worthy of the pencil of Hogarth or Cruikshank.

The room was crowded to excess. Everybody was trying to do what only one-twelfth of those present could accomplish. There were fifty claimants for every vessel.

The small messes came into collision with the large messes. The war raged with the bitterness of the contests between the houses of York and Lancaster, or the rival factions of the Guelphs and Ghibellines.

Such a conglomeration of interests and purposes ; such a chaos of voices ; such a jostling and confusion ; such an olla podrida of the absurd, the excited, the belligerent, and the profane could not well have been witnessed anywhere else.

And then the conviction that the resentments and quarrels were altogether mean and unworthy ; the idea that gentlemen should fly into a passion, and descend to the morals of the Prize Ring, about a few miserable iron skillets and tin pans ; should for no higher object imitate the fishwomen of Billingsgate, mortified all concerned when coolness and reflection came.

Every officer, when the cooking was over for the day, promised amendment, and vowed for the future he would observe decency and decorum.

But when the dreadful cooking-day came around again, those good resolutions were dispersed into thin air, and the ancient Adam asserted itself in spite of good-breeding, self-discipline, and the sense of propriety.

Through the thick smoke of the Libby Kitchen a confusion of tongues was heard that reminded one of his idea of the Tower of Babel.

Some of the foreign officers became so excited that they could not do justice to their feelings in the English vernacular, but appealed to German, French, and Italian—we had a number of nationalities in the Prison—for full expression of their fancied wrongs and woes.

Many of them declared that they would rather go through a battle than spend a day in the kitchen—and I shared their opinion fully ; for, grotesque and contemptible as those things appear at present, they were our life then, and weighed with a now incomprehensible burden on our spirit and our brain.

Who that was there will ever be able entirely to forget the Libby Kitchen ; the struggle between the small and the large messes ; the great contest of the pans and plates ; the sieges of the skillets ; the raids upon the wood-pile ; the defeats at breakfast ; the drawn battles at dinner ; the triumphant victories at supper ; the irrepressible conflict between bacon and business ; rice and rhetoric ; dried apples and despair ?

CHAPTER XXXIX.

CELL-LIFE IN RICHMOND.

Prison within a Prison.—Full Appreciation of Sterne's Starling.—Evil Destiny of the *Tribune* Correspondents.—One of our many Failures and its Result.—Interior View of a Rebel Cell.—The Rare Society we found there.—Glance at the Gross Corruption in Secessia.—Novel Means of making Confederate Currency.—Horrors of Southern Dungeons.

To dwell in a prison within a prison is one of the experiences the War Correspondents enjoyed in Richmond, and which not a few of our officers and soldiers have shared with them.

As I have mentioned, we of the *Tribune* were always endeavoring, like Sterne's Starling, to get out—by the by, I never fully felt the truth of that bit of fine writing in the "Sentimental Journey" until I had been a prisoner nearly a year—and, like the poor bird, we found it a hard task to accomplish our freedom.

At Castle Thunder we always had some plan; and as often as we failed, we formed another. We had made arrangements, through trusty messengers, where to go in the city, in the event of our breaking the bonds that fettered us; and we felt confident our escape could not be much longer delayed.

The Destinies seemed opposed to us, however. All our endeavors blossomed without fruit. We failed almost always through some other agency than our own; and at last we came to look upon ourselves as the Jonahs of any enterprise of the kind.

Any tunnel in which we were interested was sure to be exposed, or too long deferred, or to tumble in at the very moment it was ready to be tapped.

Any guard that we had gotten into a proper condition to take our money, and give us our freedom, was certain to be detailed, or fall sick, or die, or get drunk just when we needed him.

Any night on which we depended for complete darkness, proved to be decked out with at least a thousand additional stars and an extra flood of moonlight.

The Elements and Fortune both seemed to have arrayed themselves against the "historians of the War;" and we marveled much when the long night of adversity would end.

In one thing we were lucky enough. The authorities of the Prison either did not suspect us of being Catilines, or, if they did, gave us no intimation of their suspicion. That was somewhat singular; for a citizen of Maryland, who assumed to be a most earnest Unionist and a most zealous Christian, we knew was a perpetual spy upon all the inmates of the room in which we were confined; and we knew also that he was morally certain we had tried a score of times to get out.

On a certain night the thing was all arranged. There was to be no postponement on account of the weather, and positively no change of performance.

At twelve o'clock one of the *New York Herald* Correspondents, Mr. Richardson, myself, and several others, were to go out of the room—the sentinel having agreed to unlock the door—down into the street, by other guards who were in our pay and confidence.

We arose from our blankets—we had lain down for a feint—put on our clothes, and were ready to set out.

The sentinel wished to see our money.

The *Herald* man handed him a roll of bank-notes, and when they were returned, they proved to be ones instead of fives, as the Correspondent insisted. That was a palpable theft; and we concluded if the guard would cheat us on the inside of the bars, we could not depend on him on the outside.

So we fell back with maledictions on the perfidious Rebel.

The next morning the Bohemian discovered his mistake. He had given the guard the wrong roll of notes; and we lost our chances for freedom—that time at least—by our own blunder.

The subsequent afternoon we three Bohemians were called out, and informed that we would be consigned to a cell; and before evening we were transferred there.

A dismal, dirty place, that cell. It was about twenty by twelve feet; the floor incrusted with filth. But one window served to let in any light. The walls and ceiling were begrimed with smoke and years of accumulated dust.

No ventilation in the cell, which was sorely needed, as there were tubs in the den that had stood there, and infected the atmosphere for many weeks, if not months.

A temple of Cloacina was a charming abode, and a smoke-house a rosy Eden, compared to that cell. Not a box, bench, or even stick of wood, was in the place.

A small broken stove constituted its sole piece of furniture.

The cell brought to our mind the Vicksburg jail, and we laughed at the magnificent preparations made for our reception. The first thing we did was to give two or three handfuls of Rebel currency—we certainly could afford to be generous with that kind of "money"—to an *attaché* of the Castle, and ask for wood, a wash-basin, a stool, &c.

We did not relish the change, but we concluded to make the best of the worst, and immediately set about rendering ourselves—in the true Bohemian style—as little uncomfortable as possible. We lighted our pipes to improve the atmosphere, and talked of New York hotel-life; of handsome furniture, epicurean dishes, and the very opposite of our surroundings.

At a late hour we rolled ourselves in our blankets, and slept quite well, in spite of the repulsiveness of the place. In the morning, our companions in the room we had left sent us various articles of food from the boxes received from the North, and kind expressions of sympathy and hopes that we would soon be released from our prison within a prison.

The same day some seven new personages were sent into our cell for a similar offense to ours. They were decidedly *mauvais sujets*, and had all belonged to the Southern army. For two years they had been guilty of all manner of crime—theft, burglary, forgery, stabbing, shooting, and I know not what else. Their faces reflected their characters, and would have been admirable additions to the Tombs' gallery of notorious rogues.

Delightful society, thought we, for gentlemen; and we referred to Young Mirabel in the company of the bravos.

Alas! there was no Oriana to deliver us from our peculiar friends! We were obliged to await the inexorable logic of events, and we waited long.

Our bevy of fresh visitors, with all their vices, treated us with entire courtesy and kindness. They offered to do little offices, and really assisted us in many ways. One of them was extremely desirous to have me write him a love-letter to his inamorata, a bar-maid or kitchen queen residing in the city.

I gratified him, and indited a classical *billet-doux* to his proletarian mistress, with which he expressed much delight; the only objection to it being his inability to understand what it was all about.

The rogues grew very communicative, and told us how much money they used to make, twelve or fifteen months before, by "shoving a Mick," "running a kink," and other entertainments, the nature of which, from the occult language of the revealers, was entirely enigmatic.

Our friends undertook to enlighten us on the character of their speculations, informing us that "running a Mick" was to get an Irishman drunk; induce him to enlist for two or three hundred dollars; obtain five times that sum from some citizen desirous of procuring a substitute; and after sending the Hibernian to Camp Lee in the forenoon, to go out for him towards evening; bring him in again, and sell him to some other individual requiring a representative in the field.

"Coming the kink" was to steal a negro from the country, and dispose of him in town; one of the party himself pretending to be an African—having previously blacked up, and put on a wig—and a brother or near relative of the melanthrope in question. Those fellows would steal the Ethiop and sell him again; and sometimes they had bartered away the same darkey seven or eight times in one month.

Those revelations were highly edifying, of course. They gave us such a new idea of the peculiarities of trade that we have ever since confessed our ignorance of some of its branches.

Some of the rogues had been traveling through the South for two years, drawing the pay of Lieutenants, Captains, and Majors, though they never had been more than privates, and had only carried muskets until they found it convenient to run away. In the line of desertion they had been very energetic. They assured me they had belonged to twelve or thirteen regiments at different times, and had engaged themselves as substitutes whenever opportunity offered.

They were a rare *cotérie* of gentlemen, and I greatly admired the delicacy of their organization, and their sublimated ideas of honor. They furnished us with some knowledge of the corruption that existed in Secessia, by assuring us that there were hundreds of bogus officers in every State, who had swindled the Treasury out of millions of dollars.

"Confound their old rags!" said our heroes of Alsatia, in justification of their dishonesty, "what harm is there in stealing their d——d trash? They ought to pay a man for putting it in circulation."

The fellows were adventurous, too.

They had frequently made their escape, but always contrived to be brought back. They had changed their names so often that they did not recognize, or had forgotten, the one they originally bore. They had been in every department of dishonest enterprise—from watch-stuffing to garroting, and had not committed murder only because they did not believe it good policy.

I asked one of their number: "What is Mr. ——'s calling? What does he do for a livelihood?"

"He? Oh, he doesn't do much now. He's in the burglary business a little, but it hasn't paid him very well lately."

The burglary business! My question-answerer spoke as if it were an entirely legitimate avocation, and no doubts were to be expressed thereof.

The sacred seven related their manner of escape at different times, which displayed no little ingenuity, and rather interested us who had yet so much to accomplish in that way.

They had gone out of the Castle in broad daylight, with pens behind their ears and slips of paper in their hands; the guards supposing they were clerks connected with the Prison.

They had sooted their faces, and changed clothes with some of the negroes, and gone out at night to their quarters, whence they could pass over the roof of an out-house, and, dropping down into an alley, get away before the guard could fire on them.

They had slipped out behind detectives, pretending to be their deputies, and had exhausted their ingenuity in their endeavor to deceive the guard. One of them had contrived to obtain a woman's apparel, and, habiting himself in it, had passed the sentinels without exciting suspicion. They had even gotten into empty barrels, and been driven out in wagons by the negroes.

For nearly two weeks we were kept in the cell, during which we smoked a great deal, and became exceedingly disgusted with ourselves and the world at large.

How we paced the floor to and fro! How we wore smiles rather sardonic on our lips, and forced every day's bitterness of feeling into our hearts! How we grew skeptical of every one, even our nearest friends, and doubted if we had any! How we scoffed at the "disinterested motives" of the great World, and vowed that such things as affection and sympathy did not exist outside of the poet's page.

We became cynical in spite of ourselves, and reached Schopenhauer's plane—hoping nothing, expecting nothing, caring for nothing.

Few persons, unless they have had the experience, can determine how much a long captivity dries up the heart, narrows the mind, and withers all the freshness of existence.

Shut out from every refining and humanizing influence, deprived of the sight of Beauty, of the sense of Fragrance, of the sound of Melody, a man of any imagination or sensibility must be uneducated back to a condition of spiritual barbarism, and be inoculated with a moroseness and skepticism years will not eradicate, nor the assurance of love and friendship altogether remove.

His captivity leaves on his soul the shadow that is never lifted, and so rudely shatters frail barks of Hope and Beauty, which erst sailed smoothly on the unruffled sea of his Being, that they never dare venture forth in the future from the closed harbor of his isolated heart.

Out of that noisome, repulsive cell went we to our old quarters, parting from our fortnight-old companions of "Mick-shovers" and "kink-comers" without any agony of spirit, that the sumptuous splendor of that most romantic of Castles, and the deliciousness of its aromatic atmosphere would not soon remove.

In the Citizens' room, as it was called, we were greeted by those from whom we had been temporarily separated, as if we had come out of bondage to freedom; and indeed the old quarters, dreary and disagreeable as they were, opened to us on our return with a breath of the far-off fragrance of Paradise.

A brief sketch have I given here of cell-life as experienced by us; and though it presents no very attractive picture, it was bright and beautiful as a Claude or Poussin, compared to the experience of some other captives.

Some of the cells of the Libby Prison and Castle Thunder were such as we would not think to find in the present century. The former were under ground—damp, dark and dismal in the extreme, and so unwholesome that I have known officers confined there a week to sink under the infliction, and suffer from a serious illness. The brutes at the Libby—most conspicuous among whom were the Turners—have thrown Union officers into those vile cells for accidentally expectorating on the floor, for giving a piece of bread to some captive more unfortunate than they, and other trivial offenses.

When officers attempted to escape, or were recaptured after escaping, they were placed in those subterranean dens, and kept there on the smallest and most obnoxious rations for weeks, and sometimes months,—as long generally as they could be kept without imminent peril to their lives.

I have known our officers so starved there, that they caught rats, and ate them with the greatest relish; and so broken in health and constitution, that they did not recover for months, and will not, some of them, to their dying day.

The Rebels have had a great deal to say since the War, of Northern bastiles, but never a word about Southern ones. I confess to a much longer and more varied acquaintance with the Southern than those at home; but I feel confident such confinement as has been the rule in Dixie would not be tolerated in the more liberal and enlightened part of the Republic.

I have again and again seen Union captives come out of cells in Richmond pallid and emaciated as consumptive corpses—mere ghosts of men—with mouldy clothes and mildewed hair, burning with fever, bent with rheumatism, wasted with dysentery, who had been detained in those dungeons with a fiendish malignity, until their wretched existence held by a single thread.

At the Castle, too, I have often been surprised at the tenacity with which incarcerated victims clung to their frail tenements of clay in the cells and dungeons that admitted hardly a ray of light; too small for the inmates either to lie down, or sit, or stand with ease.

The air of those dens was pestiferous. They reeked

with filth and vermin. They would have delighted the Doges in the days of Venetian crime and Venetian mystery. They would have closed forever the babbling lips of those who talk of our generous but erring brothers—our brave but wayward sisters of the South.

Brave and generous people cannot be cruel, and cruelty was an inextinguishable element in the character of most of the Prison authorities of Secessia. They were malevolent without pretext, and inhuman without passion—an anomaly only to be explained by the enunciation of a truth I have long recognized, that "Slavery is barbarous, and makes barbarians."

CHAPTER XL.

CASTLE THUNDER.

Contrast between the Castle and Libby.—A Southern Bombastes.—Cruel Treatment of Prisoners.—Absurd Charges against Innocent Men.—The Prison a Regular Bastile.—Energetic and Enterprising Captives.—Difficulty of Obtaining Supplies Sent from the North.—Peculation and Plundering of the Chivalry.—Their Begging and Trading Proclivities.—Their Ridiculous Assumptions and Exposure —Bohemian Arrivals.—Comparative Comfort of the Correspondents.—Rebel Anxiety to Purchase Treasury Notes.—Campaigning with the Small-Pox.

CASTLE THUNDER, though more disagreeable on account of the character of its occupants, was preferable, on the whole, to the Libby, because there was less tyranny and contemptible malice there than at the other Richmond Prison. At the Libby we could relieve the tedium of captivity by conversation with intelligent and well-bred officers; but at the Castle we were forced to depend almost entirely on our own society,—Mr. S. T. Bulkley, of the *Herald*, had been added to the Bohemians,—as our fellow-prisoners were for the most part deserters, thieves, swindlers, and loyal but ignorant men, far more interesting abstractly than socially.

The commandant of the Castle, a regular Bombastes Furioso, happened to have some literary pretensions—they were purely pretensions—and therefore treated journalists with a certain degree of consideration. We had privileges others had not, and rather congratulated ourselves upon our transfer, albeit the Richmond authorities had designed it as an augmented severity

There, as I have said elsewhere, we first began to put in practice our ideas of escape, and, in conjunction with others, to dig tunnels, sound guards, enlist negroes in our service, and make arrangements, in the event of our exodus, for concealment in the city.

At the Castle we witnessed a great deal of suffering; though, from the causes already mentioned, and from the fact that while there we received several boxes of supplies from the North, we Bohemians were enabled to make ourselves comparatively comfortable. We were in the least bad quarters in the Prison—it was formerly a tobacco warehouse and factory—and had gathered during our long incarceration a number of such articles as are usually considered necessary to housekeeping. Compared to those about us we were the purple-robed patricians of the place. Generally, we were neither hungry nor ragged; and yet every day we saw poor devils so cold in their squalid fragments of attire, that they could hardly hold the hard corn-bread doled out to them to their pale and wasted lips.

No Union captive ever received a single garment or blanket from the Rebels: he was thrown into the prison to shift for himself as best he might. If he froze, they cared not; if he perished, they had only one less Yankee to feed. They were as indifferent to the sufferings of the prisoners as they would have been to those of the Feejee Islanders; and they made no pretense of sympathy or commiseration.

The Southern citizens were treated quite as badly as the

Yankees—even worse, sometimes, I thought—especially if they were poor and friendless. Old men, with white hair and forms bent with years, were incarcerated there on charge of having given food to their sons, who had deserted from the Army. Others were snatched from their homes on vague accusations of disloyalty to the so-called Confederacy, and allowed to die there untried and unknown.

A large number of persons were there as spies—when the Rebels could trump up no other charge against a man, they called him a spy, knowing that would hold him for an indefinite period—who had not brains, or energy, or courage enough to incur the suspicion of any sane person. They had actually thrown into the Castle as a spy, a poor lunatic who had broken out of the Jackson (Mississippi) Asylum; and when I went farther South he was still in captivity, with a prospect of ending his days there.

It was even reported among the traditions of the Prison that blind men had been there as spies, and dumb persons on charge of giving information to the enemy; but for those reports I do not vouch. Certainly, however, men were there on the most absurd grounds, and likely to remain unless they had money or friends.

There was no assumption of justice in the Castle. Any one might perish within its walls from sheer neglect, or, once confined there, all trace be lost of him. It was indeed a Southern Bastile. Almost everybody in Richmond got into the Castle some time or other, prominent Rebel officers, men, women, and children.

That it was employed for the most nefarious purposes

I cannot doubt. During the reign of General Winder and his Baltimore plug-ugly Detectives, the grossest abuses were practiced. Any man bearing malice against a citizen of Richmond had only to trump up some story, relate it to a Detective, and, presto, the unfortunate found himself in the Castle. As the nature of his offense was not stated even to him, he could make no defense, and unless some good Rebel outside interested himself in his behalf, his prospects of long imprisonment were surprisingly brilliant.

An old occupant of the Prison assured me that a Southern officer, having become enamored of a citizen's wife, breathed some secret suspicion of her husband's loyalty to Winder's ruffians, and instantly the ill-starred liege-lord was looking at Virginia's capital through iron gratings. The husband removed, the libertine officer prosecuted his suit without interruption; and when the former re-obtained his freedom, his wife had become openly the mistress of the licentious Major.

Such instances were not uncommon. The odious *lettre de cachet* was revived. The Castle was made the vehicle of personal malice and private revenge.

The commandant, Alexander, was accused of all manner of debaucheries and cruelties, and arraigned before the "Confederate" Congress on the gravest charges. Nothing came of them beyond the removal of the official, and the substitution of a much meaner man in his place, who, subsequent to our transfer to Salisbury, would not allow any of the prisoners to purchase a particle of food, or even a copy of a newspaper. That contemptible piece of malice was carried into execution until the fall of

Richmond, and the inmates of the Castle suffered greatly from the premeditated cruelty.

A more energetic set of conspirators, or more enterprising planners of escape, than were at the Castle, I have not seen. They were always contriving some means to get out, and exhausting ingenuity to that end. They dug tunnels enough to undermine the City, and worked subterraneously like moles. Whoever wanted to escape, brought himself into sympathy with the Bohemians. We were generally in league with most of the villains in the Prison, for they were more industrious and audacious than the honest fellows. Yet were we unsuccessful in our endeavors for many months, though it seemed our activity earlier merited the reward which ultimately came.

One night, some ten of the prisoners essayed to escape by digging a tunnel, but were informed upon by a traitor in their midst, and their attempt frustrated. They were taken before the Commandant, the Bobadil I have mentioned, who, with a pompous and Jupiter-Tonans air, thus delivered himself: "There is no use, men, of trying to get out of here: it is absolutely impossible! You can make no movement; you can not breathe; you can not have a thought that is unknown to me. You might as well attempt to scale Heaven as escape from the Castle; so you had better behave yourselves, and become resigned to your situation."

The very next night, the harangued captives, with twelve others, got out, and were never afterward heard of by the Rebels.

During the latter part of our confinement at the Castle,

as I have said, we were the happy recipients of several boxes. To get them was a pure piece of good fortune; for the chance of losing any thing sent from the North was as ten to one.

The officer in charge of the Rebel warehouse had known us at Vicksburg, and was unusually obliging to us. As soon as we were advised by letter of a shipment of supplies, we would obtain permission to visit the warehouse under guard, and get hold of our box before it was broken open or stolen.

If a package remained there any number of days, it was pretty certain to be pillaged. Hardly any thing ever came through unimpaired. The Union officers could obtain very little without bribery, and they frequently offered a quarter and even half the contents of a box, to procure the remainder.

No class of people I have ever met are so susceptible to a bribe as the Rebels. From the pompous, swaggering, pseudo gentleman down to the lackey, they would all, like old Trapbois, in the "Fortunes of Nigel," do almost any thing for a consideration. They outdid the stage Yankees in their fondness for bartering and exchanging, and talked of swapping and trading you out of whatever you had or wore, in a manner I had not known—often as I have been in New England—to exist, save in histrionic Solomon Swops and Solon Shingles.

They even play the mendicant almost as well as professional lazzaroni. You can not have any thing gay or striking on your person, any bright color or shining metal, but some fellow, who professes to be a gentleman, will ask you, directly or indirectly, to give it to him.

Poor devils! they have no surplus of attire or adornment; but one would imagine, with all their pretension, they might, during the present century, have learned at least the first lesson in good-breeding.

They are shams in manners, as they are in chivalry, hospitality, culture, and every thing else. They are brave, of course, because they are Americans; but they must even pretend a recklessness of life and a passion for death that is not natural to humanity, and assuredly not to them more than to any other part of the great family.

With all their braggadocio and bombast about perishing in the last ditch, and dying to the last man, woman, and child, they know when they are whipped, as thoroughly and quickly as any other people, and have no more natural appetite for coffins and graveyards than the rest of mankind.

Of course the leaders will fight while they can keep a formidable army in the field; and when they can not, they will submit quietly, or run away.

They have been prating since the War began, as if, in the event of their subjugation, which is as certain to take place as the sea to ebb, or buds to bloom, they would imitate their more generous and chivalrous brothers the Japanese, and perform a general hari-kari upon themselves. They won't do any thing of the sort: they can't be induced to do it. I wish they could. If they can endure the ripping up, I fancy we can; and as the matter-of-fact individual told the fond mamma, who informed him that her daughter was of a very gushing nature: "Let her gush, marm!" we can say, with a very commendable degree of composure, when the insurgent leaders adopt self-dissection as a business: "You never had any bowels of compassion to spare, gentlemen; but if you are so minded, let them rip."

Since the above was written, Richmond has fallen, and Lee's grand army, which was the main-stay of the Rebellion, has crumbled to pieces. Therefore what I have said may be regarded in the light of a prediction. The Rebels now *do* know they are whipped, and Jefferson Davis, his Cabinet, and the principal leaders have run away—are at this moment fugitives in the land.

The power of the great Insurrection is broken. The cause of the Secessionists is hopelessly lost, and yet we hear of no general hari-kari; no gratuitous dying of women and children; no perishing in the last ditch.

It is extremely difficult to write any thing about the War, while events are developing so rapidly as they have been in the last few weeks. The prophecy of to-day becomes the fact of to-morrow. The speculation of one hour passes into history the next.

No one can doubt at present, however much he may sympathize with the South, that the War, so far as any largeness of operations is concerned, is practically over; that the giant of Treason has been laid low. He may rave and wrestle in his chains; he may struggle to rise, and may yet do us some injury, but he has ceased to be formidable: his power for permanent evil is forever and forever gone.

To return from great to small things, let me go back

to the Castle, which is now a prison for the enemy, and not for the loyal who suffered there so long; whose sufferings are more than atoned for by the glory of the Present; the triumph of the Right; the establishment, after four years of sanguinary strife, of the integrity of the Republic, and the restoration of the Nation beyond the power of future harm.

During the month of November, if I remember rightly, two more Bohemians were added to our triad, Mr. L. A. Hendrick and Mr. George H. Hart, of the New York *Herald*. They had been captured by Colonel Mosby, while acting as safeguards at the house of a Virginia lady, who stated the circumstances, and begged that they be released, as justice and honor demanded. Mosby said he was compelled to send them to Richmond, but assured the lady they would not be detained. They were kept there for three months, and obtained their liberty at last only by securing the services of able lawyers, and by the fact that they did not belong to the *Tribune*.

Early in January, 1864, it was proposed by Commissioner Ould to exchange for them two attachés of the Richmond *Enquirer*, who had been captured in some piratical expedition on the Chesapeake, and who had no right to claim the treatment of Correspondents or journalists. Ould sent Colonel Tyler, the proprietor of *The Enquirer*, to them to arrange the exchange—ignoring *The Tribune* writers altogether—informing them if the Richmond journalists were not released from irons, in which he said they had been put—as they deserved to be, I presume—that the Southern authorities would be compelled to place two of the five Correspondents in the Castle in a similar position. Mr. Richardson and I laughed at the one-sided arrangement, knowing that if any pair were to be put in irons, it would in all probability be ourselves, although no opportunity was given us for freedom. The irons proved a mere threat, or at least there was no excuse for their employment, as Hart and Hendrick were paroled, and sent North to obtain the release of the Richmond scribes, which they did, although they had then been prisoners only about one-third the time that *The Tribune* correspondents had.

Mr. S. T. Bulkley, also of the *Herald*, was soon after released: proving conclusively, were any proof needed, that the Richmond officials had no particular animosity against War Correspondents, so long as they were not members of Horace Greeley's staff.

The five Bohemians, while together, were in the same mess, of course, and, as they were rather congenial, assisted each other not a little in relieving the tedium of prison life. With the boxes and the books we had received from the North, we continued to live with comparative comfort. The days of our cooking and playing scullion had passed; we had assistants there to perform menial offices; and, consequently, we had ample leisure for reading and indulging in our favorite amusement of whist, in which, from long practice, we attained considerable skill.

The Castle was lighted with gas, which was burned all night when we did not turn it off to hide some attempt to escape—so that we could sit up as late as we chose. We had nocturnal lunches from our bountiful supplies, and often sat over coffee, and sardines and preserves, smoking our cigars, until the sentinels beneath the grated windows called the hours of two and three in the morning.

During no period that we were in captivity, did we of *The Tribune* subsist beyond a few days at a time on the prison rations. Had we been compelled to do so, we would have been occupying long since a few feet of the sacred soil of Virginia or North Carolina. We would not have starved to death positively, perhaps; but our systems would have so run down on the meager and unwholesome diet that we would have fallen ill, and never have gained strength sufficient for restoration.

Having no expectation of release save through our own agency—and that was highly improbable—we always looked ahead, and prepared for the coming months. We managed almost always to keep in funds, receiving Treasury Notes secretly in cans of preserves, butter, and books sent us in our boxes. We experienced no difficulty in exchanging the National currency for Rebel scrip, as there was always an active demand for the former in all the prisons to which we were consigned, from Vicksburg to Salisbury, at rates varying from two to fifteen of their stuff for one of our money. The Rebel officers were ever anxious to buy, and when they did not do so openly, they employed agents to purchase the Yankee issues for them.

I remember an Israelite who had been sent to the Castle from Mobile for receiving Treasury Notes for some garment; and no sooner had he gotten inside of the Prison than a young man employed there entered the Citizens' Room, and asked in a loud tone who had any greenbacks to sell. The Hebrew opened his eyes in astonishment, and declared it "vash a tam pretty pishness to put a shentlemans in such a tam hole as dat for doing vat de tam Rebels vash doing demselves." The clothes-dealer's enunciation was somewhat at fault; but no one could controvert his logic.

At the Castle we made our first acquaintance in the South with the small-pox. We had a great many cases in the Prison—a number in the room where we were confined. In fact, we walked, ate, and slept with it for several months, there as well as in Salisbury, without contracting the disease. Persons suffering from the small-pox were permitted to lie in our quarters until they had broken out; but we had no fear of it;—why should a man in a Rebel prison fear any thing?—and to that, perchance, may be attributed our escape from infection. We even administered to those who had been seized, bent over them, and inhaled their breath and the contagion supposed to emanate from the body; yet we passed through two long campaigns with the obnoxious ailment entirely unscathed.

There was a great variety of sickness at the Castle during our five months' incarceration, and a number of our fellow-prisoners went to the hospital and died; but I always contrived to keep out of the Rebel lazar-houses, in the capacity of patient, at least; and with the exception of several desperate flirtations with the fever, I enjoyed far better health than I had any reason to expect. Indeed, I felt vexed at myself sometimes that I did preserve such an enviable hygienic position; believing no gentleman had any right to live in a Southern prison more than a month, at the furthest.

CHAPTER XLI.

EXECUTION OF A LOYAL TENNESSEAN.

Brief Account of his Antecedents.—His Attachment to the Union Cause.—His Betrayal.—His Cruel Treatment in Prison.—A Second Judas.—Conviction on False Evidence.—His Wretched Condition.—The Closing Scene.—An Inhuman Detective.—Revolting Spectacle at the Gallows.

Of the many military murders committed in the South since the inception of the War, none have been more cruel and revolting than the hanging of Captain Deaton, of East Tennessee, in the prison-yard of Castle Thunder, Richmond, Virginia, during the winter of 1864.

Deaton was a strong Union man in that most loyal part of our country, and had been very efficient in resisting the encroachments of the Secessionists from the period of the earliest troubles. He was a well-built, finely-proportioned, muscular fellow, in the prime of life and full flush of health, intelligent, courageous, determined; and, as may be supposed, a most annoying and dangerous personage for the Rebels to deal with.

As the struggle continued, the intensity of feeling increased in Tennessee, and finally Deaton was compelled to leave his home—in Knox County, I believe—and take to the bush, as it is technically termed in the South. The loyalists were outnumbered by the regular forces sent into their neighborhood, and were coerced to adopt guerrilla warfare as a means of protection.

Deaton, seeing the change in the situation, felt that organization was necessary, and soon raised a company of loyal Tennesseans, whom he was chosen to command. With these he did effective service, and he soon gained a name and fame for his daring and exploits. He was desirous of admission into the regular army, but whether he succeeded in his purpose, I am unaware.

The Rebels hated him with exceeding hatred, and, it is stated, set a price upon his head. They made every effort to ensnare him, but he was too wily for them. He had numerous hair-breadth escapes; was fired upon again and again; his clothes pierced with bullets; and yet he was unharmed. He seemed to bear a charmed life; but he had his unguarded moments, as all men have, and fell into a trap the enemy had prepared for him.

Like most of the middle and poorer classes of the South, Deaton had strong home attachments, and for a number of months he had been unable to hear directly from his wife and children, whom he most tenderly loved. His foes were aware of that, and sent him word by a person whom he deemed trustworthy, that if he would call at a certain place on an appointed night, he would obtain news of his family.

Deaton went; and while in the house, which was surrounded by armed men, he was surprised before he could use his weapons; bound hand and foot, and thrown into a wretched negro-pen. He was charged with all the crimes in the calendar, the least of which were arson, rape, and murder. But as it was not easy to prove him a person with whom Caligula would have been a saint, he was accused of being a spy, and kept in a loathsome dungeon for four or five months. His health gave way; his constitution was broken; his nervous system was shattered, and he became a wreck of himself. The Rebels were always threatening him with execution, and for many weeks he lived in hourly expectation of being put to death. No one was admitted to see him, and he fell into a condition of mental imbecility. About that time he was transferred to Richmond, where it was thought he might be treated with some humanity. Strange mistake! Humanity is not indigenous to the Rebel capital. There the meanest, and vilest, and most tyrannical of the insurgents can be ever found.

At Richmond he was thrown into the condemned cell of Castle Thunder; a cold, dark, noisome, filthy hole, next to the room in which my *confrerè* and myself were confined, and which we never passed without closing our nostrils with our fingers, in lieu of those perfumed handkerchiefs that ceased to be the mode with us soon after our capture.

Up to that period nothing had been proved against Deaton; but he there unfortunately made a confidant of a villain, formerly a Lieutenant in the old United States service, who had tried to be a Secessionist, but by his vacillations had been suspected and consigned to the Castle. The ex-Lieutenant betrayed him of course. The morning after he heard Deaton's story, he asked for an interview with the Commandant of the Prison; and soon after the Captain was loaded with irons, and treated more cruelly than ever.

A few days subsequent he was tried by Court-Martial, and convicted of being a spy upon what was declared to be false evidence. Deaton was then returned to his cell; and I have rarely witnessed a more melancholy spectacle. Haggard, emaciated, ragged, almost barefooted, bent as with a crushing weight, a strange light in his sunken eye, he seemed then more dead than alive.

We obtained for him two or three times the privilege of coming into our room, while the cell was being relieved of a portion of its filth, to warm by a poor stove his frozen feet. We gave him a seat; he took it with a vacant stare, and crouched over the fire, but spoke no word in answer to the tender pity we expressed for him. His mind wandered: his spirit was broken: long and persistent barbarity had killed in him the gallant and noble Man.

The fatal Friday came on which poor Deaton was to be executed. Certainly it was a hangman's day—dreary, lowering, bitter cold. The scaffold was erected in the yard adjoining the Prison on the west side; and into the inclosure the unfortunate victim was taken about the hour of noon. He was too weak to walk without support; and he was assisted down the stairs to the ground floor. An effort had been made to improve his external appearance; but his better clothes only made him seem more wretched. Though the thermometer was little above zero, the perspiration stood in drops upon the condemned man's brow, and a spot of crimson glowed in his ghastly cheek. He looked up at the scaffold with a leaden gaze, and when asked some question by the *attachés* of the Castle at his side, made an incoherent reply, a muttered mystery.

Detective Caphart—a gray-haired villain of sixty, who has been known to pay a large price for the privilege of hanging a man, and who boasts he has assisted at the death of all the persons executed in Richmond for many years—was very active on the occasion, and in the best of spirits. Indeed, like the laughing hangman of Louis XI., he was only happy at such a time. He pulled the Captain rudely about; cursed him for his dullness; and vented spleen on an unfortunate who had but a few minutes to live. Caphart and Warden Wiley hurried through the dreadful affair as if it were any ordinary engagement, and the scoundrel Detective glowered on the prisoners, who had been invited to witness the execution, as if he regretted very much that he could not perform the same amiable office for them.

The estimable twain having borne Deaton to the scaffold, released their hold of him, and told him to stand up. They then descended, and ordered an underling to pull the drop. The fellow had his hand upon the rope, when the Captain looked around with a ghastly, half-idiotic smile, muttered something, and sat down on the scaffold. Old Caphart flew up the scaffold again; and shaking Deaton with great fury, while his cracked and wiry voice poured forth curses upon the "d——d Yankee son of a ——," called Wiley again to his assistance.

Once more Deaton was held up; and that time he turned upon them, and smiled with a soft, sweet expression that transfigured his whole face. All the old, unsettled look fled. Courage, love, pity, benison came back to him. He tried to nerve himself to stand. The officers released him—as he seemed to desire. He staggered, and he would have fallen. The momentary inspiration passed: his head drooped: a half groan, a half sigh escaped him.

"Hurry, hurry!" cried out Caphart, in his harsh, broken tones; "the d——d Yankee will die in our arms if you don't hang him quick!"

The drop fell, and the loyal Tennessean was swaying in the air, struggling with death, and struggling hard.

So worn and wasted was he, that the tension of the rope was slight. For nearly ten minutes the victim writhed and twisted and turned.

It seemed as if he would never die. The few prisoners who had gone down to witness the tragedy were shocked; and most of them hurried away.

Caphart alone enjoyed it. He grinned like a fiend, and was evidently happy in his way.

At last the struggles ceased. The sufferings of the loyal martyr were over.

The horror of the scene impressed every one, save the gray-haired ruffian; and more than one of the Rebel officers shuddered and turned pale.

The bleak wind blew upon the scaffold, and moved the strangled corpse.

A few snow-flakes fell through the frosty atmosphere, like scattered rose-leaves on a grave.

The sun broke through the heavy clouds, and a little light streamed down, as if the path were opened, and they had parted to let a passing spirit in.

CHAPTER XLII.

SALISBURY PENITENTIARY.

Our Removal from Richmond to Salisbury.—Character of our Companions.—Troubles of Transportation.—Strange Scene and Sensation at Petersburg.—Arrival at the North Carolina Prison.—Interior View of our Quarters.—A Heavy Blow for my Confrère.—The Horrors of Southern Captivity.—Difficulty of their Realization.

ON the 2d of February, *The Tribune* correspondents were ordered from Richmond to Salisbury, and long before dawn we were standing in Carey Street, in the midst of seventy or eighty Rebel deserters and desperadoes wearing balls and chains. We were the only Northerners in the Southern shipment, and, I might say, the only persons, save a few straggling Tennessee and Virginia Unionists, who would not have picked their father's pocket, or sold their grandmother, for a sufficient pecuniary inducement.

We were not very well attired, and our nine months of captivity had not contributed to the elegance of our appearance ; but, compared to those about us, we must have seemed like robes of velvet upon hovel walls. We had a great deal of baggage in the shape of blankets, a box of provisions and cooking utensils, two old valises that we had purchased in prison ; and even after distributing our household goods to some of our retainers, we were fairly overburdened with our possessions. We very frequently asked ourselves the question Mrs. Wragge so pathetically put to herself: "What shall we do with our things?" and found no small difficulty in practically answering the query. The large box fell to our individual management. It was very heavy, and the single pole, run through the rope handles, by which we carried it, turned and twisted in our hands until they were blistered, and our muscles were sore with the weight we bore; having been compelled to carry it over a mile at Petersburg, a quarter of a mile at Weldon, and three quarters of a mile at Salisbury.

At Petersburg we stood for an hour and a half in one of the most public streets, near the railway dépôt, subject to the gaze and comment of the masculine and feminine passers-by. Rare company was that for a gentleman. I should have blushed had I not been proud—proud to be hated by the Rebels—proud that I hated them as well.

As I stood there, I saw well-dressed men and women gaze at that ragged crew with ill-concealed contempt and even disgust—I wonder if they were more disgusted than I was—and heard them utter denunciations upon "those scoundrels" that were just enough in the main.

Strange thoughts stole through my mind in that public thoroughfare. The situation was novel, and the sensation somewhat so. I had never fancied before the War that I should be a show and a spectacle in an American city—one of a crowd of ruffians and villains, from whom I could not be discriminated, passing from one prison to another—to be leered at by the vulgar and miscomprehended by my peers.

Neither my confrère nor myself felt humbled even

there, swept away as our individuality was in that unwholesome mass of humanity. The earnest conviction of what we were, elevated us above our surroundings and beyond the Present. We felt self-possessed, haughty, fearless. The blood burned in our cheek; but it was the kindling of a defiant soul; and if any close observer, any studier of countenance, had been there, he would have descried through the marble of the statue the suppressed passion of the sculptor, the repose of Art with the scorn of the Real.

The Richmond authorities had very kindly furnished us with a special detective to see that we did not escape. We had no idea of doing so on the way, having been led to believe Salisbury the best base of operations we could find. The detective proved to be a Unionist, and we told him frankly we had no intention of leaving him, so that he need give himself no trouble on the subject. We could have gotten away a number of times *en route* to Salisbury, and we regretted afterwards we had not done so on principle.

On the afternoon of the second day we reached Salisbury, and, entering the inclosure of the Penitentiary, were warmly greeted by prisoners we had known at the Castle, and officers, held like ourselves as hostages, whose acquaintance we had made at the Libby. At the Penitentiary there were Rebel convicts, Northern deserters, hostages, Southern Union men, and all persons that the enemy designed to hold for a long time. There were then but six or seven hundred inmates of the place, which we preferred either to the Castle or Libby, because we had the privilege of the yard, and had a daily opportunity to breathe the external atmosphere, and behold the over-arching sky.

The quarters in which we were confined were very undesirable, being about ninety by forty feet, with barred windows, dirty floor, partially occupied by rude bunks, and two broken stoves that gave out no heat, but a perpetual smoke of green pine-wood that made the atmosphere blue, and caused us to weep as though we had lost the dearest mistress of our soul.

There, with rags and vermin, filth and odors, as little Sabean as possible, we passed the long, cold, desolate nights, shivering in our light blankets, and striving, for many a dreary hour, in vain to sleep. What a dismal den it was!

Trophonius' famous cave, as described by Pausanias, would not have more deeply shadowed the soul of its occupant. What ages I seem to have passed there: what weary, pangful, endless nights!

How cruelly Morpheus deceived me; how he painted to my mental eye the peace and pleasantness of scenes far away! How oft I awoke from dreams of mental magnificence to the cold, staring, stony walls of that wretched abode! How frequently I was aroused from the fancied breath of roses, and the enchanting strain of unseen instruments, and the soft-sweet pressure of lips of balm and beauty, by the bite of insects and the tramp of some unfortunate tatterdemalion upon my fatigued form, steeped in half-voluptuous, half-spiritual imaginings, and surrendered quite to precious oblivion of its surroundings!

If any place more than another is the antipodes of Poetry, that surely was it.

I see it now, so barren, bleak, and squalid, so associated with the meanest bondage and the most repulsive objects; and I wonder any one can have lived there, and preserved the least sense of Beauty.

Rare old den of disorder, disgustfulness, and deformity, your form glowers through time and distance like a vision of Hades upon the distempered mind of some early Father of the superstitious Church!

I often wished I could obtain a photograph of that room, for I can give no idea of its repulsiveness and superlative squalor. A gentleman seemed more out of place there than the Angel Gabriel would in a prize-ring, or the Pope of Rome at a Five Points dance-house.

There it was my fellow-journalist, Mr. Richardson, first heard of the sudden and altogether unexpected death of his wife.

Amid all that meanness and coarseness and desolation, the heavy blow fell upon, and almost crushed him. Heavens! what a place to be informed of such a grief; of the loss of the nearest and dearest of relations; of one whose life was full of beauty and of promise! His future had been all interwoven with hers; and when cruel Fortune severed two such hearts, in his there must have seemed no bright to-morrows.

Those quarters at Salisbury and their associations, will my bereaved friend ever forget them? Can I even?

The antique junk-shop—such it seemed—was filled with odors of the most obnoxious kind, especially at night, from additional agencies that politeness will not permit me to name. Vermin swarmed everywhere; they tortured us while we tried to sleep on our coarse blankets, and kept us in torment when awake. Not a square mile of Secessia seemed free from them.

No light of any kind was furnished us; and there we sat, night after night, in the thick darkness, inhaling the foul vapors and the acrid smoke, longing for the morning, when we could again catch a glimpse of the blue beaming sky.

Think of that death-life month after month! Think of men of delicate organization, accustomed to ease and luxury, of fine taste, and a passionate love of the Beautiful, without a word of sympathy or a whisper of hope, wearing their days out amid such scenes!

Not a pleasant sound, nor a sweet odor, nor a vision of fairness ever reached them. They were buried as completely as if they lay beneath the ruins of Pompeii or Herculaneum. They breathed mechanically, but were shut out from all that renders existence endurable.

Every sense was shocked perpetually, and yet the heart, by a strange inconsistency, kept up its throbs, and preserved the physical being of a hundred and fifty wretched captives, who, no doubt, often prayed to die.

Few persons can have any idea of a long imprisonment in the South. They usually regard it merely as an absence of freedom—as a deprivation of the pleasures and excitements of ordinary life. They do not take into consideration the scant and miserable rations that no one, unless he be half famished, can eat; the necessity of going cold and hungry in the wet and wintry season; the constant torture from vermin, of which no care nor precaution will free you; the total isolation, the supreme dreariness, the dreadful monotony, the perpetual turning inward of the mind upon itself, the self-devouring of the heart, week after week, month after month, year after year.

Most strange that captives there do not lose their reason, or die of inanition and despair. How hard it is to kill a man, I had not fully learned, until fortune threw me into Rebel hands.

Frequently I thought, in prison, of the suggestive words of Glanvil: "Man does not yield to death, nor to the angels even, save through the weakness of a conquered will;" and my spirit seemed to grow stronger and control the failing flesh.

Man must be a brute or a philosopher to bear up under all the trials of confinement in Rebeldom; and I wonder now how the stoicism I had so long cultivated stood me in that period of most urgent need.

Much do I marvel that I passed through the ordeal unscathed; whether I am the same mortal who bore with outward calm and uncomplaining fortitude nearly two years of Southern captivity.

Was it my other or my actual self who passed those ages of months in Secessia? I fancy I see myself still in Richmond or Salisbury, pacing those filthy floors, and that he who dashes the pen across the page is another identical form of my developed consciousness.

More fortunate, as I was, than most of my fellow-prisoners, still am I surprised that I did not perish in pure self-defense. What motives or purpose had I to cling to the Planet? Perhaps, unwittingly, my instincts held me, and informed me vaguely of the day of deliverance.

All that sombre Past appears now like a nightmare dream, and this restoration to a free and normal condition the glad awakening. The recent realities seem shadows; and yet they were such shadows as struck terror to the soul of the tyrant-king.

While one beholds the vast, throbbing, rushing life of the great, free, enlightened North, he finds it difficult to believe but a few days divide him from the meanness and misery, the despair and death and horror, that were the constant companions of the helpless victims immured in the prison-pens of the South.

CHAPTER XLIII.

PHOTOGRAPHS OF HORROR.

Great Influx of Prisoners at Salisbury.—Barbarity of the Enemy.—Intense Suffering and Wholesale Murder of the Captives.—Pen Pictures of the Prison. —Agonizing Scenes.—Enlistment of our Soldiers in the Rebel Service. —Shuddering Strangeness of the Past.—The Secretary of War Responsible for the Sacrifice of Ten Thousand Lives.

AFTER nine months of confinement, at Salisbury, some ten thousand enlisted men were sent thither from Richmond and other points; and then began a reign of pain and horror such as I had not believed could exist in this Republic under any circumstances.

Our poor soldiers had been robbed of their blankets, overcoats, often their shoes and blouses, and were sent there in inclement weather, and turned for some weeks into the open inclosure without shelter.

After a while they were given tents capable of accommodating about half their number; and there they began to sicken and die from cold and hunger—the rations being sometimes only a piece of corn bread in forty-eight hours, until the daily mortality ranged from twenty-five to forty-five per day.

The soldiers dug holes in the earth and under the different buildings in the yard, constructed mud huts and shelters of baked clay, showing extraordinary energy and industry to shield themselves from wind and storm.

But their attire was so scant, and their diet so mean and meager, that they died necessarily by hundreds.

Hospital after hospital—by which I mean buildings with a little straw on the floor, and sometimes without any straw or other accommodation—was opened, and the poor victims of Rebel barbarity were packed into them like sardines in a box.

The hospitals were generally cold, always dirty and without ventilation, being little else than a protection from the weather.

The patients—God bless them, how patient they were! —had no change of clothes, and could not obtain water sufficient to wash themselves.

Nearly all of them suffering from bowel complaints, and many too weak to move or be moved, one can imagine to what a state they were soon reduced.

The air of those slaughter-houses, as the prisoners were wont to call them, was overpowering and pestiferous. It seemed to strike you like a pestilential force on entrance, and the marvel was it did not poison all the sources of life at once.

Imagine nine or ten thousand scantily clad, emaciated, woe-begone soldiers—unnamed heroes, who had battled for our sacred cause on twenty blood-drenched fields—in an inclosure of five or six acres, half of them without other shelter than holes they had dug in the earth, or under the small buildings employed as hospitals.

The weather is cold; perhaps a chilly rain is falling, or the ground is covered with snow. There are the soldiers—hundreds of them with naked feet, and only light blouses or shirts, hungry, feeble, despairing of the

Present and hopeless of the Future—huddling over a small and smoky fire of green wood, in a crowded tent, whose very atmosphere is poisonous; or standing shivering against the outside of the chimneys of the squalid hospitals, hoping to warm their blood a little from the partially heated bricks; or drawn up in their narrow caves, inhaling the curling emanations of the burning pine, and striving to shelter themselves from the bitter wind; or begging, with pallid and trembling lips, for shelter at the door of those lazar-houses where their companions in arms are lying in dirt, distress, and despair, breathing out their lives at the rate of thirty and forty a day.

Look into those hospitals—strange perversion of the name!—which are small brick and log buildings, twenty-five by sixty feet, and see how a people who boast of their generosity and chivalry can treat the prisoners they have taken in honorable warfare.

There lie the prisoners, in the scant and tattered clothes they were graciously permitted by the Rebels to keep, filthy from the impossibility of obtaining water to wash themselves, with no beds nor bedding, no covering even, perchance without straw; tossing and groaning their miserable lives away.

Fires blaze at one end, it may be at both ends, of the tenements; but the heat extends not far, and the cold wind rushes in from the broken windows and through the crevices in the walls; while the air is mephitic and noisome to such a degree, that when you breathe it first it is almost suffocating.

What a ghastly line of faces and of figures! To have

seen them once is to remember them always. They are more like skeletons in rags than human beings. Ever and anon some of them strive to rise and obey such calls as Nature makes; and a companion, less weak and wasted than they, bears them, as if they were children, over the dirt-incrusted floor, and lays them down again to suffer to the end.

Here lies a boy of sixteen or seventeen—whose mother, in some far-off Northern home, is praying for him every night and morning; to whom sisters are writing words of cheer and sympathy he will never see—muttering in fever, and beckoning with shrunken hands to forms no mortal eye can discover, but which may be waiting to bear his brave young spirit home.

There is a gray-haired man, who left his farm and fireside when the traitorous gun at Sumter woke a world to arms. He has passed unscathed through forty battles, to die an unrecorded hero here.

His eyes are fixed, and his minutes are numbered. Children and grand-children will look with anxious faces at all dispatches and letters from the Army of the Potomac, but will not learn, for months, the fate of one who was only a private.

"Is this man here?" carefully inquires a soldier, looking in at the door and reading the address of a letter. The answer is in the affirmative, and the ward-master calls out, "Mr.——, here's a Northern letter for you."

There is no eagerness to hear. The person addressed does not even turn his head.

Strange, for he has waited many weary weeks to see the characters of that well-known hand; has dreamed night after night, amid the pauses of his pain, of reading the sweet assurances of his dear wife's love.

These are the words: "Dearest Husband: I have not heard from you for months. I can not believe any harm has befallen you; for I have faith that Heaven will restore you to me at once. I feel sure my deep and earnest prayers have been answered; that my affection will be as a shield to you, and my fond bosom again be your pillow."

Blessed words! what would he give if he could behold them. Alas! they have come too late. Her love has been lost in a greater love, and the life that is in a life to come.

Through all the day and night corpses are carried from the hospitals to the dead-house, where the bodies are piled up like logs of wood, until the rude cart into which they are thrown is driven off with its ghastly freight.

At any hour one may see men bearing across the inclosure the pallid and wasted figure of a soldier, whom the Rebels had starved or frozen to death with malice prepense.

There goes into the dead-house a young man who, four years ago, was the idol of his circle.

Possessed of beauty, genius, fortune, friends—all that could make Earth sweet—he quitted the attractions of a life of ease and a luxurious home, and took up his musket that his country might be truly free.

Not even she who loved him better than a sister, more intensely than a mother, would recognize him among the heaped up dead.

The unclosed eye and gaping jaw make that once handsome face hideous to view; and suffering, and neglect, and cruelty, have changed it into a vision of repulsiveness and horror.

But why seek to paint these scenes which defy description? Everywhere is pain, squalor, and horror.

All day long, one sees wretched, haggard, sick, and dying men in every part of the inclosure. Their faces tell their story—an unwritten epic in the saddest numbers. Their wasted forms reveal the inhumanity and barbarity of a savage foe. Amid all that assemblage of thousands of men, though the sun shines, and the birds sing in the groves near by, not a laugh nor a jest is heard—not the faintest sound of merrymaking.

Not a single face relaxes into a smile; every eye is dull with despondency; every cheek sunken with want; every lip trembling with unuttered pain.

Disease and Death there hold high carnival, and the mirror of misery is held up to every vacant stare.

The air is heavy with plaints, and prayers, and groans, and over that accursed camp hangs the pall of despair. Guercino could paint no darker picture. Indeed, no limner, no artist in words or colors, could give a just idea of the scenes of that terrestrial Tophet.

Suffering everywhere, and no power to relieve it. In every tent and hole in the ground, wherever you tread or turn, gaunt and ghastly men, perishing by inches, glare on you like accusing spectres, until you find yourself forced to exclaim, "Thank God, I am not responsible for this!"

Little, if any thing, could be done for them medically. Hunger and exposure could not be remedied by the materia medica; and to seek to heal them by ordinary means was like endeavoring to animate the grave.

What advantage had quinine and opium when they could get neither bread nor raiment? The sending of physicians into the Prison limits was a ghastly farce, for the Rebel officers premeditatedly starved and froze our brave men, hoping to compel the Government to exchange, or to force the soldiers into the Southern service.

Hundreds of the privates, anxious to save their lives, joined the enemy, trusting to the future to escape. I can not blame them. Who could demand that they should await certain destruction in the form of disease, and cold, and hunger, when relief was offered them even by a cruel and barbarous foe? No, I cannot censure those who forgot in such fearful hours all but their own salvation; yet I can find no language too strong to praise the heroes that stood firm when they seemed deserted by their friends, their country, and their God.

The Rebels, apparently not content with the ravages of disease, almost entirely superinduced by starvation and cold, fired upon the wretched prisoners whenever the humor seized them; killing and wounding them without reason or pretext. The guards seemed influenced by a diabolical spirit, shooting men in their tents, and in holes in the ground, seemingly in the merest wantonness.

No one was safe. Whenever a sentinel felt in the mood, he would murder a "Yankee" without being removed from his post, or even asked why he did it. Again, and again, I myself saw soldiers fired upon by the guard, and that too when they were transgressing no rule, and violating no order whatever.

My readers may well ask, what motive had the enemy for such nefarious crimes? I can only answer, that I have often put that question to myself; that I am utterly at a loss to conceive his motive; that he seemed actuated only by a fiendish malignity, to maim and murder as many Yankees as possible.

On the 25th of November last, a few of the prisoners, perhaps a hundred or two, feeling that their condition was entirely desperate; that they were being deliberately murdered by starvation and exposure, determined to attempt an outbreak; knowing they could, at the worst, only be killed, and that death was almost certain if they remained in prison. Such arrangements as were practicable they speedily made, without giving any intimation to the other captives; and, about one o'clock in the afternoon, fell upon the relief-guard, some twenty in number, when they entered the inclosure, and seized their muskets.

Some of the guard resisted, and a fight occurred, in which two of the Rebels were killed and five or six wounded, with about the same loss on the part of the insurgents.

The alarm was immediately given. The whole garrison mounted the parapet; and though, in a minute, the *émeute* was suppressed, the effort to get out of the gate having failed, they began firing indiscriminately upon the prisoners, albeit it was evident to the dullest observer that the great majority had nothing whatever to do with what was called the insurrection.

The prisoners, seeing they were to be shot down in cold blood, took refuge in the tents, behind the outbuildings and hospitals, and in the caves they had dug. But that made no difference. The Rebels discharged two of the field-pieces bearing on the camp, and continued firing into the tents upon the poor captives, who were trying to screen themselves from the murderous balls.

For fully half an hour the shooting went on, and, in that time, some seventy men were killed and wounded, not one of whom, I venture to say, had any intimation of the outbreak before it was undertaken, and who were as guiltless of any attempt at insurrection as infants unborn.

That was a fair example of the animus of the foe. He found a pretext for wholesale slaughter, and availed himself of it to the uttermost.

Woe to those who are responsible for all that hideous suffering; to the inhuman Rebels who plundered our poor soldiers of their clothing, and turned them into that filthy pen to die; who had store-houses full of provisions, and yet starved their unfortunate captives with a fiendish persistency which one must be a believer in total depravity to understand!

The truth is, the minds of the Southern people have for many years been so abused by their leaders and newspapers; their source of information respecting the North has been so poisoned; the feelings, opinions, habits, and intentions of the Free States have been so grossly misrepresented, that it is not singular the loyal citizens of the Republic should be regarded by those dupes as thieves and assassins, barbarians and monsters.

The Southern people, as a class, have had no means of judging of the Northerners, for they rarely traveled, or met socially those who had traveled; and the consequence was, they believed whatever absurd and infamous statements they heard from their demagogues, or read in their newspapers.

For at least ten years—twenty-five would be nearer the truth—the South has been carefully and constantly stimulated and goaded into the bitterest hatred of, and direct enmity to, the North. The Southern leaders had long prepared for the overthrow of the Government, and believing the time ripe when Mr. Lincoln was elected, undertook the aggressive form of treason.

Secession became a mania. It drove the embracers of the doctrine mad. All their worst passions were enkindled by it, and they swept through four years of agony and war to break themselves in pieces at the feet of the magnanimous and triumphant Nation.

Now that I have escaped from that Hades of Salisbury, I marvel how I ever endured to breathe that pestilential air; how I continued, week after week and month after month, to keep my hold upon that dark point of the Planet.

Truly, it seems like a nightmare dream; and I can hardly realize I ever lived, and walked, and labored, in that place of shuddering horrors.

While I sit writing in an easy-chair, glancing out of the window at the gay throng of the ever-changing Broadway, hear the peals of Trinity and the vast roar of the Metropolis, I wonder if I have not been drowsing, after reading Poe, and following his ghastly fancies into the mystic sphere of sleep.

It is not real, I think. With all this bustle, and energy, and beauty, and plenty, and enlightenment, and Christianity about me, it cannot be that a thousand miles away hundreds of heroes, who had borne our flag on dozens of immortal fields, died every week from the premeditated cruelty of the Rebels.

Surely it cannot be, for the Government was aware of all the atrocities of Southern prisons: it had heard the story over and over again from the lips of sufferers; and, if it had been as was represented, the Government would certainly have made some effort to relieve its stanch supporters and its brave defenders.

Alas! the story is too true; it is written in thousands of unknown graves, whose occupants, when alive, cried to the Government for redress, and yet cried in vain!

As soon as Mr. Richardson and myself reached our lines, we determined to visit Washington even before returning to New York, to see what could be done for the poor prisoners we had left behind, and determine what obstacles there had been in the way of an exchange. We were entirely free. We owed nothing to the Rebels nor to the Government for our release. We had obtained our own liberty, and were very glad of it; for we believed our captives had been so unfairly, not to say inhumanly, treated at Washington, that we were unwilling to be indebted to authorities of that city for our emancipation.

We went to Washington—deferring every thing else to move in the matter of prisoners—and did what we thought most effective for the end we had in view. During our sojourn there, we made it our special business to inquire into the causes of the detention of Union prisoners in the South, although it was known they were being deliberately starved and frozen by the Rebels. We particularly endeavored to learn who was responsible for the murder—for it was nothing else—of thousands of our brave soldiers; and we did learn. There was but one answer to all our questions; and that was, Edwin M. Stanton, Secretary of War.

Although he knew the exact condition of affairs in the Rebel prisons, he always insisted that we could not afford to exchange captives with the South; that it was not policy. Perhaps it was not; but it was humanity, and possibly that is almost as good as policy in other eyes than Mr. Stanton's.

After our departure from Washington, such a storm was raised about the Secretary's ears—such a tremendous outside feeling was created—that he was compelled to make an exchange.

The greater part of the Northern prisoners have now been released, I believe; but there was no more reason why they should have been paroled or exchanged since February than there was ten or twelve months ago. No complications, no obstacles had been removed in the mean time. Our prisoners might just as well have been released a year since as a month since; and if they had been, thousands of lives would have been saved to the Republic, not to speak of those near and dear ones who were materially and spiritually dependent upon them.

Dreadful responsibility for some one; and that some one, so far as I can learn, is the Secretary of War. I hope I may be in error, but I cannot believe I am. If I am right, Heaven forgive him! for the people will not. The ghosts of the thousand needlessly sacrificed heroes will haunt him to his grave.

CHAPTER XLIV.

TUNNELS AND TUNNELING.

Respect for Tunnels.—Their attractive and absorbing Power.—Tunneling at Castle Thunder.—Difficulty of their construction.—The Libby Prison Enterprise.—Uncertainty of their Completion.—Frequency of Excavations at Salisbury.—Desires to Obtain Subterranean Freedom.—Ideal Regrets.

SINCE my incarceration in Rebel Prisons I have had a profound respect for the Thames Tunnel; because, unlike those with which I had the fortune to be connected in Secessia, it was an established success.

Well was it for the fame of Brunnell I had no interest in his great enterprise, which in that event would, I am confident, never have been carried out.

Tunnels were my thought by day and my dream by night for nearly twenty months.

I was always a large stockholder in some Tunnel contemplated, begun, or completed.

I helped to plan Tunnels; watched over them; sat up with them; crept into them and out of them; but, alas! never crept through one of them.

Freedom was in some way associated in my mind with a Tunnel.

I fancied Adam must have crawled into Paradise through a Tunnel.

A Tunnel to me was the greatest work of Man.

Dig a Tunnel, and get out of it, appeared the injunction of the Gods!

With attent ear I heard the divine injunction; and yet its latter portion I could not obey. Witness all those weary, dreary months, how often and how energetically I tried, and only tried to fail!

In the Libby Prison the Union officers had no opportunity to dig a Tunnel while I was there, their quarters being too far removed from mother Earth. But when I was removed to Castle Thunder I fell in with a number of amateur engineers, who believed the way to Liberty lay through the sacred soil of Virginia.

They so believed, and acted upon their belief. Tunnel after Tunnel was made there; but they were always so long in its construction, that it was either exposed by traitors, or discovered by the officials.

It is singular how much the prisoners accomplished with slender means. They rarely had more than a case knife or an old hinge; and yet with that they would dig, in a few days, a hole large enough to admit the body of a man, through ten and even twenty feet of earth.

The greatest difficulties in the construction of a Tunnel are the disposition of the dirt and the lack of fresh air, which, as soon as the excavation is carried to a distance, very soon becomes exhausted.

A Tunnel is so old and well-known a means of egress from Prison, that the authorities are ever on the alert to find one; and the appearance of any quantity of dirt would at once excite suspicion. Hence the greatest precaution is necessary. Haversacks and small bags are brought into requisition, and the dirt is carried, little by little, from the mouth of the Tunnel to some place where it will not attract attention.

Operators usually select some spot where they think they will not be interrupted, near the outside limits of the Prison, and go to work. They toil like beavers, laboring often day and night with changes of hands, because they feel the danger of delay. I have known numerous Tunnels to be discovered because their completion had been deferred over a single night.

At Castle Thunder, by getting down into an old storeroom below the Court-Martial room, as it was termed, one could begin his Tunnel beside the rear wall of the Prison, skirting an alley fifteen feet wide; and as few persons went there, the prospect of disturbance was small.

The design was to commence digging in the morning, and finish it before dawn the following day. That never could be accomplished, or at least never was while I remained there. If it had been, I should have gotten out certainly; for I frequently sat up watching the progress of the subterranean bore, all ready to wake my companions, and depart at a moment's notice.

During the five months I was at the Castle, more than a dozen Tunnels must have been constructed, all running under the alley mentioned, and designed to come up the other side of the fence, out of sight of the sentinels, where one could have walked through a military-hospital yard to Main-street, and made good his retreat.

The most extensive and successful Tunnel in the South, during my compulsory sojourn there, was that made by the officers at the Libby Prison, in the month of February,

'63, by which over one hundred and twenty escaped, and some sixty-five got through into our lines.

There the officers had ample leisure to work, and were engaged three or four weeks in the enterprise. They removed the bricks of a hearth in a store-room on the ground floor, cut through a stone wall two feet thick, and then began the Tunnel proper, which was carried some fifty or sixty feet into an inclosure, passing the prisoners under, and placing them beyond, the beat of the sentinels.

The officers relieved each other constantly, and conducted their labor so adroitly that Major Turner had not the faintest suspicion of what was going on.

When so large a number was missed, the morning after the escape, the Rebel authorities were nonplused. They could not imagine, for an hour, what had become of them. They went to the store-room and searched carefully, but still could find nothing of the Tunnel; nor was it till late in the afternoon that they made the discovery.

The nature of Tunnels is such, that the work necessarily makes slow progress. As soon as they are fairly started, and the operator is below the surface, he is compelled to lie flat on his face, at full length, and, using his knife, or whatever implement he may have, he throws the dirt behind him, which is gathered up by an assistant, and removed in a pan or bag.

The mole performance is continued day after day until it is supposed the Tunnel is ready to be tapped or opened. That is an important matter, and it is requisite that the distance be accurately measured. Awkward mistakes and needless discoveries have been made by neglect of proper precautions in that respect.

I remember distinctly a Tunnel by which the Correspondent of the *Cincinnati Gazette* and myself expected to escape at Salisbury, during the month of November. We were assured it would be ready for opening at ten o'clock; but after examining it, and sitting up with it until after twelve, we concluded there was no hope for it that night, and we went disappointed to our bunks. The next morning, about daylight, it was tapped, and came up nearly two feet this side of the inclosure instead of the other side. And, to complete the ill fortune, a Rebel officer stepped into it before noon the same day.

A woman's humor is not more uncertain than a Tunnel.

I never knew any man to make a correct calculation of the time of a Tunnel's completion. But you can always conclude, when its engineers declare positively that it will be done in two days, that it will still require some finishing strokes at the close of a week. Tunnels linger longer than rich relatives whom expectant heirs are waiting to bury.

Two or three begun at Salisbury, that were to be completed by November 1st, were only half dug in the middle of December.

The truth is, that the operators are so anxious to finish a Tunnel that they calculate their capacity for performance, even with their wretched implements, by the intensity of their desire.

When we three Bohemians escaped from Salisbury, there were four Tunnels completed, and at least seven more in a half-finished state. The former would have been tapped weeks before, had not some wretches who had been interested in them enlisted in the Rebel service, and exposed them to the authorities.

The officers of the prison could not find where they were located, or exactly where they were to come out; but they placed extra guards at all the points designated, so preventing any chance of escape.

We regretted that greatly, because we preferred to pass out of a Tunnel, as we could then have carried with us blankets and provisions; but, going in the way we did, we were compelled to travel light.

I was anxious to realize my long dream, and pass to the outer World, from which I had been so long separated, by a Tunnel; but when I found myself fairly free, I ceased to mourn that my long-cherished hopes as to the means of exit had been blasted.

A Tunnel is a Tunnel; but Liberty is Liberty; and the latter is acceptable in any form, while the former alone is but an abstraction.

Possessing Freedom, I have small general regrets that a Tunnel did not help me to it; though in my loftiest moods I lament in spirit that a Tunnel, on whose tawny bosom I had lain, like a subterranean Antony hanging upon an earthy Cleopatra's lips, bore me not to the upper air and the blessings of the disenthralled.

In my rapt moments of the Future, in my visions of the Night, I shall still dwell on the perfidy of Tunnels—the Elfridas of excavations. I shall, perhaps, endeavor—my mind going back to the dreariness and horror I have left behind—to pass out of some Broadway Hotel by undermining the Brussels carpet, and carrying out the ottoman in an imaginary haversack, and so realize in sleep the passionate prompting of Prison hours, distant, thank Heaven! and departed, I trust, forever.

CHAPTER XLV.

MUGGING.

The Meaning of the Term.—Who the Muggers were.—Their Plan of Operation.—Character of their Victims.—Indifference of the Authorities on the Subject.—Flogging of Northern Deserters.—Their Cruel Treatment.—Mugging in Richmond and Salisbury.—Its Reduction to a System.—Our Own Soldiers in the Business.—A Vigilance Committee Proposed.

FEW of our readers who have enjoyed the blessings of freedom all their lives will understand the meaning of the caption of this chapter, the purpose of which is to explain in detail what the term represents.

Mugging is the argot expression for robbing, and one of the most popular words in the Southern-Prison lexicon. Every place in Secessia where miscellaneous captives are held contains its Muggers in abundance. They were originally Rebels, but so demoralizing was their example, and so extensive their practice, that they added quite a number of our own men to their ranks.

In the Libby, being in the officers' quarters, we saw no mugging, although a great deal of it was going on in other parts of the Prison; and after we were removed to Castle Thunder and the Salisbury Penitentiary, we were daily witnesses of its operations.

The chief Muggers in every instance were Rebels,—natural thieves, born bullies, and thoroughly-developed ruffians,—who had lost their liberty by deserting, swindling, stealing, and violating in various ways the military as well as the civil law. A few of them formed the nucleus for all the rascals who might be consigned to the Prison from time to time; and as they were organized, they had strength, and large capacity for mischief.

The Muggers, like most bullies and ruffians, manifested a fine discrimination respecting the party they attacked, selecting those they thought they could rob with little resistance and entire impunity.

Any person they saw fit to make their victim had small chance of escape. They would fall on him at night in numbers, throw a blanket over his head, hold him down, and rifle his clothes at will, the surrounding darkness preventing him from determining who were the robbers. If he resisted, he was cruelly beaten, and often was so served when he submitted quietly to the plunderers.

They generally selected some unsophisticated fellow or ruralist to "go through," as they termed it, and did it most effectually. The unfortunate, at first taken by surprise, and then terrified by the terrible threats they would make in the event of his raising an alarm, would permit himself to be robbed without an outward protest or murmur; and in the morning would find himself moneyless, coatless, shoeless, and hatless.

Sometimes I have known men to be completely stripped of their clothing, and cruelly belabored beside. Probably the victim would not be aware who the Muggers were; and if he did, would be afraid to expose them to the authorities, on account of the sanguinary menaces promulgated against all informers.

That honest men should be plundered and beaten by

scoundrels who were notorious, and be prevented by apprehension of physical consequences from giving their names, is a hardship, independent of the severity of Prison, which must be difficult to endure. The principal Muggers were very well known in Richmond and Salisbury to the commandants there; but only in a few instances were they punished.

As the "Yankees" were for the most part the sufferers,—the Southern captives had little to lose,—perhaps the authorities felt no disposition to cast over them the mantle of protection. Whatever the cause, they most shamefully failed to perform their duty. They said, if they could obtain the Muggers' names, they should be severely punished; but made no effort to ferret out the perpetrators of the outrages. They could have put a stop to the nefarious practice in forty-eight hours, if they would have done so, as was shown by the flogging at Salisbury of a dozen Northern deserters who had been guilty of mugging their own class.

Captain G. W. Alexander, who inflicted the punishment, refrained from bestowing it upon the Rebel convicts, although they were far worse than our deserters,—proving that his conduct arose from passion instead of principle. Indeed, he afterwards ordered a number of lashes given to the unfortunate deserters because an attempt had been made to escape from their quarters, and they would not expose the parties who had participated in the enterprise.

That was infamous; and plainly indicated that Alexander, who was at heart a brute and bully,—and, if the opinion of his intimates might be trusted, not possessed of that extraordinary courage to which he pretended,—would have flogged every prisoner at Salisbury, if he had dared, for the smallest infraction of discipline. The deserters had no friends, North or South, and he fell on them for that reason.

Little love have I for our deserters or for Muggers; but when I saw them tied to a whipping-post, and lashed with a leather thong by a muscular Sergeant, my blood boiled with indignation, and every nerve in my body thrilled.

The punishment seemed an insult to the Race, and degraded, I thought, all who witnessed it.

Although Alexander, when he whipped the deserters, sent armed soldiers to all the Prison quarters to compel attendance in the yard, for the purpose of witnessing the revolting spectacle, I always contrived to avoid being present.

Years before, my pulses had throbbed and my blood leaped to my cheek when I had accidentally seen negroes lashed in the South,—thank Heaven, I shall see no more of that ignominious brutality in this fair country!—and I was in no better frame of mind, years after, to witness the beating of members of the Caucasian family.

When the mugging continued; when old and innocent men were pounded so severely that they could not be removed from the hospital for weeks, merely because they were unwilling to be robbed of what served for their physical salvation; when, night after night, the most brutal assaults were made by the worst of ruffians upon all who had any thing to lose, I changed my opinion somewhat; concluding that if whipping were the only remedy for mugging,—which I did not believe,—it ought to be well laid on.

Our deserters I rather pitied, when I found they were made the scapegoats for others' offenses; that the Rebels took advantage of their position to treat them with undeserved harshness. Who ever heard of a people, unless they were "chivalrous," imprisoning and persecuting the soldiers who, they were bound to suppose, had fled from our Army to theirs out of sympathy with the Southern cause?

At Castle Thunder, in Richmond, the Mugging was mainly confined to two of the rooms of the Prison, one of them immediately above the apartment in which I was confined.

Almost nightly a rush would be made on the floor above; several bodies would be heard to fall; perhaps a loud outcry, with "murder, murder, murder" attachments; then a heavy struggle and a general confusion, followed by a return of quietude.

Those were the mugging demonstrations, and rarely attracted any attention.

In the morning, several new men would report that they had been robbed and beaten; though they would be entirely ignorant of the perpetrators, as the assault had been committed in the darkness.

No investigation would be made, no inquiry established. The whole thing would be taken as a matter of course, and repeated as soon as any fresh subjects presented themselves.

At the Penitentiary in Salisbury, Mugging was reduced to a system.

Men were frequently mugged in the Prison-yard. Several of the band would gather round the intended victim, who on a sudden would be thrown to the ground; his pockets turned inside out; his coat and hat, sometimes his shoes, taken; after which he would be let alone until he obtained more money or clothes to invite a fresh attack.

The Rebel room, in the third story, where the convicts were confined, was the principal field for mugging. The wildest cries of pain and terror emanated from that quarter every night or two; and daylight would reveal some poor fellow with black eyes, swelled lip, and badly cut face, deprived of all his valuables and a large portion of his clothes.

The Rebels would be abroad at an early hour, and dispose of their stolen goods to some of the guards who were in league with them; thus removing all traces of the theft.

Complaint, as I have said, proved of no avail.

The authorities would return the stereotyped answer: Point out the men who robbed you, and they shall be punished.

The victims, even if they knew the thieves, were afraid to give the names, knowing they would be beaten half to death as soon as they were shut up again with the convicts.

So far as my observation extended, the officers of the Prison seemed to favor the most notorious scoundrels of the place, provided they were on their side. They reserved their wrath for the Northern deserters, who soon became weary of the mugging business, from the fact that they were made to answer for the sins of all the other thieves without reaping any fair proportion of the ill-gotten gains.

No attempt was ever made to mug either my *confrère* or myself, although we frequently anticipated and prepared ourselves for an attack, in conjunction with some more muscular allies, offensive and defensive.

Frequently we lay down with clubs under our heads, and slept, as the phrase is, with one eye open.

Amiable as we were by nature, the constant repetition of such outrages made us feel a trifle bellicose; and we concluded, if we were mugged, we would endeavor to give the muggers something to show for it.

Well perhaps for our expectations and our physical condition, the experiment was never tried on us. We were not sorry, for we did not regard it as an experience we particularly needed.

When the nine or ten thousand Union soldiers were sent to Salisbury, many of the most worthless formed a league with the Rebels, and the two forces carried matters with a high hand up to the time of our escape. Robberies continually occurred. Men were stabbed, and their skulls cracked; some thrown out of the windows, and their necks broken; but the authorities in no manner interfered.

The better class of prisoners talked seriously of instituting a "Vigilance Committee," and hanging some of the principal Muggers, as had been done at Andersonville, Georgia, a few months before—by the by, four of the individuals executed there had gone from Salisbury, where they had been held as deserters,—but no definite plan of action had been agreed upon at the period of our hegira.

Justice, which had long slumbered at Salisbury, fell, I fear, into a sleep too deep for waking.

UNION BUSHWHACKERS ATTACKING REBEL CAVALRY.

CHAPTER XLVI.

DESPERATE ESCAPE.

Constant Effort of Prisoners for Freedom.—Practicability *versus* Planning.—A Trio of Desperadoes.—Cause of their Extraordinary Gayety.—Their Remarkable Exodus.

In Prison, the inmates think and talk of little beside escape.

To them, freedom is everything; all else, nothing.

By day and night they revolve one plan and another in their mind; hope and despond; try and are frustrated; attempt and are punished. Yet they return to their favorite idea, and endeavor and re-endeavor, though failure ever follows. Dungeons and bayonets have little restraining influence.

Few men who will not brave the possibilities of death, when freedom beckons, and they are encircled by the horrors of a Rebel Prison.

How well I remember the numerous trials and failures of my *confrère* and myself to escape! It seemed as if we never could get out. Our genius, we thought, did not lie in that direction. Our plans were elaborate, and so were our preparations. We speculated constantly on what we might do; talked of the feasible in our blankets far into the night, amid the pulsings of the stars and the ravages of insects.

While we theorized grandly, some dull fellow, with

only one idea, but that in the right direction, got out, and brought us, with our fine reasoning and subtile calculations, to overwhelming shame.

Was the fault with us, or with the Gods?

It matters not now, for at last the Gods were kind.

While at Castle Thunder, we were taught what enterprise and nerve will accomplish.

Three prisoners on capital charges were in the condemned cell, heavily ironed. They were desperate fellows, no doubt, and endured their situations very cheerfully—laughing, singing, and howling in the most uproarious style.

Their gayety seemed to increase daily; for they soon began dancing in their chains, and dropping their iron balls on the floor as if sporting with their misfortunes.

This latter entertainment they kept up so regularly, I began to suspect there was meaning in it, and that it covered a design.

Nor was I mistaken, as the sequel proved.

About two o'clock we heard a row and a rush below; the discharge of several muskets, and the general indications of a disturbance. We could learn nothing then; but after breakfast,—the eating of a piece of corn-bread, the throwing away of a bit of fat, rancid bacon, and the swallowing of a cup of water, was so denominated in the Castle,—we were apprised of the adventure of the turbulent trio.

It appears they had made all the noise to drown the sawing through of the floor which was over a store-room; and at an hour of the night or morning when the sentinels were apt to be careless, they took up a part of the boards, and slowly and silently slipped into the under apartment, having let themselves down by strips of a blanket they had torn up for that purpose.

The enterprising scoundrels then quietly forced open a window into a passage leading to the street door of the Prison; and in the shadow of that quarter seized three muskets placed against the wall on racks. They then rushed upon the guard nearest them, and struck him with the butt of the piece, knocking him senseless over an iron railing that ran across the passage.

The outer sentinel saw this movement, and prepared for it, bringing his gun to the position of a charge. He had mistaken his men, if he supposed that would stop them. They dashed upon him, and he was just on the point of firing, when the nearest prisoner discharged the contents of his musket into the breast of the guard, literally tearing his breast to pieces, and of course killing him instantly.

They then ran into the street, past the outer sentinels, who were too much surprised to act, and who forgot to use their muskets until too late. The fugitives were nearly to Seventeenth street, when the Rebels gave a dropping fire as harmless as it was useless. The alarm was given, and the garrison of the Prison beaten to arms, but no traces of the bold prisoners could be found. Where they went, how they went, and by what route, was never known; but a week or ten days after, their arrival at Fortress Monroe was publicly announced.

They had gallantly earned their freedom, and I hope they enjoyed it more honestly and worthily than I fear they did before they became inmates of the Castle.

CHAPTER XLVII.

UNION BUSHWHACKERS.

Cause of Bushwhackers.—Repulsiveness of the Custom.—Its Excuse.—Their Sufferings and Wrongs.—Collisions with Home-Guards.—Victories of Union Men.—Terror of their Name.—The Vendetta in the Mountains.—Virtues of the Southern Royalists.—War of Extermination.—A Fearful Avenger.

BUSHWHACKERS are peculiar features of this War, which indeed gave them birth. So much has been said, and so little is known, of them, that a chapter on their life, manners, and habits, cannot be out of place in a volume like this. During my long march from Salisbury to Strawberry Plains, I had abundance of opportunities to make their acquaintance, learn their history, and observe their idiosyncrasies.

This great struggle has made Bushwhackers on both sides; but it is of the Union class I propose to speak. They are confined to the Border States, or to those sections where political feeling is greatly divided; where military power has usurped the right of the people, and compelled them to resist aggression by the most stealthy and deadly means.

It is difficult for an honorable or a courageous man, who has seen aught of military life, to endure, much less sanction, bushwhacking. All one's instincts revolt at it. It is slaughter without any of the palliating circumstances of hot blood, generous passion, struggle for principle.

It is treacherous, coldly calculating, brutal; and yet, believing all that, I cannot find it in my heart to blame many of the men who resort to it in the mountainous regions of North Carolina and Tennessee.

They were quiet, peaceable, industrious, loyal; opposed to the doctrine of Secession, and all its attendant heresies; the natural antagonists of the Slaveholders; lovers of the Union for the Union's sake, and regarded as an enemy whoever would seek its destruction.

When the Rebels brought on the War, those loyalists held themselves aloof, determined to take no part in it unless on the side of the Republic.

The contest continued, and the Conscription Act was passed. Then those innocent and patriotic citizens were forced either to enter the insurgent army or run away; leaving their property and wives and children—all they held most dear—behind them, and seek some new locality that, to their slender observation and limited knowledge, appeared like another sphere.

Domestic by nature and habits, they were unwilling to quit their firesides and the few acres that had been and were their World. They would rather die than surrender all they valued in life. Yet they could not stay at home. If not carried off to the army, they were hunted, harried, persecuted; driven into the woods and mountains like wild beasts. Frequently they were killed or wounded by the Home-Guards; oftener captured and sent bound to Richmond, where they were put into the field.

At the earliest opportunity they would desert, of course, and return to their humble dwellings. Then would begin the persecution anew. They had forfeited their lives by desertion. Whenever the Guard saw them, they would be fired on.

It is not difficult to conceive how a few months of such experience would transform a man from an enduring saint to an aggressive demon.

Amiable, gentle, merciful at first, the process by which they were transformed into Bushwhackers rendered them vicious, passionate, bloodthirsty. They were coerced to live in caves, or pits dug in the earth; and while they were absent, the Guards or Rebel cavalry would visit the houses of the fugitives, and steal whatever could be found. The wives and children of the Unionists were robbed of horses, mules, and even personal attire and small sums of money—all because they were loyal. In addition to that, they were occasionally abused corporeally. Terrible threats were made against them unless they disclosed where certain property or articles were concealed. Their barns and even dwellings were burned down; and in many instances Bushwhackers have found only smouldering embers or a heap of ashes where they looked for a pleasant home.

In North Carolina and Tennessee I met men who had not slept under their own roof for two and even three years. All that time they had been "lying out," as it is termed. When there was no danger, they would go to their houses for an hour or two, but would not venture to remain there overnight.

If the Home-Guards were in the neighborhood, or approaching, word was sent immediately to the Bushwhackers, or some signal given which was understood. Horns would be blown, cowbells rung, peculiar cries given, and in less than a minute all the Bushwhackers in the neighborhood would be on the wing towards mountain-tops, caves, or some secure hiding-place.

In the Union settlements, every one is trained to be a messenger. The children of ten and twelve years, if they see persons resembling the Guards or Rebel cavalry, bear the tidings at full speed to the nearest house, and so the intelligence is spread far and wide.

If there be any number of Unionists compared to the Rebels, the former give them battle; and so often have they proved victorious, that the latter shrink from an engagement unless in greatly superior force. Those small fights are of common occurrence, and I encountered many families who had lost near relatives in such warfare.

When the Rebels pass through a section of country favorable to bushwhacking, the persecuted loyalists profit by the opportunity of revenge to the fullest extent. All may be quiet, and outwardly peaceful; the enemy will be walking or riding down a mountain-road, or through a gap, or past a thicket of laurel, when half a dozen rifles will crack, and perhaps two or three of his squad be shot dead or wounded.

All men, however brave, have a natural dread of being attacked by a concealed foe. It is like stabbing in the dark. The mystery and uncertainty of the character and strength of the assailant lend a horror to the surprise; and well disciplined must be the courage and firm the nerves which do not take refuge in flight.

The Bushwhackers have not infrequently frightened away thrice their number. Many of them have Spencer,

Henry, and other carbines, which discharge from six to sixteen times without reloading, giving the party attacked a very vivid idea of the strength of the attackers.

In Wilkes County, North Carolina, twelve determined Union men have compelled from seventy to a hundred Guards to flight. And in Carter County, Tennessee, they tell a story of a declaration by the "Confederates" that those tories (meaning loyalists) have guns they can wind up Sunday morning, and fire all the week.

Of course, the Bushwhackers are held in great dread. The Rebel cavalry are in perpetual fear of them, and never pass a turn in the road, or by a sheltering rock, or a heavy undergrowth, without extreme caution. The breaking of a twig alarms, and the projection of a branch startles them. Where there is so much fear, there must be a corresponding hatred. Alas, for the poor Bushwhacker who falls into Rebel hands! Short will be his shriving, and speedy his exit from the Planet. His capture is synonymous with his execution. He is shot through the head as coolly as a bullock would be, and probably before the week is over, his executioner is a corpse also.

The war in the mountainous regions of the two States I have mentioned is a war of extermination, and has already become a kind of Vendetta. Oaths of vengeance are sworn against those who have killed relatives and friends, and the oaths are most bloodily kept. A son shoots a father, and the son of that father shoots the father of the first son. One brother kills another brother in an adjacent family, and in turn loses his brother by violence. These feuds are handed down season after season, and year after year, as in the medieval time. Life is paid with life, and death answers to death.

I remember meeting in Castle Thunder, Richmond, Virginia, two Tennesseans who had vowed revenge upon certain parties in their section. They obtained their freedom long before I did; and when I passed through the neighborhood where the former captives resided, they had redeemed their word. The men who had wronged them had ceased to live. They were killed in their own homes.

In Western North Carolina, particularly in Wilkes and Watauga, and in the northern counties of East Tennessee, few prisoners are taken. The black flag is ever raised there. No quarter is given or asked by the inhabitants; and the escaped prisoners who travel in that quarter, understand that "liberty or death" is no mere figure of speech, but a dreadful reality.

Everywhere we were told if we were captured that we would be pushed off the precipice of Time very summarily, and doubtless we would have been. Had we not succeeded in our search after liberty, no one, I presume, would have ever known our fate. Our bones would have whitened on some mountain-side; and though it would have been unpleasant at the time, we would have rested as peacefully there as under a marble shaft in Greenwood.

One would expect to find the Bushwhackers fierce, cruel men; yet many of them are quiet, though determined—warm-hearted, but excitable. Their peculiar life has quickened all their senses, and perpetual anxiety and frequent alarm have given them a certain wild expression of face, especially of the eye, that belongs to hunted men. They are as much attached to Northerners, as they are opposed to the Rebels. They received us with kindness, and even welcomed us to their homely fare. They piloted us in many places, and would have protected us at the risk of their lives.

When we had crossed the Yadkin, and were within twenty miles of the Blue Ridge, a party of Bushwhackers informed us we could not get over on account of the snow; that we would be tracked and murdered. After learning that, we thought seriously of waiting where we were, even until Summer, if necessary, and the generous fellows, poor as they were, offered to take us to their dwellings, and provide for us as best they could.

In Johnson County, Tennessee, we encountered a bevy of Bushwhackers of the most reckless character. One day, while lying in a barn, we heard a tremendous yelling, and soon discovered that it proceeded from three of the fraternity. Instead of remaining concealed, they were using their lungs to the utmost to attract attention. They defied the Rebels, and as they were armed to the teeth, they would have proved formidable foes.

One of the trio, known as Canada Guy, was a type of the most savage class. He had been arrested as a Bushwhacker nearly two years before; was sent to Richmond to be tried for several murders; and yet contrived to deceive the authorities to such an extent that he was transferred to Belle Isle as a prisoner of war, and exchanged soon after.

Reaching Annapolis, Guy told the Provost-Marshal he wished to resume operations in Tennessee. The Provost gave him a certain sum of money, and bade him go on his way rejoicing.

Guy, on his return, had many old scores to wipe off; and the sole erasive compound he knew was blood. In less than six months he killed seven men, all bitter Secessionists, and vowed he would not forego the pleasure of killing more of the number for any consideration on earth.

No wonder he was ferocious. The Rebels hanged his father, some sixty years old, because he would be loyal in spite of threats, and shot four of his brothers. "But I'll be even with them," he exclaimed; "I'll kill at least twenty for every one of my kinsmen." He bids fair to keep his word. He delights in exterminating the Secessionists, and his glee is almost fiendish at times.

I could not sympathize with or like such a man, though I doubt not his wrongs had rendered him the reckless, bloodthirsty creature he was. Guy believed religiously that no Rebel had any right to property or life; so he robbed the enemy wherever found, and was only too desirous of generating a difficulty that would give him a pretext for adding another to his list of victims.

To the Bushwhackers I am indebted for many kindnesses which I shall not forget. I found in them virtues that are rare in civilization, and possibilities of far better things. They have been compelled in self-defence to take the course they have; and I am not at all sure that many of us who have loftier aims, and larger culture, and higher instincts, would not do worse if we had been so foully wronged as those hardy and naturally humane mountaineers.

CHAPTER XLVIII.

THE ESCAPE.

Our Efforts Useless in the Salisbury Hospital.—Bohemian Talent for Forgery.—Mode of our Exodus from the Penitentiary.—Sensations of Freedom.—Our First Night in a Barn.—A Long Fast.—A Rebel Officer Sound on the Main Question.—Commencement of the Journey toward Liberty.—Our First Two Nights' March.—Hunger, Cold, and Exhaustion.—Our Assistance from the Negroes.

Two of my journalistic friends and myself, as soon as the large influx of Union soldiers had been made into the Prison, entered the hospitals, hoping to be of some service to the sick. We found the task extremely difficult, because there was no co-operation on the part of the authorities; and the longer we remained, although we worked very hard, the more fruitless we perceived our labor. We concluded, therefore, to try another plan of escape. We had been very industrious in that way, for months, at Salisbury, but had met with our old ill-fortune. The tunnels in which we had been interested had been exposed; the schemes we had formed had been frustrated; the agencies on which we had depended failed in the moment of need. We resolved thereafter to trust only Fortune and ourselves, and we prepared to make our exodus on the evening of Sunday, December 18.

Two of us Bohemians—Mr. William E. Davis, of the

Cincinnatti *Gazette*, and myself—had passes to the Rebel hospital, outside of the first inclosure and the first line of guards, and we spent an hour of Saturday night in forging a pass for my associate of *The Tribune.*

It was my first essay in that department of the Fine Arts, and I congratulated myself I had done well; nor was I without a lingering suspicion that if my talents in that direction had been properly developed, I might have been a rival of Monroe Edwards. There was this difference, however, in his chirographical experiments and mine: his resulted in getting him into, while mine were designed to get a friend out of, a Penitentiary.

Our graphical labors went for naught.

My confrère, the following morning, concluded it would be wiser to use my genuine pass, and let me trust to going by the sentinel without any. We agreed to that; and so, a little before dusk, the night promising to be dark and stormy, two of us went out to the Rebel hospital, to wait for the development of events.

Mr. Richardson took a box employed for carrying medicines, and, filling it with empty bottles, walked boldly up to the guard, who stopped him, and asked if he had a pass.

"Certainly," was the reply; "you have seen it often enough; have you not?"

"I do not remember," responded the Rebel. "Let me look at it."

It was handed him, and, after scrutinizing it carefully, he returned it to Mr. Richardson, with the remark that it was "all right."

My confrère walked out, and met, in the second inclosure, the Adjutant of the garrison and a paroled Rebel convict, both of whom knew him intimately.

Feeling that assurance alone would prevent suspicion, he accosted them both, exchanged some ordinary remarks about the weather, and passed on.

A fourth prisoner, Thomas E. Wolfe, captain of a merchant vessel taken by the Rebels off the Balize—who also had a pass, and, just before we started, had concluded to try the adventure with us—was looking on, determined, if Mr. Richardson failed, to notify Mr. Davis and myself, that we might be off before the whole plan was apparent.

Richardson's coolness had disarmed suspicion. He walked quietly to a vacant office at the end of the hospital, placed his box and bottles therein, and moved leisurely by the guards, who were on the parapet at his right, to a small out-house, into which he stepped for concealment until it became darker.

Having loitered about the hospital as long as it seemed prudent, I walked by the guards—who supposed, no doubt, we belonged to the garrison—to the outhouse in question.

There I talked with Richardson in a low tone of voice, and agreed, as it was quite dusk, to go out to the gate in the fence skirting the road, and which was unguarded; and, if I were discovered, to return to the hospital. If I continued on, he was to follow.

I started, and just as I put my hand on the bar of the gate, to force it open, I felt it move from the other side.

Our old ill-fortune, I thought. We are discovered, and our hope of freedom once more blighted.

The gate opened, and I was vastly relieved to see Mr.

Davis, of the *Gazette*, and the Captain. They believed it hardly dark enough; but I pushed on across a small bridge over the railway; having told them I would meet them at the appointed place, on a public road about a quarter of a mile from the Prison.

Richardson followed, and in half an hour we were all four together, lying down in the rain in a fence corner.

While there, a man crossed the field, and walked so near us that we thought he would step on us. We held our breath, and heard our hearts beat, as we had so often done before, believing we must be discovered. He conjectured not our presence, however, and walked off into the thick and all-enshrouding darkness.

In another hour we had crawled into a barn, and were lying under the straw and fodder, waiting for the next night, when a Union man had agreed to procure us a guide, of whom we stood in great need, as not one of our party had any knowledge of woodcraft, or of the country we had to travel through.

Long shall I remember the fresh, free air that greeted me like a benison when I stepped out of the Prison limits on that murky, rainy evening. The old worn-out feeling, the inertia, the sense of suppression, seemed to fall from me as a cast-off garment; and I believed I could walk to the ends of the Earth, if I could but find the sweet goddess of Liberty—dearest and best of women—at the end of my long, long journeying.

To the barn, in which we lay concealed, we were aware a number of small negroes came every few hours of the day; and it was therefore necessary for us to keep very still lest they should discover and betray us, not from perfidy, but through indiscretion. We covered ourselves entirely over with the fodder, and never spoke a word above our breath.

We were in sight of the grim and cruel Prison where we had passed almost eleven months of anxiety and agony, and we had, you may imagine, a most wholesome horror of being taken back there before we had fairly started on our travels.

From the time we escaped, on Sunday evening, until Monday night, we had not a drop of water, and we had no food, save a few broken mouthfuls, from Sunday noon until Tuesday evening.

Yet we did not seem to suffer. Our ardor for freedom was such that it displaced all other desires, even those of a physical nature. We hardly knew we were thirsty until a Captain in the Rebel service gave us a canteen of water, after we quitted the barn. He had been several times wounded, having fought through nearly all the great battles in Virginia; and yet was a Union man at heart. In our presence he anathematized the Rebels, and expressed the pious wish that they were all plunged so deep in a certain igneous region that even the Petro leum-seekers could not reach them. We had become acquainted with him while in Prison, and knew, when we got out, we could depend upon such aid as it was in his power to give us.

It no doubt seems anomalous that loyal men should be in the Southern armies, and fight for a cause in which they do not believe. Yet the instance of our friend the Captain was one of many.

Hundreds of persons, at the beginning of the troubles,

rushed into the War, believing it would be only a kind of parade of arms, with perhaps a few skirmishes, followed by a recognition of the independence of the "Confederacy."

How fearfully they were deceived, let the mourning in every Southern home, and the countless graves in every insurgent State, from Virginia to Texas, testify in terror and in tears! Four years of devastating conflict have taught them the great issues at stake, and the hopelessness of the struggle; the weakness and the woe, the crime and penalty of Slavery; and the day has dawned at last, when the South will, for the first time, be truly free.

To resume: after leaving the barn and repairing to the place appointed, we met the Lieutenant of militia I have mentioned, and waited for the guide who, he said, would soon be along. An hour or more passed, and the guide coming not, we concluded he had already gone on, or had failed to redeem his promise, and set out upon our journey, with Wilkes County as an objective point, where a number of relatives of the Lieutenant resided, and who, he assured us, would welcome us with warm and loyal hearts.

We went at a rapid pace through two miles of mud from six to twelve inches deep, almost losing our boots often in the adhesive loam, the blood bounding in our veins, and the perspiration starting through our pores, until we reached the Statesville and Morganton Railway, which we proposed to follow for at least twenty-five miles, and then strike a more Northerly direction.

We had not gone more than three miles before we espied a camp and a fire before it, and, thinking they might be pickets, we concluded to flank the locality, and did so, but not without much difficulty. We made a wide circuit through the woods, and as the night was very dark, we fell over logs and stumps; got into thorn-bushes and tore our clothes; tumbled into bogs and ditches; had the skin brushed from our noses and cheeks, and our eyes nearly put out by sharp twigs and swinging branches.

That first flanking was truly amusing; I could hear my companions plunging over logs, and occasionally uttering expletives more forcible than orthodox, as they struck their heads against trees, or had their mouths rudely opened by an entering twig. Splash, splash we went, through the water and mire, and then crackled through the sodden leaves and dead branches, and then crept noiselessly by some wayside tenement, and then halted with suspended breath at some actual or imaginary sound.

Whenever we observed a camp or fire near the railway we made a flank movement, to the serious detriment of our boots and clothes, and then struck the road again, thus vastly increasing the distance and time of our journeying. The first night we made only eleven miles in a direct line—how much in détours, it would be impossible to conjecture—when one of my companions declaring himself utterly exhausted, we endeavored to find a place of concealment.

That was very difficult, as there was, during the Winter, no undergrowth to furnish a hiding-place. We tried haystacks in vain. We penetrated into woods, and could not get out of sight. Everywhere we went, we found ourselves too near some road, and the out-houses too unsafe.

We walked farther and farther from the railway, through one piece of timber and then another, and yet were ever likely to be seen from the highways or some wagon-way.

At last the early dawn had deepened into broad day. We could go no farther. We crept into a pinery and lay there, not more than a hundred yards from the road, within sound of the voices of men at work, and the babble of children at the farm-house.

The day was very raw and cold, but we durst not light a fire. So we lay flat on the ground, never speaking in other than the lowest *sotto voce* tone, shivering, and anxious and longing for the shades of evening.

I was very thinly clad, having no other coat than a light blouse; and, unable to move about to start the circulation of the blood, I suffered much from the cold, as did my companions. "If we are not captured to-day," we said, "the Gods who have been so long opposed must be on our side."

The welcome dusk came at last. No one of those who had been in our immediate vicinity had seen us; and with glad hearts we went forth, like the beasts of prey, in search of food. We repaired to the quarters of the slaves on an adjoining plantation, and soon obtained a promise from one of them, if we would go to a barn on the place, that he would send us food. Before this time a chilly, penetrating rain had begun to descend, and as we were quite wet, a roof was very acceptable.

The master of the plantation had company that night,

and consequently we were compelled to wait until nearly midnight before we obtained any provisions. We did not know how hungry we were until a liberal supply of corn bread and bacon was handed us by the negro.

Those are means of sustenance I naturally abhor; but no Fifth Avenue dinner, however recherché, ever pleased my palate so much as those Southern staples. When we were ready to resume our march, a negro offered to guide us back to the railway; and we set forth in a driving, drenching storm, through such a pall-like darkness, that we could not see the nearest object. We walked in what is known as Indian file, sometimes one leading, and sometimes another, with preconcerted signals for doubt, danger, and recognition.

When our leader paused we stopped, and a motion of the hand, if it were light enough to see, or, if it were not, a low "hush!" brought us to an instantaneous halt. If we were scattered, a sudden quick cough was the sign of recognition, and a low whistle, in imitation of a night-bird, brought us together.

Through that tempestuous night we marched wearily on, our clothes dripping, like a jealous woman's eyes when the storm is subsiding, and running into our boots, until they were full of water. Harder and harder the rain fell, and colder and colder it grew.

We were chilled from head to heel, and our saturated garments became a burden, chafing our limbs and clogging our steps.

How often I thought of the line of Shakspeare about "biding the peltings of this pitiless storm," and marveled if even old Lear had encountered a rougher and a drearier night.

There were a number of cattle-guards and pits along the road, filled with mire and water; and as we had to walk over them on the rails, the condition of our boots and clothes, added to our chilliness and fatigue, made our pace unsteady, and frequently we fell, waist-deep, into those turbid and ungrateful baths.

The ties, too, were slippery, and often we lost our equilibrium, and wounded our weary and paining feet. The sea-Captain badly sprained his foot, and could barely hobble along; occasionally requiring our support for a mile or two.

One of the greatest sources of our anxiety was the fear of a sprain, or some manner of maiming, knowing that such an accident must greatly diminish our prospect of freedom. In the superlative darkness, and in a region entirely unknown, we were liable at any moment to make a misstep that would place us beyond the power of marching farther. How we prayed, in our Bohemian way, for sound feet and strong limbs, for continued health and the favor of Fortune.

The negro who had guided us to the railway had told us of another of his color to whom we could apply for shelter and food at the terminus of our second stage. Him we could not find until nearly dawn, and when we did, he directed us to a large barn filled with wet corn-husks.

Into that we crept with our dripping garments, and lay there for fifteen hours, until we could again venture forth. Floundering about in the husks, we lost our haversacks, pipes, and a hat that belonged to the speaker, and deprived of which, he was, indeed, uncovered.

About nine o'clock we procured a hearty supper from the generous negro, who even gave me his unique head-covering—an appropriate presentation, as one of my companions remarked, by an "intelligent contraband" to the "reliable gentleman" of The N. Y. *Tribune*—and did picket-duty while we hastily ate our meal and stood against his blazing fire. The old African and his wife gave us "God bless you, massas!" with trembling voice and moistened eyes, as we parted from them with grateful hearts.

"God bless the negroes!" say I, with earnest lips. During our entire captivity, and after our escape, they were ever our firm, brave, unflinching friends. We never made an appeal to them they did not answer. They never hesitated to do us a service at the risk even of life, and under the most trying circumstances revealed a devotion and a spirit of self-sacrifice that were heroic. The magic word "Yankee" opened all their hearts, and elicited the loftiest virtues. They were ignorant, oppressed, enslaved; but they always cherished a simple and beautiful faith in the cause of the Union and its ultimate triumph, and never abandoned or turned aside from a man who sought food or shelter on his way to Freedom.

CHAPTER XLIX.

THE MARCH TO FREEDOM.

The Third, Fourth, and Fifth Nights Out.—Missing the Road.—Extremely Cold Weather.—Our Sufferings in a Barn.—The Slaves our Faithful Friends.—Torture of the Boot Revived.—Our Pursuit and Masterly Retreat.—Our Re-enforcement with Mules and Whisky.—Incidents along the Route.—Arrival in Wilkes County.

A New Hampshire soldier, Charles Thurston, a sergeant of the Sixth regiment, had joined us before we left Salisbury. He had been a fellow-conspirator for many weeks, and had been going out with us through various tunnels; but when they were all exposed, we were compelled to resort to some other mode of exodus. Having heard privately that we had gone, on Sunday night, he managed to slip out of the hospital bakery, where he was employed, behind one of the Prison Detectives, about four hours after our escape, and get into the town unobserved.

Our party then consisted of five, and we continued our march on the railway in better condition, having gotten our clothes partially dry, and satisfied our hunger. That was our third night, and we were only seventeen miles from Salisbury. We were desirous to go nearly to Statesville—eight miles to the west—and then, flanking the town, move in a northwesterly direction toward

Wilkes County. We had been directed by the negro, at the last stopping-place, to Allison's Mill, which was to be our guide in the way we wanted to go. We flanked Statesville, and found Allison's Mill, which proved afterward to be the wrong one—we had not been told there were two—and therefore missed the road entirely.

We knew not where we were going, but we took first one road and then another; marching very rapidly, as we needed to do, for the wind had veered round to the North, and the night had grown very cold. We climbed fences, examined haystacks and dilapidated cabins, but found no negro tenements, nor any place where we could stay without danger of freezing.

Our limbs became stiff and our lips blue when we paused; and as we were afraid to light a fire, we went on in the teeth of the biting wind, until the tears streamed from our eyes, and our faces and hands and feet were like ice.

It was nearly dawn when we descried, by the light of the moon, a plantation at a distance. One of us went to the negro quarters, and returned with the information that we could go to a large barn near by, and cover ourselves with hay until the principal house-servant had an opportunity to bring us food.

All five of us climbed into the barn, built of logs piled "cob-house" fashion, and consequently very cold; the wind driving through the open spaces, and chilling us through and through. We buried ourselves completely in the hay; but there was no possibility of getting warm. I shivered against Mr. Richardson's side, and he against mine. We put our arms around each other, and snug-

THE ESCAPED CORRESPONDENTS ENJOYING THE NEGRO'S HOSPITALITY.

gled up, as children say, to no purpose. We thought we would freeze to death if we fell asleep; so we crawled out of the hay, and began moving about in the loft, and soon induced our companions to come out also. We were still very cold, but we suffered less than we had done, because our blood circulated more.

About eleven o'clock the negro came to us with a basket of pork and corn-bread, which we ate with great relish. He was delighted to see us, and was very intelligent, having been a servant to a Rebel officer in the field. He said his master was a violent Secessionist, and would kill him, and us too, if he knew we were there; but that he was not afraid. He had helped the Yankees before, and would help them again.

After dark the negro took us to his cabin, gave us our supper, and let us thaw before his fire, guided us to *the* Allison's Mill—when we learned we had walked about fifteen miles and accomplished only half a mile in the right direction—and there told us what road to follow, piloting us a mile and a half on our way.

When I escaped I had been compelled to wear a very large, coarse, stiff pair of boots—the sole ones I could procure in the Prison—which I could keep on only because they were tight across the instep and around the ankles. They tortured me at every step, and wore holes in my ankles that resembled wounds from buck-shot; while their weight and clumsiness tired me greatly, and made me stumble as if I were intoxicated. They had become soaking wet again and again, and frozen on my feet, so that they were like wooden shoes, entirely without elasticity or power of expansion. Mr. Richardson's foot-coverings were very much of the same kind; and as we marched along through the darkness over the rough and broken ground, it was with great difficulty we could often suppress cries of pain. When we slipped, or stepped into ruts, our feet were wrenched as if they were in a vice; and still we had but begun our march of four hundred miles; and the most arduous and toilsome part was yet to come.

What were boots, or pain, or cold, or hardship, compared to freedom?

We marched on through the moonless night until we reached Rocky Creek, in Rowan County, where we paused, very cold and fatigued, and built a fire—we had taken the precaution to supply ourselves with matches—in an adjacent pinery. There we warmed ourselves as well as we could, and about four o'clock Friday morning, crossed the creek on a log on our hands and knees; the frost having made it so slippery there was no security in walking.

We then struck a dirt road going from Statesville to Jonesville; and about six o'clock began to think we were off the direct route.

Sergeant Thurston determined to apply for information at a house standing at the forks of the road, and did so. When he returned, we concluded the man he had seen was a Rebel, and might raise the dogs, old men, and boys, armed with rifles and shot-guns, and hunt us down, as is the custom in Secessia.

Our conclusion was correct.

When daylight came, one of us perceived the old fellow following us, and the Sergeant ran back toward him in a threatening manner that frightened him into a rapid retreat. We had no fear of him alone, but apprehended that he would excite an alarm, and bring the whole human and canine neighborhood upon us.

We thought we were so tired we could go no farther; but the prospect of pursuit so strengthened our limbs that we started upon a run; darting into woods, over fences, through quagmires; crossing and re-crossing fields; moving to every point of the compass so rapidly that an African blood-hound would have found it difficult to scent out our progress.

At last we paused, about nine o'clock, in a pinery, and soon had a blazing fire of dry wood, which caused very little smoke. We would not have made the fire, but, as we were freezing, it was a military necessity. We were quite anxious all day; but we heard and saw nothing that led us to believe we were pursued. If we were, our pursuers must have lost the trail, which would not have been singular, as we were at least two miles from any road or even footpath, so far as we could determine.

We then concluded that another night's march would take us to the settlement in Wilkes County, to which the Lieutenant of militia had directed. Then I first began to have some well-defined hope that we would get through.

When I escaped, I did so on principle, trusting that we might at least be out a week, or possibly two, and believing if we were shot we would have the satisfaction of dying in the laudable effort to obtain our freedom, as became American citizens.

We had but fifteen miles further to go before we should find a haven of rest, which we sorely needed. We resumed our march in excellent spirits, though greatly worn and exhausted ; and no wonder, as we had been unable to sleep more than a few minutes at a time, on account of the cold. Indeed, I do not know that I had lost my consciousness after our exodus from the Penitentiary.

I struck out boldly, however, and summoned all my will. The miles seemed endless, and every step increased my fatigue.

At last I was forced to lean on my confrère's arm, as he had done on mine the first night out. My breath was short and hot, my head was heavy, and my limbs trembled.

My associate insisted upon it that I was on the eve of a severe typhoid fever.

I knew I merely wanted rest. He urged me to stop at a way-side public-house, the only one we encountered in all our journey, and said he would remain with me. I would not consent, fearing my doing so would endanger the whole party. Therefore I endeavored to go on, telling my companions to leave me if I failed. To that they would not agree. Mr. Richardson, with characteristic generosity, declared he would not separate from me.

At the public house, or shanty rather, we procured some food, and learned to our satisfaction that the proprietor was a Unionist. Hearing we were all greatly fatigued, he offered for a certain sum—and we had abundance of money in our party—to loan us two mules to help us onward.

We accepted his proposition, and Captain Wolfe, still suffering from his sprain, and myself, mounted the animals. Their equipments were very inferior. My mule was saddleless, and the sharp backbone almost bisected me, while my legs pained me excessively, and seemed as if they would part company with my body.

After proceeding two or three miles, we halted at a cabin to get two or three more mules, and while there the host pressed us to drink some whisky. The distillation of corn is very repulsive to me ; but I thought it might give me temporary strength, and I swallowed a large quantity before we resumed our journey. It improved my condition at first ; but very soon I began to grow very ill. The liquor had nauseated me, and for three hours I swayed from side to side, and resembled Vesuvius in a constant state of eruption.

Jove ! but I was sick ; I almost lost my senses. Every atom of my frame ached. It seemed as if I would fall to pieces. Riding on that mule was purgatorial. I dismounted, and stumbled over the road.

Finally, we reached the vicinity of the settlement in Wilkes County. We parted with our mule-owners, and Mr. Richardson went in quest of the Lieutenant's mother, leaving me lying on the ground, begging to be let alone. He returned after a long search, and half supported, half carried me, with genuine tenderness, to the cabin where the good woman lived.

There the other three preceded me, and were leaning against the chimney corner fast asleep. I was soon undressed, and in a soft, warm bed.

What a luxury it was, after twenty months of lying on hard floors and rude bunks ! Hardly had my head touched the pillow before I lapsed into a slumber as sweet and deep as if I lay a child again upon my mother's bosom.

In four hours I awoke, entirely refreshed and healed, to find my associate by my bedside, with a cup of rye coffee and a plate of fritters in his hand, asking me to eat something. I had a good appetite, and gratified it, and went to bed again, to sleep once more a dreamless and delicious sleep.

CHAPTER L.

THE HAVEN OF REST.

The Union Settlement in Wilkes County.—Frequent Change of Base.—Christmas Spent in a Barn.—Ghostly Marches.—Alarms and Adventures in Yadkin County.—A Bohemian Model Artist.—An Eventful Night.—Storm and Sentiment.—Love-Making in a Tempest.—Parting with our Loyal Friends.—Their Devotion and Regret.—Battles between Unionists and Rebel Home Guards.—Inextinguishable Fidelity of the People.

THE settlement we had reached was chiefly composed of relatives of the loyal Lieutenant, who gave us a most cordial and generous welcome. They could not do enough for us—some of them had never seen a "Yankee" before—and they were delighted to meet us. They were very demonstrative, and asked us more questions in a minute than we could answer in a day.

Though entire strangers, we were regarded from the first as their dearest friends. Men, women, and children were anxious to serve us; and we felt, indeed, as if our lines had fallen in pleasant places. They offered us their fullest store, and would have given us half of what they possessed if we had needed it.

More kindness, affection, devotion, I have never seen. Those noble-hearted people—for the most part poor—gave me a higher idea of humanity; and their efforts in our behalf, and their spirit of sacrifice, filled me with the deepest sense of gratitude, which I long for an opportunity to display in something more than words.

The loyal Lieutenant had requested us to tarry in the settlement for two or three days, and he would join our party and go through with us to our lines.

The evening of the day—Saturday, December 24—we arrived in the county, we left Mrs. ——'s house, and repaired to the barn, about a quarter of a mile distant, of a relative of the family, for increased security, and from unwillingness to jeopardize the good people who so generously sheltered us. We remained there that night and the next day (Christmas), when a number of men and women visited us to congratulate us on our escape, and to assure us of their unswerving fidelity, of which we had no doubt.

Christmas night, one of our friends told us it had been whispered about that there were five Yankees in the settlement; and, fearing the Rebel Home Guards might be apprised of the fact, deemed it prudent to remove us to the adjoining County of Yadkin, where the wife of the Lieutenant resided.

Under the man's guidance we walked through the woods by by-paths to the new place of shelter, a distance of four or five miles. The night was dark as Egypt, and we moved along as cautiously and noiselessly as if we stepped about the couch of our dying mistress.

We called those nocturnal journeys the marches of death. We spoke not a syllable; we suppressed our breath, and moved as lightly as if our life depended—and perhaps it did—upon our perfect quietude.

Not a twig broke beneath our careful feet. The

silence was almost painful in its impressiveness. The stirring of the dry leaves, as the wind swept through them, sounded loudly to our strained ears. Every sense was on the rack of apprehension; every nerve at its highest tension. We seemed like unquiet ghosts as we stalked along—disembodied spirits wandering on the Stygian shore.

In an hour and a half we reached the desired habitation, and the same generous welcome greeted us as before. The wife of the Lieutenant assured us we would not endanger her home by resting beneath her humble roof, and that night we lay in comfortable beds. She was a native of Virginia, an intelligent, calm, brave, quick-witted woman, fruitful in expedients and resources.

In the morning her children, two of them little girls of four and six years, stood picket while their mother and their elder sister prepared our breakfast.

Strange and thorough teachers are danger and devotion. Those children, as all others we met, were unnaturally developed; their senses acute; their secretiveness perfect; their self-possession complete. We could trust them as we could matured persons. We had no fear of their indiscretion: we relied on them fully. Custom and order were reversed. Strong, self-reliant men who had passed two years in the field, who had often looked death in the face, who had stood by countless couches of suffering and death, to aid, to comfort, and console, were protected by, and leaned on, women and children. They could do for us what our own sex could not, and they did it with a silent and unconscious heroism that made it all the more beautiful.

Soon after breakfast a squad of Breckinridge's cavalry were reported coming up the road—the house stood at the roadside—and we were advised to conceal ourselves under the beds. We were not long in taking our positions, and then the Lieutenant's wife went out on the porch with an unconcerned air. The cavalry men stopped, and she talked to them in a quiet, easy way, well calculated to disarm suspicion, if any had been excited. They did not enter the dwelling, as we feared, and after a few minutes rode on.

She then called us to come out, saying, "All is safe, boys." But we had hardly assumed an erect position when several suspicious-looking characters were announced, and again we crept under the beds. Some of our party may have been compelled to indulge in that kind of thing before; but I conjecture it was under very different circumstances.

The pursuit of gallantry had nothing to do with the recreation there; and I confess I did not like it altogether, although it was for the sake of that dear woman who holds the shield of the Republic, and wears the garment embroidered with stars.

The precaution was unnecessary that time. The suspicious-looking characters proved to be rude hinds who went quietly by the dwelling.

Once more we went forth in a vertical form, ascended to the corn-loft and removed our clothes—for what purpose, those who have been in Rebel Prisons need not be told. I was still lingering over my poetic toil when two tithe-officers knocked at the door, to collect their dues in corn.

Mr. Davis cried out: "Hurry, Junius, those men are coming up!" and immediately darted below. Poor me! But a single garment graced my slender form at that juncture, and, seizing the remainder of my wardrobe, I rushed into the apartment we had quitted a few moments before. There I found the kind-hearted woman, who a third time told us to get under the bed.

My companions laughed at my costume; but I declared with imperturbable sang-froid that I did not care.

My feminine friend smiled, and very sensibly remarked that it made no difference whatever; that such things would happen sometimes; and that she had seen men in that guise before, which, as she was the mother of four children, is not at all improbable.

The same night, Monday, we concluded that Yadkin County was not as safe as it might be, judging from our single day's experience in it; so we marched back, the same dark, silent, breath-bated march as before, to Wilkes County, and the friendly barn we had quitted. We lay there concealed in the corn-husks and hay until Tuesday evening. Then we heard the guards were searching for us, and we divided; three going to the habitation of the Lieutenant's mother, and two to his sister's.

Wednesday morning, while at breakfast, two men entered the cabin, taking us by surprise. The dog on which we had depended had gone away, and therefore the strangers came unannounced.

There was no means of retreat, as the cabin had but one door, and we knew our greatest safety would be in a calm manner. We continued our humble meal, therefore, very deliberately and unconcernedly, and at its close were not displeased to learn the strangers were deserters from the Rebel army, and entirely trustworthy.

The day we spent in a barn, and at night we returned to the cabin. We were at supper when a low whistle was heard outside, indicating a surprise, perhaps a surrounding of the house by the enemy, with the intention of shooting down whoever attempted to escape—the custom in that section of country.

The wife and her adopted daughter, a girl of sixteen or seventeen—we will call her Lucy—were greatly alarmed. They threw ashes on the burning logs in great haste, to extinguish the glare of the fire, and told us to get under the bed and to go out of the door at the same time. We chose the latter, and out we dashed into the dark and stormy night, more than half expecting to be greeted with several rifle-flashes as we emerged from the dwelling.

A minute after I felt some one clinging to my arm, and a voice saying, in a suppressed tone: "Come this way!" I could hardly see the face, it was so dark, but I knew it was the black-eyed, black-haired, intensely loyal Lucy, who took as much interest in our welfare as if we were lovers and brothers combined.

"What are you doing here, my dear child?" I inquired whisperingly. "Why don't you go in out of the storm, and let me care for myself?"

"O, I want to stay with you," she answered earnestly. "Do come with me. I will show you where to hide. I wouldn't have any thing happen to you for the world. I'd rather die than have harm come to you."

Poor girl! Her appeal was resistless. I forgot the

danger of the situation in my pity and regard for her. Her voice and manner had touched even my worn-out heart.

The rain was falling in torrents, and the thunder bellowing through the sable vault overhead; but still Lucy clung to my arm. The other, disengaged, I threw about her waist—a taper one, even though she had always lived in North Carolina, and had never worn a corset—and drawing her plump figure to my bosom, kissed her long and closely—more for gratitude than gallantry, more from a sense of duty than affection; and yet duty just at that moment appeared not disagreeable to discharge.

The sensation was not unpleasant to me.

I do not believe it would have been to any man who had not touched a woman's lips for at least two years.

In the midst of that rather sentimental scene we learned that the whistle we had heard proceeded from a Rebel deserter who had come to the house to see Lucy—she said she liked him because he had shot two Home Guards; but as a man he was not agreeable to her—and who had given the signal, fearing the masculine voices he had heard inside might be those of enemies.

In less than an hour we had another alarm, and once more we ran out into the rain; but that alarm was also causeless and returning to the cabin, we went to bed—the members of the family and ourselves all in one room, which was indeed the whole house.

I slept quite well, and dreamed that Lucy was a princess in disguise, who introduced me to a black-robed magician, that furnished us with a winged dragon, that mounted, with us on his back, and flew away to New

York, and set us down to an elegant supper at the Maison Dorée.

About that time I awoke, and Lucy was sitting demurely in the chimney corner, preparing our plain breakfast before the fire. So Lucy was no princess, and the dragon could not be procured, and the magician was absent; and as I could not have any of those fine things, I took a piece of corn bread instead, and swallowed it with relish, and a new longing after the Ideal.

The next night, believing the Lieutenant would not come, and that our delay was dangerous, we parted from our good friends with saddened hearts. Old men took us in their arms and blessed us; women, young and old, wept at our departure, and children nestled to our bosom as if we were the nearest and dearest of their kin.

All that was not for us personally. It was the outpouring of loyalty from those noble spirits toward the representatives of that element in the great Republic; the homage paid to the principle of patriotism; the gushing forth of suppressed Unionism toward those who had suffered in its cause.

Wilkes is one of the strongest Union counties—probably the strongest—in North Carolina. The Rebels call it old United States, and declare it irrepressible. Deserters from the Southern service went about there with impunity, but generally carried their weapons. Often fights took place between them and the Home Guards, and the latter were generally worsted.

At Traphill, some twenty miles from the settlement in which we were, the Unionists and Rebels had had a dozen fights, the former being intrenched, and capable of defending themselves against large odds.

The Guards were tolerably quiet when we were there, so far as deserters were concerned, but they would have been very glad to capture or shoot an escaping Yankee.

The Union men were increasing every month, and the insurgents diminishing. Some of the latter had undergone a great revolution during the year. A man who had been a prominent Secessionist invited us to his house, but we went not.

The loyal population had suffered greatly. The War had deprived them of their property, their protectors, and their peace; but still they clung to the belief that the cause of the Republic must prevail; that all would be well with those who held out to the last.

CHAPTER LI.

THE MARCH ONWARD.

Accession of Escaped Prisoners.—Resumption of our Journey.—Excessive Roughness of the Route.—Character of the North Carolina Roads.—Flanking of Wilkesboro.—Losing our Way.—Crossing the Yadkin.—Skeptical Women. —Interview with Bushwhackers.—Consoling Counsel.—Passage of the Blue Ridge.—A Severe March over Mountains.—Safety ever Retreating.—Narrow Escapes from Union Rifles.—Contradictory Reports about our Lines.

WHILE in Wilkes County, two of our fellow-prisoners, a captain of a small trading-vessel from Philadelphia, and a North Carolina Unionist, having escaped by bribing the guard at Salisbury, arrived in the settlement, and sent us word they would like to journey in our company; but, deeming it prudent for us to travel in small parties, we declined, and Sergeant Thurston joined the other two, who, with a deserter from Lee's army, set out toward Wilkesboro, the capital of the county, the day before we did.

Wednesday night, December 28, we resumed our march. It was very dark and stormy, and one of our many loyal friends guiding us for five miles to the cabin of a free mulatto, who in turn piloted us on, we reached Glass's mill, a distance of fourteen miles, without fatigue.

Our long rest had materially benefited us, and we felt

CONFERENCE OF THE CORRESPONDENTS WITH BUSHWHACKERS.

much fresher than when we quitted the Penitentiary so abruptly. At the mill we found the other party of four, and going to the habitation of a Unionist, he directed us to his corn-crib, where we lay concealed until the following night. After dark we obtained a substantial meal, and continued our progress toward Wilkesboro, having secured the services of a guide.

The road was extremely rough, being so excessively cut up and frozen that we stumbled along like men in the last stage of intoxication, frequently falling on our knees and at full length.

One who has not traveled in North Carolina since the War can form no idea of the state of the roads, which deserve not the name. They have not been repaired for years, and were never in a good condition. There are ruts, gullies, embankments, ridges, cuts, over which no ordinary wagon could move beyond a snail's pace without upsetting half a dozen times every mile. And then, traveling upon them at night vastly augments the labor and the difficulty.

The march is exhausting to the last degree. Cold as the weather often was, our bodies were bathed in perspiration; our blood burned; our limbs ached; our feet were twisted and strained until they seemed as if they must refuse their office. They became numb and sore, fevered and frozen by turns. The frozen earth cut through our boots like knives, and lacerated the tender flesh.

It appeared often as if we must sink down by the wayside—that even the strong magnet of Liberty could draw us no farther. Yet we exercised our Will. We thought of the prisons we had left; of the wretched death that might overtake us if we lagged behind in that wild and dreary country; and then of the beloved North and the dear friends from whom we had been so long separated, and who would greet us there as if we had risen from the tomb; and the contrast spurred us on. Our strength revived, and our sinews were braced afresh.

About midnight we were within a mile of Wilkesboro. We essayed to flank the town, and, losing our way, were compelled to retrace our steps for several miles. We were all tired out, and obliged to halt when we had finally passed around and beyond the place. Our blood was chilled; our limbs were stiff; our frame shook as in an ague-fit.

We paused and lighted a fire, knowing not where we were, for our guide had lost his reckoning entirely. We lay down on the frozen ground, but, exhausted as we were, we could not sleep. While one side of our bodies was hot from the flames, we were icy cold on the other.

We suffered more from the sharp, frosty air and the wintry wind than when in motion. We must go on, and on we went for five miles, until we reached the banks of the Yadkin River. It was then broad day, but it was highly important we should cross the stream at once; for we had been assured that when we were on the other side we would be safe.

Fortunately, we met a Unionist who directed us to the ford, which we found, after wandering up and down for an hour. A woman was crossing the river in a canoe, and when she reached the eastern bank we asked for a man who had been recommended to us. The woman was wary, fearing we were Home Guards in search of her husband, the person for whom we inquired. We soon succeeded in convincing her of her error, when she told us she was his wife, on her way to Wilkesboro to sell some butter. We crossed the stream, but before we could reach the habitation we were seeking, we heard a horn blow, and knew it was a signal to the "liers-out."

Having arrived at the dwelling, not a man was visible, and an elderly woman there proved as absolute a know-nothing as it was possible to conceive. She declared she was utterly destitute of information of any kind on any subject. We assured her we were friends; that we were escaped Yankee prisoners; but she could not be convinced; remarking that the Rebels often went about in disguise, pretending to be what they were not, and plainly intimating that she did not believe a word of what we said.

Almost an hour's argument was requisite to prove to the female skeptic that we were what we had stated. Then she offered us something to eat—fat pork, butter-milk, and corn-bread, which, as we were very hungry, we consumed voraciously. She told us to hide in the bushes, and that the man we wished to see would soon join us, as she had sent a messenger for him.

We did so, and ere long the bushwhacker made his appearance, and was very glad to see us. He introduced us to several others of his class, and three or four of Colonel Kirk's regiment. We inquired about the prospect of crossing the Blue Ridge, twenty miles to the West, and the answer was, that it was useless to make the attempt; that the mountains were covered with snow; that, if we endeavored to go over them, we would certainly be tracked, caught, and killed. "It is two hundred miles to Knoxville," continued the spokesman, "and no one ever reaches there. All who try it are murdered on the way."

That was encouraging, certainly, to us, who had been assured our peril would be past when we had crossed the Yadkin. I laughed at the consolation we had received; though, I confess, the laugh was not from the heart.

We told the bushwhackers we were willing to take the risk; that we would pay any of them liberally who would undertake to guide us across the mountains. None of them would consent; but informed us, if we would wait until the snow had disappeared, they would pilot us, but not till then; and that we could live with them until that time arrived.

Knowing from past experiences, that dangers and difficulties generally diminish when we confront, or as we approach them, we resolved to push on at least to the base of the Blue Ridge. That night we started, although we had been told the passes were guarded, and accomplished seven North-Carolina miles—the longest in the world, except those of Tennessee—when we found another Union family. We went into an open corn-crib, and thinking we could sleep, as the weather had moderated, we threw ourselves on the ground.

We had barely lain down before the wind veered round to the North, and blew so coldly on our thinly attired bodies that sleep was impossible. We had little or no protection from the blast; and believing I would freeze there, I removed to another out-house, and was endeavoring to bury myself among the ears of corn, when the Unionist came up and said: "Boys, it's too cold here. I'll put you in my store-house. There's a good deal of fodder there. My wife will send you food and quilts, and I reckon you can make yourselves comfortable."

In a few minutes our party of eight—we had discovered and greatly frightened a couple of deserters from Alabama and Florida, who had traveled on foot all the way from Richmond, by coming suddenly upon them in the corn-crib, but whom we left there asleep—were in the store-house, and very agreeably situated, comparatively. I rested very little that night, but my companions slumbered soundly; and the next morning—the last day of the year—we told the other four they had better go on, and that we would wait until January 1st.

So we divided again, and after passing New-Year's Day in the store-house, we started again that night—clear, bright, and cold—but not before I had exchanged the cape of an army over-coat for a quilt—and walked ten miles, crossing Wilson's Fork at least twenty-five times, and falling into it at least twelve, arriving about four o'clock in the morning in Watauga County.

The Laurel Spur of the Blue Ridge we ascended with little difficulty, and were taken in by a Unionist, who put us in the upper part of a store-house, on a feather-bed, and gave us several coverlets. Strange! I could not sleep; I never tried more energetically in all my life; but I lay there stark wide awake all day; the infernal vermin, of which we had not gotten rid, torturing us exceedingly, and driving away repose; our inability to bathe and change our under-clothes, as we had done regularly in Prison, rendering our condition very uncomfortable in that respect.

On the night of January 2, we engaged the loyal man who had sheltered us to take us over the Blue Ridge, which, he informed us, there was no difficulty in crossing, as the passes were not guarded, and the snow was not deep enough to impede our progress.

We had anticipated vast difficulty and extreme fatigue from that part of the journey, and we were greatly pleased to hear him express himself so encouragingly, particularly as we fancied, once beyond that range of mountains, we would have a fair prospect of getting through.

Experience proved the correctness of our guide's observation. We found the ascent far easier than some of the roads we had traveled, and we enjoyed a fine view of the surrounding country at the summit, twenty-five hundred feet above sea-level.

We were in fine condition. We descended, obtaining very picturesque views of mountain scenery, which we were hardly in a proper frame of mind fully to appreciate, and reached and crossed New River. We were very glad to see a river sensible enough to run North, as that did, and we knelt down and kissed and quaffed its limpid waters in token of our admiration for its judgment.

Made fifteen miles that night, much of it very hard traveling. Fell into a number of mountain streams, and were quite wet when we reached our destination. The weather cold and wind cutting, as we crawled into our usual place of shelter and concealment—a barn. Were very hungry, and ate a piece of corn bread with exceeding relish, as we lay covered up, but shivering, in the hay. My note-book reads: "How I long for the snowy sheets and soft pillows—shall I say the softer snowy arms?—I have known in the beloved and blessed North!" I presume, as the feeling is very natural, that the wish must have come from the heart.

January 3, we made the first march by day, having been assured it was perfectly safe. No doubt it was, for it was by foot-paths over very steep, rough mountains, through laurel thickets and rocky streams, and over fallen timber. The snow was ten to twelve inches deep on the mountains, and we were eight hours in going ten miles. We often fell head over heels in descending, and sometimes hurt ourselves not a little, by striking trees and stumps; and in ascending we had to drag ourselves up by the branches of trees, and with the aid of our staffs almost constantly.

At the end of our stage we learned we were in Johnson County, Tennessee, three miles from the North-Carolina line. Out of that State we were at last; and much we felicitated ourselves on the fact. That began to look like successful escape—like a reward for all our endurance and suffering.

We had been told when we arrived in Tennessee we would be perfectly safe. In fact, those stories were repeated to us all along the route. The place we chanced to be in was very dangerous; but just beyond—ten, twenty, or thirty miles—there was another place, where there was no danger whatever.

When we left Salisbury, to reach Wilkes County was to be secure. When we quitted the Union settlement, all we needed for safety was to get beyond Wilkesboro. Then, when we had crossed the Yadkin, we could lay aside all apprehension ; and beyond the Yadkin we met reckless bushwhackers and hardy mountaineers, who would not venture to go with us over the Blue Ridge, but told us it was madness to make the attempt.

Our natural deduction was, from all this, that no locality was safe except that over which the blessed Banner of Stars waved ; and to see that once more was our aim, our anxiety, our aspiration.

In Johnson County we obtained an excellent supper for that region—the best we had had—and we ate ravenously after our mountain climbing, and a fast of fifteen hours.

The Union people to whom we went put us in their barn, advising us to be very cautious, as the North Carolina Home Guards frequently came into that county, and robbed and burned without the least regard to person or property.

The loyalists of that section had suffered fearfully. Marauders had frequently been through there, and stolen women's and children's clothes, broken open trunks and drawers, and carried off articles of which they had no need. They had stolen provisions, until the poor people were sometimes compelled to beg ; had applied the torch to the dwellings of honest farmers before their eyes, and threatened to hang them if they complained of the outrage.

We assured our protector, if we were discovered, that we would fully exculpate him ; that we would make

THE BOHEMIANS CLIMBING THE MOUNTAINS.

oath, if need there were, that he knew nothing of our being in his barn.

We crept under some fodder, and slept at intervals until morning, when we returned to the house and ate breakfast, while two of the old man's daughters stood picket. We then learned we had had several narrow escapes in coming down the mountain. We had been mistaken for Home Guards; and several of the bushwhackers had had their rifles leveled at us, when some fortunate circumstance intervened to prevent them from pulling the trigger.

None of us were anxious to be shot, but if that was our destiny, we preferred to be perforated by a genuine Rebel rather than by our natural allies and political friends.

Our boots being cut and burst out, we set forth to find a cobbler, and did so. While we were waiting for the return of our foot-coverings, in a hay-loft, we were visited by a number of bushwhackers, who wanted us to stay with them; assuring us we would make excellent members of the profession. They related many of their adventures, and entertained us for some time, though we did not feel inclined to accept their proposition. Received a great deal of advice as to the best course for us to pursue; and if the adage be sound, that in multiplicity of counselors there is safety, we should have been entirely out of danger.

Heard a great deal about Home Guards, Rebel scouts, and cavalry; were advised to stay where we were, and depart at once; but as we could not do both, we concluded to remain in the neighborhood of Drake's Creek until we could learn something of the situation further on. The other party were in the vicinity, waiting, as we were, for information, which was very difficult of obtainment.

We were naturally very anxious to learn where our forces were, having heard some miles back that they were at Peach Orchard, Tenn. It was then reported they were not there, but were certainly at Carter's Dépôt, in Carter County, and that the cars were running to Greenville, on the East Tennessee and Virginia Railway. Our hearts leaped at that intelligence; for we could make Greenville in three or four days more. Our hope of getting through to our lines became something tangible, and we had no higher boon to ask than Freedom, which, after the repair of our boots, we had less fear of losing through any failure of leather.

After burrowing in the corn-husks of a barn, on the night of January 4th, we were informed by our Unionist friend that some hundreds of the enemy's cavalry were reported coming down the road, and that, as they would certainly search all the stables and outhouses for fodder and horses, we had better flee to the mountains for concealment. We had had so many alarms that *The Tribune* scribes put little faith in the story, and were disposed to lie still; but as the others were uneasy, and extreme prudence is the best policy of unarmed men, we crawled out of our nests, and sallied forth into a bright, still, cold night, resembling, with the snow, the mountains, and the frosted pines, the Polar regions far more than the sunny South.

The more we reflected on the report of the Rebel cavalry the less we believed it; and therefore, instead of climbing the mountains, we elected to invade some other shed, in a more secluded place. We roamed about for two hours, like Scandinavian specters, over the rough, frozen, snow-covered ground, and at last crept into a barn, where I lay sleepless until morning, and almost frozen, being barely able to stand when I rose to my feet.

Very weary and wearing was that species of existence; but through the heavy clouds we had faith the sun would ere long break in golden glory. Referring to my note-book, I find these words: "This experience will be pleasant some day to look back on, and talk about; but it is difficult to undergo, requiring all the patience and philosophy I can master. Any thing for freedom! Though I perish in the effort to regain it, I shall not regret it, I am sure, if conscious in a future state of what has occurred in the present."

That very day, January 5, we made preparations to go forward, having found an individual who said he would guide us to Carter's Dépôt. Very glad were we to be on the march once more, as we were tired enough of freezing in haystacks and corn-lofts, and skulking from barn to barn, from valley to mountain, from ridge to ravine.

We met the second party, consisting of Sergeant Thurston, the other two escaped prisoners, and the three Rebel deserters, at the cabin of a loyal woman, whose husband had gone to the Yankees; and after obtaining a hearty meal, and taking rations enough in our haversacks for two days, we waited for the guide.

While we were waiting, several of us ascended an

adjacent mountain, to see a party of Unionists who were lying out. Some of them had been in the Rebel service, and others had fled from home to avoid conscription. They had been living in rude huts or holes in the ground for twelve, some for twenty-four months, obtaining provisions from their relatives or friends, but never remaining at home or sleeping in a bed for a single night.

The men were hardy, determined fellows, only violent when they spoke of the enemies of the country and the wrong they had suffered at their hands. They all had their stories of outrage and wrong to relate; and no one who heard them could refrain from pitying their condition, and sharing their hatred of the Rebels.

CHAPTER LII.

THE HEGIRA IN EAST TENNESSEE.

Traveling in that Region.—Passage of the Piney and Stone Mountains.—Crossing the Watauga River.—Invitation to a Frolic.—Peculiar Reason for our Declination.—Recklessness Engendered by our Situation.—Meeting with Dan Ellis, the Pilot, and his Party.—His Kindness and Generosity.—The Effect of Apple Brandy.—Mysterious Disappearance of a Bohemian.—Severe Marching.—Strain on the Nervous System.—Reports of Rebels in our Vicinity.—A Valuable Steed and his Fate.—Anxiety of our Guides to Meet the Enemy.

THE guide arrived at the cabin about three o'clock in the afternoon, and we set out at once for Carter's dépôt. We crossed Piney and Stone Mountains, the steepest and most difficult we had encountered, and had a fine view of the Alleghanies from their summit. They reminded me of an earth-storm; the barren peaks looking like vast billows frozen into stone. The snow was some twelve inches deep, and the march arduous, but romantic. We slipped, tumbled, and fell along in the most ludicrous style, and tore our newly mended boots worse than ever. Leather appeared to have no power to endure those mountain marches. It was like paper against the sharp stones and rough rocks.

We had not proceeded more than twelve miles before our pilot said he must return. We told him he had promised to take us to Carter's dépôt; but he vowed he had not; though he would do it if his wife were not sick, and in need of his attention. We offered him any remuneration if he would accompany us ; even proposed to pay for his consort should she die in his absence ; but he would not be persuaded or hired, and we were compelled to give him up, though very reluctantly.

Kindling a fire in one of the gorges, we sat by it until dark, when we continued our march under our own supervision. We stopped at the house of a Tennessee clergyman about ten o'clock, and there had an ample meal. He was a fine specimen of an upright, bold, outspoken loyalist. He had four sons in the Union service; said he wished he had four more, and that he would have been there himself if his years and health would have allowed him to be. He congratulated us on our escape, and said he would pray for our safe arrival within our lines ; told us what direction to take, and what people to see, regretting he could not pilot us himself on account of his rheumatism.

After resting we proceeded, and about three o'clock the next morning reached the farm to which we had been directed, and, as usual, went to the barn—having made some eighteen miles from the last settlement. No sleep worthy the name, of course ; arose from our couch of hay about eight o'clock, January 6, and accepted our host's invitation to breakfast with remarkable promptness. He told us we were in quite a secure region, and that there would be little danger in traveling to and along the Watauga River by daylight.

We took him at his word, bathed in Roan's Creek, and felt refreshed and lighter-spirited. We had a pleasant ramble along the Watauga, which reminded me of the

Kentucky River, being quite picturesque and romantic, for eight miles, when we crossed in a canoe to Carter County, and, going to one of our cordon of Union men, received a warm welcome, and the best and freest of his hospitality. We slept in a bed, with more comfort than usual, undetermined whether to wait for some time or push on the next day. We heard all the Rebels had left below, and were once more assured that our forces held Greenville, but not Carter's dépôt. We breathed more and more freely as we progressed, the prospect of freedom growing brighter every day.

Where we then were we met a number of Union Tennessee soldiers, who had come home on furlough, some of whom were soon to return to their regiments. They were going about very openly, giving us an idea there was not much danger in that neighborhood from the enemy.

They even had what they called a "frolic" one night, and invited us; but, as we had no arms, we did not deem it prudent to go; for it was not unusual for the Home Guards to surround the houses in which the company gathered, and shoot the men as they went out.

Several cases of the kind had occurred a few weeks before our arrival in Wilkes County; and when the deserters were gathered in force, they would invite the Guard to call again; but, when expected and prepared for, they invariably stayed away.

I remember some years ago, in New Orleans, I was amused to see in the papers advertisements of masquerades, to the effect that gentlemen were requested to leave their weapons at the door. But not until I became a fugitive in Secessia had I ever declined an invitation to join a social circle because I had no weapons to take there with me.

Unique country that, and peculiar state of society down there, particularly since the War!

Our party had been entertained, from the time of its escape, by assurances of people we met along the road that we were likely to be shot at any time by our friends from the brush, or in the mountain passages.

Life was evidently of no value in the sections through which we passed, as we learned from the stories of murders and butcheries almost daily told. That wild mountain life generated recklessness and indifference, no doubt, as we ourselves experienced. Though seemingly in the midst of perpetual danger, we cared little, if any thing, for the possibilities or probabilities of the future; but often amused ourselves with representing how "our special Correspondent" would appear with a rope about his neck, or a bullet through his brain.

On the whole, that nervousness we expected to have on the march through the enemy's country, and that constant anxiety about our capture or massacre, we did not feel to any extent. We determined to do all that lay in our power to effect our escape and reach our lines, and left the result in the hands of the Gods. We became for the time being fatalists, as most men are prone to who lead hazardous lives, and were resolved not to worry ourselves about the Unseen, or entertain grave apprehensions respecting the Untried.

About noon of January 7, our host agreed to take us across the country by a secret path to a relative of his, residing on the banks of the Watauga; telling us that a famous guide, Dan Ellis, of whom we had heard a great deal, was soon to go through to our lines with a party, and that, if we could strike him, there would be little danger of our failure to seeing our freedom. That was exactly what we wanted, and we marched off very briskly; crossed the river about three o'clock in the afternoon, and were soon comfortably ensconced by the fireside of the most comfortable dwelling we had seen on our journey.

At that resting-place we converted ourselves into washer-women, going out on the bank of the river, lighting a huge fire under an iron kettle, and abluting our under-clothes with more energy than skill; and all night, though it was frosty, denuding and bathing ourselves in the stream. Of course we must have felt quite secure to do those things, and we did, from the fact that the house where we were stopping was on the other side of the river from the road—the stream was so high, too, as to be unfordable, and situated in front of a gap between the mountains, furnishing an excellent means of retreat if we were pursued. It was really an intrenched position, and we could afford to expose ourselves there.

Sunday, January 8, we deemed it well to push forward to the rendezvous from which Dan Ellis was to start that night. We crossed the river in the morning, and after going five miles found the other party, and took a bountiful luncheon, furnished by a generous-hearted Unionist, in an open field. We then set out for the rendezvous, and heard that Ellis would certainly be there. Soon after he sent word for the footmen to move on; that he would speedily be along and overtake us. That was sufficient; for Ellis's word was not to be doubted.

Our united party of seven escaped prisoners and three deserters started with some fifteen more that had assembled to join Ellis, but had not gone more than two miles before the famous pilot was up with us. We three Correspondents were presented to Ellis, who assured us we should be put through in the right kind of style; that all we had to do was to keep with him, if we wanted to see the Stars and Stripes again.

His party was very miscellaneous, made up of Tennessee Union soldiers, Rebel deserters, loyal Southern citizens, conscripts who would not serve, and escaped prisoners. He had about twenty horses and mules, and he offered us Bohemians an opportunity to ride, which we accepted; but I found the animal that I strode so slow and indolent that it tired me more to urge him along than to walk, and I dismounted after a mile of persevering toil to little purpose.

Ellis loaned his mule to Mr. Richardson, and, carrying his carbine, which fired sixteen times without re-loading, walked more rapidly than almost any horse could. Most of his party were mountaineers, and quite fresh, while we had been twenty months in prison, and had then accomplished over two hundred miles under very adverse circumstances. I for one found it very difficult to keep up with the party at first, having fallen behind by being on that Rosinante. On several occasions I was compelled to run for more than a mile at a time, falling over logs and into streams in my usual fashion.

I had grown so accustomed to falling in that mountain

travel that it interfered very little with my progress. I found I could get along about as well by standing on my head, turning somersaults, and performing acts of ground and lofty tumbling generally, as by regular pedestrianizing.

That night's march was tremendous. We went twenty-seven miles long before dawn, and found, after crossing the Nolechucky, that we had lost several of our party, three mules, most of the rations, and I know not what else. The truth was, some of Ellis's men had drank too much apple brandy, becoming so intoxicated that they parted with their reason, and, when asked, could not tell where any thing was. One of them, indeed, really lost his identity, and declared he was somebody else; that the other fellow—giving his own name—was so d—d drunk that they had left him behind.

Among the mysterious disappearances was Mr. Richardson. It was supposed he had gotten behind, and that the mule had taken the wrong road. We were unwilling to go on without *The Tribune* scribe, so we bivouacked, and sent scouts out to obtain tidings of the missing individuals. They all came to light, having run off the track by some means unknown to themselves. My associate trusted to his mule, and the mule, having delightfully original instincts, wandered off in a North-Easterly instead of a South-Westerly direction. The journalist, discovering his confidence in the animal had been betrayed, concluded to suspend operations, and put up for the night on a log. When the morning dawned, he found a farmer who informed him of the right road, and in four hours after he was in our camp. The other mules were discovered, but the rations never revealed themselves.

Monday, January 9, we quitted camp in Washington County about eleven o'clock in the morning, and set out to cross the mountains, Big Butt being the highest and hardest to climb of any we had seen. It is seven thousand feet above sea-level, and seven miles from summit to base. By Jove! how we did toil up that steep! It seemed as if we never would get up, and, once up, as if we never would get down. The horses and mules could hardly be dragged to the top, though they had nothing to carry. My strength and endurance were augmenting, although I rarely was able to sleep; and that day I followed immediately behind Ellis until we had descended to the valley in Greene County.

The rain and sleet had been falling for hours when we paused for the night; we had had nothing to eat and we were quite wet. We had no shelter, but tried to arrange an old roof of a house, that had fallen down, for that purpose; and failing to effect it, Messrs. Davis and Richardson, and myself, undertook to discover some farm-house where we could procure food. We were successful in that, as well as in engaging a few bundles of corn-husks for a couch in a wretched fodder-loft. We rested far better than we had expected, owing, no doubt, to the extreme hardships we had undergone.

For the first time, I felt a tremendous strain on my nervous system, caused by the fact that it was always on the rack while with Ellis, for fear, from his rapid movements, I should be left behind and lost, which was equivalent to forfeiting all hope of freedom, if not of life. Those mountain men never halted; they rushed on without looking back or waiting for any one. They would go through a ravine or gorge, leap across a creek, dart into a laurel or an ivy thicket, and all trace of them be gone, though you were behind them only five seconds. I remember, after keeping at the head of the file for a number of hours, I stopped to give a soldier a drink from my canteen, and I lost nearly a mile. So it was. There was little resting, and instead of marching steadily and leisurely, they would go at a break-neck pace that fatigued all of us more in a mile than three miles would have done at an ordinary and regular gait.

My boots became more broken than ever on the 9th, and, having split across the joint of the foot, when they grew wet and shrank they gave me much pain in walking. I began to be very anxious about getting through after my seven-leaguers showed such unmistakable signs of complete dissolution, knowing that to lose their usefulness was to lose all else.

January 10.—We three procured a light breakfast at a farm-house, proving much more fortunate than most of our companions, who were half famished. Heard an immense deal about Rebels—that there were several squads in the neighborhood, and so many scouting the country that it was hardly possible to get through. Two men who had come from North Carolina with us became alarmed and turned back, selling their horses to the highest bidder.

Mr. Richardson purchased one of the steeds, and though neither very fleet nor handsome, he had qualities to wear—out his rider. My confrère was much exhausted, and needed an animal to ride, even if it did not appear well, or evince any indications of patrician lineage. He rode the beast through to Strawberry Plains, and then paid a negro ten dollars to give him Christian burial, which he deserved, for the service he had rendered. The poor horse did not wish to defer his obsequies, for, having eaten several bushels of corn, he exploded into so many pieces that they could not be collected for interment.

Poor Rosinante was not a serious loss; for, although my associate paid fifty dollars in treasury notes for him, his original cost, with eleven other animals like him, was at the rate of five dollars per dozen in Rebel currency.

The rain continued to fall steadily, and we were all drenched; the roads becoming almost impassable from mud. About eleven o'clock the sky cleared, and we resumed our march on the alert for the enemy; having no fear of any small squad, for there were eight or ten carbines in Ellis's party, and as many revolvers, which the owners knew how to use, as the Rebels had learned in past times to their cost. At least ten of the Unionists were old scouts and rangers, who had frequently engaged the "Confederates," and, so far from being desirous to avoid them, were extremely anxious to come in collision with any thing like their own number; feeling confident, as they expressed it, that they could "sweeten their coffee" for them in a very few minutes.

CHAPTER LIII.

DAN ELLIS, THE FAMOUS PILOT.

Sketch of his Life and Career.—His uncompromising Loyalty.—Efforts to Suppress him.—His success as a Pilot.—Mode of Joining his Expeditions.—His Adventures and Narrow Escapes.—His Attachment to his Carbine.—His Opinion of the Confederacy.—A Rebel Officer's Views of his Usefulness to the Union Cause.

DAN ELLIS, or Captain Dan Ellis, as he is often called, is one of the notabilities of East Tennesee. He is a native of Carter County, and one of the most ultra and irrepressible Unionists in that extremely loyal section. From the beginning of the troubles, he took a most decided stand for the Government, and has maintained it ever since. He was at all times open, bold, and decided in his opposition to, and hatred of, the Rebels, and declared, whatever temporary success they might have, they would be ultimately crushed, and the so-called "Confederacy" with them.

Ellis is about thirty-five years old; rather slight, but muscular, and agile as a cat; of vigorous constitution and immense endurance; brave as Belisarius, but prudent and cunning; entirely familiar with the country within a radius of four or five hundred miles; accustomed to all the hardships and adventures of frontier life; candid, generous, and amiable to everybody but the Rebels, whose right to existence he does not clearly perceive.

Though uneducated, Ellis is intelligent, a close observer, a good judge of men, strictly honest and abstemious, and, with all his fondness for a wild and reckless life, tenderly attached to his wife and children. He has the greatest regard for his word, and all who know him accept his simple statement with the most implicit faith. His promises every one relies on ; and among the people of his county, "Dan Ellis says so" is an indubitable evidence of truthfulness.

His outspoken sentiments at the inception of the Rebellion, and his uncompromising hatred of the enemies of his country, soon made him a marked man, and excited against him the most violent hatred of the Secessionists. He was rather an unpleasant person to draw into a quarrel, and therefore many of the traitors, who would have been delighted to find an excuse for attacking him, hesitated to do so, knowing his courage and determination, and the violence of his passions when once aroused.

His foes tried to intimidate him, sending him warnings, and making the most sanguinary menaces. He heeded them not, but continued his labor on his farm, neither seeking nor avoiding quarrels if they were thrust upon him. Before the Summer of 1861 ended, he had several rencounters with Secessionists, and had been shot and stabbed once or twice, but not seriously.

At last, so bitter was the feeling against Ellis, that numerous plots were formed to murder him ; and he would certainly have fallen a victim to some of them, had the designs of the villains not been revealed to him in season for his own security. Yielding to the solicitations of his wife and friends, he quitted his home, and resided in Kentucky for a while, but soon returned in the capacity of guide or pilot to those who wished to reach our lines.

The qualities we have named admirably fitted him for that business; and though he frequently took charge of parties of one and two hundred at a time, he always conducted them through safely. For many months Ellis piloted Unionists and Southern deserters all the way from Carter County to Louisville, Kentucky; and, after the fall of Donelson, to Nashville, Tennessee.

For a year and a half previous to our meeting him, he had been piloting parties to Knoxville; and so well was he acquainted with the men, women, and children belonging to every loyal family in Western North Carolina and East Tennessee, and with every by-road and bridle-path and mountain way and ford of river and of stream, that there was little fear of his failing to take those under his guidance to their destination. Indeed, those who knew Ellis best, said the Captain had never lost but one man, and that he was captured through his own indiscretion.

Since the beginning of the war, Ellis, it is said, has conducted to our lines fully five thousand men, most of whom would have been forced into the Rebel service if they had remained in Secessia. His name is known all over Tennessee. He makes regular journeys between Knoxville and Carter County, and the time when he proposes to move from his own home to our lines is understood for miles around. All who want to go join his party on the way, he and his experienced scouts being in advance, and giving directions to the rest.

Old men and boys, conscripts and deserters, sometimes

women and children, flock to Ellis's cavalcade as it moves by, and he takes the best care of them, often purchasing provisions for those who have not the means. He makes no charge for his services, though they who wish to remunerate him can do so. He has supplied a number of soldiers to the Tennessee Union regiments, and the Government has paid him for many that he has furnished, which, with the horses and mules he buys and sells, and not unfrequently confiscates, when they prove the property of Rebels, enables him to live; and I understand he has accumulated a fair amount of property.

The "Confederates" have declared he should not live in Tennessee; but he has sworn he would, whether they like it or not, and he has kept his word. He is often absent from his home in the mountains for months at a time; but he generally sees his wife and children every few weeks, sometimes being compelled to steal into and out of the house. The Rebels have threatened to burn his house frequently, but have not carried their menaces into execution,—whether from the fact that his wife is a very amiable and kind-hearted woman, though as loyal, and almost as courageous, as her husband, or that they fear the vengeance of her liege-lord, I cannot say. I presume it is from the latter reason.

Ellis's house has been surrounded a number of times by armed bands, on several occasions when he was there; but he has either hidden where they could not find him, or gotten out surreptitiously, or run the gantlet of their fire without injury to himself. Few men have had more narrow escapes; though he says the traitors have been trying to put his light out for four years, but that he does not think he was born to be hurt by them. He has become a predestinarian in the fullest sense of the term.

All kinds of ingenious plans have been laid to entrap Ellis, but he has had so many friends among the people who would give him timely information, that he always contrived to defeat the purpose of his foes. They even set a price upon his head at one time, and Rebels skulked about his farm, for weeks, to shoot him. But, as several of them were shot while they were watching for Dan, they concluded it would not be worth their while to engage in the business permanently, and at once embraced safer and more profitable avocations.

The poor and loyal people of East Tennessee have a most enthusiastic admiration for Ellis, and would secrete him, or work or fight for him, under any circumstances. He has been extremely kind to them ever; has given them provisions and money when they were in need; brought dresses for the women and children, and endeared himself to the loyal community in the most extraordinary manner. They all regard him as a very near friend, and if he were to be a candidate for any office in that section, I venture to say he would obtain every vote of the laboring classes.

The number of adventures Dan has had would make a large and very readable volume. He says little of them himself; but his companions informed me how many chases the Rebels had given him; how they had emptied their cartridge-boxes at him again and again; how they had shot through his hat, coat, and boots; killed his horse, and pursued him on foot without injuring him seriously, or making him prisoner. They would not capture him, or if they did, they would dispatch him, as they have often threatened. They sent him word, once, that they would never take him prisoner, unless he ceased to assist "citizens and soldiers of the Confederacy" through to the Union lines; and his answer was, that he did not design to give them any opportunity; but that he would put every Union man in God's country who wanted to go there, if the Rebels built a wall round the State five hundred feet high.

Dan's carbine he never allows to go out of his hands, sleeping with it in his arms, and setting it at his side when he takes his meals. On one occasion he was pursued for at least ten miles, through a mountainous region, and had emptied his piece of its sixteen cartridges; but still, though his life depended on his rapid flight, he would not throw away his beloved carbine, heavy as it was, and much as it impeded his progress.

"That old gun," said Ellis, "has saved me a dozen times; and if the Rebels ever kill me, that carbine shall be the last thing I will hold on earth."

"Give that up! throw that away!" exclaimed Dan, passionately, holding up the piece; "why, it's my best friend! I'd as soon think of giving up my wife as that old blazer; without that, I'd have been under the sod long ago. Oh no, I can't let that go;" and he drew his carbine to his breast as if it had been a woman, and his keen gray eye glistened with emotion at the very idea of parting with so old and faithful a companion.

During 1863, Ellis went to Knoxville, and was elected Captain of a company of one of the loyal Tennessee regiments, mainly composed of men he had brought through the lines; but after being in the service a few months, the Commandant of the post told him he thought he could be of much more advantage to the cause and country by resuming his old avocation. Dan thought so too, saying the Army was rather dull after scouting, and gladly resigned to return to the wilder, more exciting, and daring life he had before followed.

Many of Ellis's friends were anxious he should remove his family from Carter County to Knoxville; but he declared he would remain just where he was. "I worked and paid for that patch of ground," he remarked, "and I'm going to stay until the 'Confederacy' is moved down to the Gulf, and towed out to sea and sunk where there's no bottom. What's the use of my moving when the Rebels are moving so fast? Why, if I were to dodge around as the 'Confederacy' is doing, rolling up and growing thinner every day, I'd have no place to stand on —not even the last ditch. No, sir, I can't move a bit. Let the 'Confederacy' move off of my farm, where it has no business. I've only got to stay there a little while longer, and there won't be any 'Confederacy' to move out of."

Dan was right, as recent events have proved.

No one man, I venture to say, in all Tennessee, has done more to injure the Rebels and the Rebel cause than Ellis. He has taken away their deserters and conscripts; spread disaffection and despondency among the half-secessionists; confiscated their horses and mules; bushwhacked their soldiers and officers, and more or less demoralized the entire community in which he lived.

Hundreds of persons, less strong and self-reliant than

he, looked up to him for support and counsel. When the days of the Republic were darkest, he bade them be of good cheer; when they were about to yield and go over to the enemy, he strengthened their weak knees, and pointed to a radiant future they could not see.

One of the insurgent leaders said: "Ellis is worse than a Yankee regiment, and I would rather have one stationed in Carter County than have Dan there. Confound the Tory scoundrel! he must be in league with the devil. We have hunted him, shot at him, put a price on his head, watched his house, and had him surrounded and almost in our hands a score of times; and yet he always contrives to give us the slip.

"D—— him to H——! I'd rather hang him than Andy Johnson or old Brownlow. He's done us more harm, I believe, than both of those Tories, for he comes right into our midst, and finds out what we are doing; and before we learn he is among us, he's off to Knoxville again, giving information to the Yankee authorities. If I could hang him, I'd die easier, I believe; and I'd give my last nigger for the privilege; I would, by G——!"

CHAPTER LIV.

THE NAMELESS HEROINE.—UNDER THE STARS AND STRIPES ONCE MORE.

Pursuit of the Enemy.—Alarm and Separation of our Party.—Our Fair Guide.—Her Appearance and Antecedents.—Our Continued March.—Confiscation of Horses.—Our Last Night Out.—Sensations on Approaching the Union Lines.—Chagrin of the Rebels at our Escape.—Their Absurd Stories about the Departed Bohemians.

Early in the afternoon of January 10, we hear five or six of the hostile cavalry are in advance of us only a few miles. Ellis immediately calls for those who have arms to follow him, and away they dash in pursuit of the foe; while the rest of us, who are on foot and weaponless, trudge along the road toward Kelly's Gap in the Nolechucky mountains, arriving there just before sunset.

That was the appointed rendezvous, and Ellis and his party reached there about dusk, after a long and useless chase, and we prepared to camp for the night. Dan went to one of the Union houses, a few miles distant, and returned with the information that we were almost surrounded by the Rebels; that it would be necessary for the horsemen to separate from the footmen, so that in the event of pursuit the latter would not be taken.

All was activity at once. Those who had lain down, in the deserted and dilapidated cabins of the abandoned plantation to which we had repaired, were aroused.

Horses and mules were saddled, fires extinguished, and every preparation made for speedy departure.

The cavalry were to move first, the infantry to follow, after the others had gone far enough in advance. Ellis offered me a mule—Richardson and Davis were mounted—but as it had no saddle, and I remembered my partial bisection the night we journeyed to the Union settlement in Wilkes County, I respectfully declined; preferring to walk rather than to undergo a repetition of those tortures. I even gave Davis my quilt to use as a saddle-cloth, and bade my friends good-by, fully expecting to see them again in the morning, at the furthest.

After they had been gone about half an hour, a scout named Treadway, who had been placed in charge of the footmen, told us to fall in; that we were to cross a mountain and descend into a ravine, where we would camp until the next night.

"But where are we to meet the other party?" inquired I. "O, we won't see them again until we reach Knoxville, if we ever have the good luck to get there."

We had learned the day before, that all the stories about our forces being at Greenville and other adjacent points were without foundation; that our lines were at Strawberry Plains, fifteen miles East of Knoxville; and that we must go there before we could have any hope of freedom.

That was nearly a hundred miles farther, and the intelligence was rather disheartening, for we had been imagining our journey was nearly at an end. No doubt many of us felt like the North Carolinian of the party, who had been in prison nearly three years, when asked if he was tired. "Tired?" echoed he, with a mingled air of disgust and contempt. "Why this would wear out an iron man."

The reply of the scout: "We won't see them until we reach Knoxville," smote on my heart like the sound of my death-knell.

Separation from my friends—the three companions with whom I had escaped, with whom I had endured so much in prison and on the march to freedom—seemed a calamity I could not bear. It foreshadowed to me every thing gloomy and horrible—recapture, dungeons, despair, and death.

And while I stood there in the darkness—not to advance for twenty-four hours—they were every minute hurrying away, making the distance greater between us. They are going to freedom, I thought, and I am left behind. My doom is written. Liberty is not for me. I shall perish here in these mountains, and the few who feel an interest in me will never know my fate.

Materially considered, too, I had lost my quilt, which had saved me much suffering, and I was penniless, my Bohemian brothers having all the money there was in our party.

The record in my note-book is: "I have no more hope now of getting through; yet will I do my utmost, and compel the strong spirit to rule the weak flesh. I will march till I fall fainting on the road from hunger, cold, and exhaustion. I am resolved never to give up. Still am I most worn, weary, and wretched; and all my dark views of Human Life and Experience come up mentally darker and grimmer than before."

The pedestrians proceeded to the ravine, and built a big fire; the weather was too cold to sleep. We were hungry, having had nothing to eat for twenty-four hours, and there was little prospect of getting any thing.

The scout went off somewhere, and left us alone, most of the party being ignorant, silly, coarse, imprudent fellows—mere children in character, whom I could not induce to stand picket, or act cautiously about any thing. They disgusted me greatly, and I saw there was little safety with such simpletons.

The scout returned, having visited a number of Unionists, who reported us in a very dangerous vicinity; that we yet had many perils to encounter, and must be extremely cautious if we wanted to reach our lines. The worst of our perils, it seemed to me, were hunger, cold, and exhaustion.

About noon we had an alarm from some Rebel cavalry, who passed along a road so near us that we distinctly heard their words. Supposing they had seen us, we precipitately left our camp fire, and ran up the mountain in fine confusion. After running at high speed for some hundreds of yards, I paused to observe if any one was following us; and perceiving no one, I called out, and we all stopped; then reconnoitered; then returned to our camping-place. The fire of dry wood was still burning in the chilly, crisp air, and several haversacks and blankets, left in the rapidity of retreat, lay there undisturbed. It was evident the enemy had not known of our whereabouts, and had passed on unconscious of our presence.

Toward evening I began to be resigned to my new situation, having the consolation of knowing that the separation between me and my companions would prevent the probability of the recapture or extermination of all of us. The fate of *The Tribune* Correspondents was at least likely, under existing circumstances, to be different. If Mr. Richardson were retaken, I might get through; if I were retaken, he might.

Just before leaving the ravine the scout obtained some provisions for us, which we enjoyed after our long fast. We then started at a break-neck pace over the ridges, falling every few hundred yards so violently that I marveled some of us did not break our limbs. Once my knee came in contact with the root of a tree so forcibly that it seemed shattered, and I did not recover from the soreness and lameness occasioned by the fall for days after.

About sunset our party was on the summit of a ridge looking down into the valley where resided a girl who, the night previous, had guided Dan Ellis and his companions, by a private path, out of the way of the Rebels believed to be in the vicinity. For more than an hour we sat there watching the house in which she lived, and seeing ten or twelve Rebel cavalrymen ride up to the dwelling, and then depart in squads of two or three. At dusk we descended to the valley cautiously, and met her at the appointed place, mounted, and ready to act as our guide. That girl, not more than sixteen or seventeen, belonging to one of the stanchest loyal families in East Tennessee, was known to all the Unionists in the county. She had assisted many true men out of awkward predicaments and dangerous situations, and had shown herself willing at all times to aid them. She had often arisen at night when she obtained intelligence of importance, and communicated it to loyalists some miles distant, preventing their capture or murder by the enemy.

Ellis had known her from childhood, and depended on her for information whenever he was anywhere in her neighborhood. She had told him the preceding night of the presence of the enemy, and recommended the division of his band, as pursuit was possible ; assuring him that she would guide the footmen, as she would him, if they would be at a certain place at a certain hour.

The girl, whose name I will not give—though I can state, for the benefit of the romantic, that it is a pretty one, and would sound well in a novel—was decidedly fair, intelligent, of graceful figure, and possessed of that indispensable requisite to an agreeable woman—a sweet voice.

I confess I looked at her with some degree of admiration as she sat there, calm, smiling, comely, with the warm blood of youth flushing in her cheek, under the flood of mellow moonlight that bathed all the landscape in poetic softness and picturesque beauty.

It was natural that almost any man of gallantry and imagination should idealize her, under the circumstances; but I did not.

I gazed at her as I do at most of her sex, with the cold eye of Art, and at the unvarying angle of æsthetic criticism.

That scene was a good theme for a picture. The girl mounted, and the central figure, with some eighteen men in half military, half civil garb, with bronzed faces and a certain wild appearance, travel-stained, ragged, anxious-eyed, standing around her in groups, listening to what she said in a low but earnest and pleasantly modulated tone

She gave directions as quietly and composedly as a veteran commander in the field, requesting us to keep some distance behind her ; saying that, if she were halted, we should stop, and lie down ; that, when all was safe, she would cough ; and that, if she saw any danger, she would sneeze to give us warning.

All ready, she struck her horse, a spirited animal, and darted off at a pace that we pedestrians could hardly sustain, even running. Confound that girl ! I thought. What does she rush along at this rate for ? I have not had much experience in following in women's lead ; and if this is a specimen, I want no more of it.

We were out of breath, all of us, and had fallen so often in our haste, that we were suffering from numerous bruises and abrasions ; but she dashed on mercilessly, dragging us after her.

I reached her side once, and told her to go a little slower ; that we were greatly fatigued, and that some of us must fall hopelessly behind if she did not check her pace. She drew in her rein until those who had been nearly distanced came up, and then only walked her impatient steed for the remainder of the distance.

She guided us seven miles through woods and ravines, over mountains and along valleys, away from the frequented roads and paths, until we came to a long bridge over the Nolechucky River. We were fearful that might be guarded. So we waited on one side, while she crossed to the other. If she went on, we were to follow. If she stopped, we were to wait on the ridge where we lay concealed until she returned to tell us what was in the way.

Silently we crouched on the frosty ground, hearing her horse's hoofs ring out clearly and sharply upon the cold night on the planks of the bridge. But no challenging voice greeted our attentive ear. The bridge must be unobstructed, we thought, as the hoofs grew fainter and fainter; and, at last, when they were no longer audible, we knew she was on the road riding toward her sister's house—as she had told us she would—and that, her mission accomplished, we had parted with our fair guide, and would see her no more.

For the sake of my romantic readers, if I have any, I wish I could relate the occurrence of some sentimental scene between one of the Bohemians and the nameless heroine. It would look well on paper, and read well, too; but, so far as I can learn, neither of my fellow-journalists exchanged a word with her the night before; and as for myself, my only feeling toward her was one of irritation at her extreme haste, and my sole words—"Do go a little slower!"

Nothing like sensational coloring, and sentimental glitter in composition. If I were not a conscientious journalist and a veracious historian, I should relate a parting interview with the fair stranger much after the manner of Contarini Fleming's separation from the pretty gipsy.

I should tell how I, or somebody else, took her hand, and kissed her lips in the moonlight, and saw the tears start to her eyes; how my heart, or some other person's heart, beat wildly for a moment, as that vision of beauty, more beautiful in its sorrow, beamed upon the wintry, Luna-lighted night, and then faded away forever.

But, as nothing of the kind occurred, I shall say nothing of the kind. I shall only wish the dear, devoted girl the truest and tenderest of lovers, and the brightest and happiest of lives. Upon her youthful head may the choicest benisons of Heaven fall unstinted! May violets of beauty and lilies of sweetness bloom ever in her pathway, and fill with fragrance all her coming days.

What was remarkable about the girl was, that none of the Rebels suspected her of giving active aid to the Unionists. They knew she was loyal; indeed, she did not deny her loyalty; but, on the contrary, told them her sympathies were all with the North, and her most earnest wishes for the suppression of the Rebellion.

She said what she pleased with impunity. She was young, pretty, and intelligent. Everybody liked and petted her as if she were a child, when she had the feelings, the earnestness, the convictions of a woman; and, from her openness and candor, they presumed she told them all she did. They never dreamed of her secret excursions, her nightly expeditions, her communications with their enemies.

The Southern officers were half in love with her, and told her, with great indiscretion, all their plans and expectations, never imagining she would make use of them, which, of course, she did most effectually. No doubt, being feminine, and possessing feminine tact, she encouraged her admirers sufficiently to elicit from them what information she needed, and, in that way, was enabled to be of invaluable service to her friends.

For nearly four years, she had devoted her time to the service of the Republic ; had risked her liberty, perhaps her life ; had acted the heroine on the stage of our great National Drama without the least self-consciousness, or any other inducement than her attachment to the cause.

Her parents were in comfortable circumstances, quite wealthy, indeed, for that region, and had given her a very fair education, and some accomplishments which were very remarkable for a girl reared in the rural regions of the South. She had been petted and flattered by Secessionists of both sexes, who had in vain attempted to seduce her from her allegiance ; but she ever remained true to her country, and to those who befriended it in the time of its extremest need.

That she may some day be generously compensated in a higher than material form for her services, is my earnest hope and desire ; though I feel assured that recent events, establishing the integrity of the Republic, will be to her the most precious reward she could receive.

After leaving the heroic girl we marched seventeen miles, camping on top of a mountain about two o'clock in the morning, and kindling a fire, when I crept under a blanket that one of my companions kindly offered me.

Before reaching our camp, I had been an involuntary witness and apparent sharer in an enterprise which I did not anticipate and could not countenance. The scout who was our guide had heard that a notorious Rebel was at the house of his father-in-law, and accordingly went there in search of him. He told us to surround the house, and we did so—for what purpose I did not know. He then began beating on the door, and crying to the "d——d scoundrel"—that was the mildest of his epithets—to come forth, or he would blow out his brains.

An old man and woman came to the door, and declared their son-in-law was not at home. They were greatly frightened, and I felt very sorry for them, and would not have seen them hurt if I could have prevented it. No one threatened them; but many of the Tennesseeans swore and bellowed so loudly, that I do not wonder the poor people were alarmed.

"Where are that d——d traitor's horses?" was roared out a dozen times in a quarter of a minute. The old man showed the way to the stable, and in a brief while the two animals were bridled and saddled, and two of the Tennesseeans on their backs riding away.

The horses belonged to the Rebel, who was an officer in some guerrilla band, and no doubt ought to have been confiscated, but I could not reconcile myself to the confiscation, which seemed to me very much like vulgar horse-stealing; and I inwardly determined, if my fellow-travelers designed making a general business of that department of fine art, that I should separate from them, and journey towards freedom on my own account.

I had quitted Salisbury to obtain liberty, not horses; and it did not appear that my prospects for the former would be materially augmented by any acquisition of the latter. Fortunately, however, there were no more confiscations on the route; and consequently I had no occasion to put my determination in practice.

That equine appropriation was about the last adventure we had. At dusk on the evening of January 12, we set out for Russellville—eighteen miles distant—crossing

Lick Creek, and passing into the corner of Hawkins and into Granger Counties before four o'clock the following morning.

We struck the Virginia and East Tennessee Railway at Cheek's Cross Roads, and walked at a rapid rate to our camp, where we bivouacked. We learned after dawn that Ellis's party were safe, and had camped where we were the night previous. Our guide told me that the coming night (Friday, January 13th) would probably be the last we would be out; I truly hoped so. My boots were worn out; my attire in rags; my nervous system strangely sensitive, and perhaps deranged, from absence of sleep and constant exertion, with long fasts and perpetual anxiety. Yet I felt a degree of strength and freshness that was extraordinary, under the circumstances. I was calm withal, and unagitated, although freedom seemed so near at hand. Indeed, the idea of Liberty I could not realize—it seemed too great a blessing to be enjoyed. I often asked myself: "Shall I indeed see the dear old flag, and breathe the free air of the North once more?"

We had nothing throughout Friday but a little corn, which we parched in the ashes of our camp-fires, until just before setting out, when we procured the best meal we had had. The Tennessee scout accompanied us until we struck the railway again, and there left us, having, as he said, some important business to transact on the morrow.

Always before, Freedom, as I have said, had seemed too blissful to be realized; but when I found myself within one night's march of our glorious destination, I could no longer doubt that on the morrow I might plant my foot on loyal soil, and again behold the glitter of Union bayonets.

I was filled with a new life: I could not be restrained: my blood tingled: my pulses leaped: my whole being glowed.

Rapidly I walked along the broken railway. The mile-stones seemed to whirl by me as if I were on an express-train.

The wind was from the North—keen, cutting, penetrating; I loved it because it was from the North—and I still was very thinly clad.

But I felt not the low temperature: a blast from an iceberg would not have chilled me.

Within me was the sacred fire that has made martyrs and heroes through ages,—the fire which the love of Liberty has lighted, and which will burn forever.

My companions, fatigued and exhausted and half-frozen, fell off one by one, and in little squads. But a single man remained, a tall, stalwart, muscular fellow; and he declared he would go with me to the end.

On, on, on we went, faster, faster, faster.

The mile-stones still whirled by like ghosts of departed fears and expired miseries.

Colder and colder blew the wind; but it was more grateful than breezes from Araby the Blest. The night was dark and lowering; but to me the heavens were lighted as with an auroral splendor.

Through the encompassing shadows I fancied visions of beauty and landscapes of delight. The arid plain blossomed with association, and the bow of promise spanned every accomplished mile.

Just before the dawn, the fires of the Union pickets crimsoned the somber sky in our front, and a few minutes of hurried striding brought us within the voice of the challenging sentinel.

"Who comes there?"—"Friends without the countersign—escaped prisoners from Salisbury," was the answer. "All right, boys; glad to see you," again awoke the silence; and I walked within the lines that divided Freedom, Enlightenment, Loyalty, from Slavery, Bigotry, Treachery; was once more an American citizen, emancipated, regenerated, and disenthralled.

Still from habit I looked to the West, whither the pole of my spirit so many anxious days had pointed, and I beheld there, as in the East, the coming dawn, typified in the dawn of a better and prouder day for the Republic after its purifying baptism of blood; and saw the star that all along our toilsome march had beamed toward us as the harbinger of the glorious to-morrow, when the tide of War that has swept over the regenerated Nation will have washed clean as polished amethyst the Slavery-stained record of ninety years.

* * * * * * *

Some weeks after our arrival in the North, we learned that all kinds of stories were in circulation in the Penitentiary about our escape. One was that a Rebel General had come for us in a carriage, and borne us away—quite after the manner of the good princes in the Fairy Tales; another, that we had obtained Southern officers' uniforms and passed the guard; a third, that we had bribed the sentinels; a fourth, that we had tunneled out; and I know not how many more, all of them equally untrue.

As many of those stories came from head-quarters, no doubt they were believed by the Rebel officers there, who probably had no correct idea of our mode of exit.

They seemed greatly agitated on the subject, and made every effort to recapture us; sending out scouts to the East and West; believing, I presume, that we had gone directly to Newbern or Morganton.

We lay over the first night—Tuesday—that we got out, and, on the third night after the commencement of the march, quitted the railway near Statesville; and to one of those facts, perhaps, we owe our avoidance of the scouts, who, however, hardly attempted to travel after dark, as we did almost constantly.

When the scouts returned to the Penitentiary, after their unsuccessful search, some of the Rebel officers, both in Richmond and Salisbury, declared we had been caught, and sent farther South; while others swore we had been shot by guerrillas. They seemed very unwilling to admit that we had gotten through, even after the Richmond papers had published the fact; and from the tenacity with which they had held *The Tribune* Correspondents, it was natural they should feel a little chagrined that we were fairly out of their clutches.

With thanks to none but ourselves we did re-obtain our liberty, making the journey from Salisbury to Knoxville in eighteen traveling days, being the best time on record by the over-the-mountains-pedestrian-prisoner-line —one of the least convenient and comfortable routes while in progress, but the most satisfactory and delightful after its completion, in the known World.

CHAPTER LV.

THE SOUTH AND THE WAR.

The Popular Idea of the South.—Its Fallaciousness.—Character of the Southerners.—Their Best Society.—Slavery and its Pernicious Influence.—The Real Cause of the Rebellion.—The Great Revolution in Public Opinion.—Disgraceful History of the Past.—Our National Atonement.

THE popular idea of the South in the North is, or used to be, rather, as singular as erroneous. The South was excessively idealized, even in the minds of persons little troubled with imagination. They believed the country lying the other side of Mason and Dixon's line, especially the Cotton States, the home of Refinement and Culture, Beauty and Luxury, Elegance and Ease.

Few Northern travelers had journeyed to or dwelt in the farther sections of the South; and those who had, had done so to little purpose, seeing with the eyes of people among whom they went, rather than with their own.

Southerners had gasconaded so persistently and perpetually about their sunny homes, their floral fields, their orange groves, their statue-bordered walks, their sparkling fountains, and their palatial residences, with many other highly colored phrases that might have dropped out of Claude Melnotte's sophomorical description of the Lake of Como, that those who heard and read what they said, actually believed them literally.

Northerners, living in a region comparatively unfertile, to be sure, but cultivated and useful, productive and picturesque far beyond that of their rodomontadic neighbors, really began to think, even came to the settled conviction, that they were little blessed; that their school-houses and academies and daily newspapers and galleries of art went for nothing, brought in juxtaposition with the sandy cotton and unwholesome rice-fields, the miasmatic marshes and muddy lagunes of the Gulf States.

They knew there were fine men and lovable women among the hills of New England and on the prairies of the great West; but the most exquisite gentlemen and the most charming ladies must be sought in the Southern plantations.

Marvelous mistake, extraordinary delusion! The hundreds of thousands of our soldiers who have "invaded" Dixie have had ample opportunities to undeceive themselves since the War. They have found out, what the unbiased and observing found out long before, that the South is a large sham; that the beauty of its scenery, the generosity of its people, the splendor of its homes, the luxury of its surroundings, exist only in the imagination; that negroes and indolence, swagger and ignorance, are the poor bits of glass which have assumed such attractive forms in the kaleidoscope of Fancy.

Of course there are a few genuine gentlemen and ladies in the South—or were at least, before the War—who are such in spite, not on account of the peculiar institution; whom even that great wrong and unnatural condition have not blunted or brutalized.

But as for the many, what are they?

Uneducated, coarse, ignorant, vulgar people, who have no idea of comfort or convenience; but live in wretched cabins, on pork, corn-bread, and hominy, thanking God they are not negroes, but having no conception of a higher or worthier existence.

Even the oligarchs, the privileged few, who hold slaves, and rule the whites as thoroughly, though in a different way, as they do their human chattels, have little to boast of.

They have wealth and education, generally. They have expanded their area of observation. They have been in the North, and sometimes in Europe. They have learned there is a World outside of plantation limits and negro quarters. They are as broad, perhaps, as men can be who are born, and reared, and pass their lives in the midst of Slavery and its narrowing and blighting influences.

Yet, their best Civilization is of a mediæval character. Compared to the free North, they are a half a century behind the age. They are semi-barbarians. Their generosity is carelessness; their hospitality, vanity; their frankness a lack of self-discipline; their bravery physical rather than mental, and fostered by a false standard of honor and a pernicious notion of chivalry.

The virtues that appertain to them are the virtues of an imperfectly developed race, and peculiar to their form of society. They are self-loving to a degree of morbidity; amiable and anxious to be agreeable while they are wheedled and flattered; but impatient of contradiction and restraint, and violent, unjust, and cruel when opposed or thwarted, even by those they have assumed to regard as their dearest friends.

They are a little more than intelligent barbarians, the best of them ; nor is it strange, when we reflect that they are ever exposed to the baleful influences of Slavery.

What can be expected of men who found their ideas of superiority upon their elevation above an ignorant, persecuted, servile race, who are in the habit of beating, or seeing beaten, men, women, and children ; of indulging their basest passions with the unfortunate females who dare not oppose their desires ; and in whose embraces they degrade themselves even more than the sable partners of their lust.

Respecting the mode of living, how unwise they are! They have profusion, but not propriety ; liberality, but not taste ; abundance, but not fineness. Nothing is complete with them. Elegance and fitness are things unknown, and aught like harmony is ignored.

Their dwellings, grounds, furniture, and table show this. There is ever somewhat lacking in one place, and somewhat of excess in another. Nothing is finished ; nothing is repaired. The trail of the negro is over them all.

They imbibe all the defects of the slaves, with none of their virtues. They seem indeed to be ruled, rather than the ruling race, since they take hue, and tone, and habit, from their dusky bondsmen. They have their deceitfulness, indolence, animalism, and even their accent.

On them, and their section, the negro is indelibly stamped, and all their interests, purposes, and performances are made subservient to the peculiar institution. It is that which has mildewed the South, which has drained the spirit of progress, and has made her the disloyal, purblind, violent wrong-doer she long ago became, and which generated in her the culminating folly and crime of Secession.

I remember, when the War first broke out, a Virginian of education and wealth, and a slaveholder in Missouri, but still a Unionist, who, deprecating the Rebellion, told me how, in that State, every interest had been made subservient to Slavery.

When the thinking and progressive people wanted schools, the Pro-Slavery party opposed the measure, because, if they had schools, they must have teachers, and teachers must be brought from the Abolition Free States.

When manufactures were advocated in Missouri, they were decried, because the operatives must be Northerners, and haters of the peculiar institution.

Railways were unpopular with the men who afterward blossomed into Secessionists, for the reason that the roads would furnish facilities to fugitive slaves for escape.

So, through and for Slavery, every measure for the development and prosperity of the State was discouraged, misrepresented, and counteracted as far as possible, and all advocates of reform and advancement denounced as Abolitionists. The history of Missouri has been the history of every other Southern State, except that the feeling of opposition and the determination to stagnancy have been augmented in the Cotton regions.

Slavery, from the beginning, has been the curse of the Republic, and the sole cause that threatened its dissolution. It is, and always was, this very War in a state of suppression. No one need say that the Rebellion has proved the impracticability of self-government. It has merely proved that two irreconcilable elements—two utterly different systems of labor, engendering opposite customs and conditions of society—must sooner or later clash, and struggle with each other for the mastery.

All the talk and theories in the Rebel papers about the difference of race—about the Cavaliers and Puritans—in the early settlers of Southern and Northern States, is the merest gallimatia. The only difference there is between the two sections has been made by Slavery.

And as to the War, it was certain to come. Every possible effort was made to stave it off—as the history of our compromises—compromises too often of principle with temporary interest—abundantly shows ; but human endeavor was useless. The cause lay deeper than it was thought, and could not be reached by public enactments or plausible harangues.

Our forefathers, for mere expediency, had compromised with a palpable injustice, a grievous wrong; and we were compelled to pay the penalty. They, no doubt, regarded Slavery as a temporary thing, which would be abrogated in the South, as it was in the North, after a few years.

They did not see—nor could any one then have seen—what an immense interest cotton would become, through the invention of the cotton-gin, and how millions of people would be made insane, by consulting what they conceived to be their pecuniary advantages.

To Slavery—and it alone—we may justly ascribe all

the calamities of the Nation, all the horrors of this War.

The loyal people did not perceive this at first; but now their minds have been illumined by remorselessly logical events and indubitable facts. Hence they have grown Abolitionists; not so much, I am sorry to say, out of their sympathy with the negroes, as out of a cold and calm consideration that, inasmuch as Slavery generated the Rebellion, there never can be a permanent peace, so long as any part of the territory embraced within the United States is cursed with the power to hold human beings in bondage. So feeling and believing, they have determined to have no more of it, and they have done wisely.

Very useless and idle is it, therefore, to speculate on the immediate causes of the War.

Mr. Lincoln's election was made the pretext by the South; but if the advocates of State Rights had not had that pretext, they would have found another. They had remained in the Union so long as they held the political power.

When they lost it—when they saw the progress of the Anti-Slavery sentiment had been such that they never could hope to regain what had slipped away from them, they resolved to destroy the Government they could no longer control. They tried it, and they have destroyed —themselves.

What a wonderful revolution has taken place in public opinion in a few years! Few of my readers, I fancy, who do not remember when they would have felt grossly insulted if they had been called "Abolitionists." But,

I opine, there are still fewer at present who are not proud to know that they are Abolitionists.

That once huge bugbear has lost its power to frighten. Men are no longer children, to be terrified by a word. The term of odium has become an expression of praise; and men of this age and generation will be proud to say, in the future: "I was an Abolitionist in the days of the great Rebellion."

The scales have but begun to fall from the eyes of the people. They have just commenced to perceive the anomaly, the anachronism, the enormity and crime of Slavery. "The land of the free and the home of the brave," shouted on every possible occasion, for half a century, and containing the most bitter satire on the institutions of the country, means something at last; and an American can sing it now without a shame.

Unborn generations will wonder at the fact that the model Republic, for nearly a century, not only permitted Slavery, but went down on its knees before the Slave power, and prayed for a deeper humiliation.

Whose cheek does not tingle when he thinks for how long a time the North succumbed to the South; how long its representatives in Congress were insulted, bullied, and even assaulted, for words spoken in debate; how long its Press played the sycophant, and groveled in the dust that the Slave State leaders shook with disgust from their feet?

No history of a great Nation is more disgraceful than ours was for the twenty-five years previous to the War. Thank Heaven! it will never be repeated, and that we bore all the ignominy and shame to preserve the Republic and the Constitution as we received them from those we had been taught to honor as something more than mortal.

If we were too conservative and reverential, it was only natural. When the first gun from Sumter sounded, our false scruples were scattered. We all became iconoclasts. Right then began to rule over Precedent, and Justice grew stronger than Authority.

We have atoned for the errors of the Past by the sacrifices of the Present. We have hidden the fatal blunder of our ancestors behind the glory of our struggle for a people degraded and enslaved.

We have lifted the age of romance and chivalry to a hight it never knew, from the time of Cœur de Lion to Francis I., by a long, obstinate, unyielding war, not for an idea only, but for humanity and freedom, for the very principle that underlies the foundations of our Republic.

CHAPTER LVI.

THE FUTURE OF THE SOUTH.

Its Undeveloped Resources.—Its Wealthy Planters and the Northern Farmers.—Slave Labor and its Defects.—The Blighting Effect of the Peculiar Institution.—Contrast betw en the Free and Slave States.—Occupation of Secessia by the Yankees.—The Changes Consequent Thereupon.—The Much-Vexed Negro Question.—The Rights of the Freedman.

In the preceding chapter, I have spoken of the undeveloped resources of the South; of the uncomfortable manner of living there; of the lack of accommodation and ease among the people; which all who have traveled in what has since the War received the name of Secessia must have observed.

The people were contented enough, with their slender means and small resources, because they had no higher ideas of living; because they had not, to any extent, obtained a loftier standard from communication with the North.

The prosperous and educated Southerners, having visited our leading cities and principal watering-places, of course learned something; and their knowledge was made apparent by the improved order of architecture and laying-out of grounds which began to reveal themselves, particularly a few years before the Rebellion.

Yet, as I have remarked, there was almost always a lack of completeness and taste, even in the houses of the wealthiest planters—a kind of barbaric profusion without fitness, a sort of ostentation, without a just adaptation of means to the end.

A species of coarseness ran through their mode of living; and one witnessed, in the dwellings of the cotton lords and sugar barons, less genuine comfort and elegance than could be found in the far less pretentious homes of New England, New York, or Ohio farmers.

All the labor was performed by negroes, and consequently but half done. No reforms were introduced, and no changes made. All the improved methods of agriculture, the new implements, the advantageous innovations of the North, were neglected at the South, and, where they were known, were regarded suspiciously, as the result of Yankee ideas, and therefore not to be adopted.

If patent plows, reapers, thrashing-machines, or what not were introduced at the South, they soon got out of order, on account of the ignorance of the slaves, and were of course never repaired.

The South did very little, until compelled by necessity, to establish manufactures of any kind, because they depended wholly upon the inventive genius and extraordinary energy of the "Yankees."

The South was purely agricultural, and they believed they could do better by raising cotton, rice, tobacco, and sugar, than by attempting to make mills, engines, or locomotives.

They could not summon practical energy enough to

furnish for themselves what they needed, and they lacked the inventive faculty almost altogether.

They had untold wealth at their very doors, in coal, iron, lead, and other minerals; yet in very few of their States were the mines worked to any extent.

Whatever passed into their possession seemed affected by the mildew of Slavery. A splendid carriage, purchased by a planter in the North, would very soon lose its polish and freshness, very probably a hub, and two or three spokes; and these would hardly be replaced.

A fine set of harness would soon part company with some of its buckles, which would be supplied with a broken twig and a tow string.

A beautiful span of horses, all symmetry, mettle, and sleekness, would, in a few weeks after exchanging owners, appear rough, lean, and broken down.

Babiecas would be transformed into Rosinantes, almost as suddenly as Cinderella's mice into prancing steeds.

A grand piano required but a brief sojourn in a Southern home, to be deprived of its gloss and its tone, and mayhap one of its legs.

And so with every thing else. Importation from the North to the South proved destructive to fine qualities, material as well as mental.

Unremunerated compulsory labor manifested itself in every part of the South, in the way of stupidity, blunders, and inexcusable carelessness.

Who that has ever steamed down the river, between Kentucky and Ohio, needed to be told which State was free, and which was Slave? On one bank, neat, comfortable dwellings and stirring farms looked across the beautiful river at poor cabins or dilapidated frame tenements, with uncleared fields, partially tilled, as if they wondered at the unfinished appearance of their opposite neighbors.

In descending the Mississippi, low, bleak, and barren are the shores of the mighty stream, with their unvarying sand and their ghastly cotton-woods! Even after reaching the coast country below Baton Rouge, the much-talked-of beauty disappoints him sorely. It is an agreeable contrast to what met his eye above, and to that fact I have always attributed the exaggerated notion of the delightfulness of the Louisiana coast.

When the Rebellion is crushed; when Slavery no longer blights the soil of the South; when that section is settled, as it will be, by a new people, possessed of industry, energy, and perseverance, how metamorphosed all that region will be!

The "barbarous Yankees" will supersede the chivalrous sons of the Cavaliers, and desert places will blossom like the rose. The mining and agricultural interests will be developed to their fullest, and wealth will be poured into the lap of the new-comers.

Elegant villas, such as adorn the Hudson, will beam out of handsome groves, and marble fountains will sparkle where turbid pools have stood poisoning the atmosphere, and diffusing fever and ague to all the country round.

Factories, and school-houses, and graceful churches, will rise where cabins crumbled, and hay-ricks grew moldy in the pestilential air.

The song of cheerful laborers will go gladly up to Heaven where the dusky Slave bent to his irksome toil beneath the overseer's lash.

The South, in that not distant future, will be actualized into the ideal through which it has been seen.

I perceive it now, fruitful and glorious because of its freedom; gathering the harvest of abundance after its long period of bondage has passed away forever.

Then, indeed, will it be the sunny South—sunny with sweet associations and happy memories; beautiful with peace and benison; grand with its history of an emancipated race and a regenerated Republic.

Very many of us have perplexed ourselves with the question, so often asked me while a prisoner, What will we do with the negroes? What will we do with the Rebels? is the first and most important interrogatory. That once settled—and it seems rapidly settling—the other will arrange itself in due season, as do all other things, by the force of Circumstance and the consequence of Universal Law.

Nothing, however, let me remark, seems more inconsistent and irrational than the supposition that the negroes, who have for generations raised the products of the South, while enslaved, will be unable to do so when emancipated.

The theory of the necessity for compulsory labor is a false one.

There is no human creature living, black or white, who can not work as well, and far better, when free than when in bonds; when he has the genuine instincts of manhood in his breast, in place of the haunting and hopeless conviction of perpetual slavery; when he is cheered with a golden future instead of being burdened with a rayless past.

To declare the contrary is the worst form of doubt, the darkest shade of disbelief, the repudiation of Nature and her generous promptings.

Whatever the fate of the Rebels, the land they once possessed will not be destroyed; and the freedmen can certainly till, with their unshackled hands, the soil they have watered with their scalding tears and bloody sweat.

The experiment will doubtless be tried, and it will be proved that the yield of rice and tobacco, and sugar and cotton, under the new system, will be far greater than under the old and degrading one.

The climate of the South is favorable and congenial to the negro. Why should he not remain there if he so elects?

Let him, in the name of justice and humanity, reap something of the harvest for which he has suffered and fought, has bled and died!

The true principle of a free Government is to give every man a chance, whatever his station or antecedents. That we will give to the negro, as his right. No bugbear about negro equality will deter the people from meting out to the emancipated slave the long-demanded justice of making to him that late atonement for what the country has compelled him to endure.

The man who fears the African will become his equal, must have a shuddering conviction within that he merely needs an opportunity to become such. Away with the base apprehension!

The World was given to us all, to do the best work of which we are capable; to try for its rewards; to make endeavors for its happiness.

Unworthy and ungenerous is he who asks what he is unwilling another should have.

Life, Liberty, and the Pursuit of Happiness, are our natural rights, the African's as well as the Caucasian's; and I, for one, welcome the negro on the threshold of his new career, and bid him God speed in whatever he is able honestly to obtain!

CONCLUSION.

WHILE this volume has been in press, and the proof-sheets has been undergoing revision, the great Rebellion has been hastening to its close, and may now be considered fairly ended. Few weeks in ancient or modern times have been more eventful, more prolific of History than those of April and May, 1865.

When the first chapters of this book, which were very irregularly furnished, were written, the Rebellion still looked extremely formidable, and caused very grave doubts whether it might not survive the year, and linger on until the returning spring; whether thousands of lives might not be required for sacrifice upon the altar of the Republic before the colossal insurrection was completely crushed.

Thanks to Fortune, those days of darkness and anxiety and doubt have gone forever. The dawn has come at last. After that long and fearful night, shaken with tempest, and pregnant with terror, watched with throbbing hearts and suspended breath by every loyal American, the sun of Freedom has re-arisen, and its glory is streaming over a regenerated Land.

Within a few weeks, Richmond, the key-stone of the arch of the bastard "Confederacy," has crumbled; Lee, the head and front of traitorous opposition, has surrendered, and Johnston, and Taylor, and others of less importance, have imitated his example through force of necessity.

Amid all the radiance of victory there was a sudden eclipse. In the highest hour of rejoicing a chill was struck to every gladdened heart.

The Chief of the Nation, the great and good man who had steadily and conscientiously, and skillfully guided the Country through the terrible trial of battle, fell a martyr to Freedom by the hand of an assassin, a desperate, but wretched tool in the hands of his masters in treason and in crime. He fell, but not an hour too soon for his glory: his cup of honor was full: his immortality was determined; and if it had not been, the explosion of the murderous pistol would have rendered it secure.

While the Republic still weeps, the death of the assassin, and the capture of the arch traitor (Jefferson Davis), are announced. There seems a destiny in all the closing scenes of the grand drama which for four thrilling years has kept possession of the American stage, and held all civilized Nations in painful suspense.

It appears as if no relic of the Rebellion were fated to escape; as if no part of the vast crime against Nature and Liberty were to be left unanswered for; as if all the vile falsehoods of the enemy were to be exposed beyond capacity to doubt, and his braggart insolence and ridiculous swagger forever humbled in the dust.

What a bitter mortification it must be to the Southerners who for fifty years have filled the air with their vaporings, and disgusted the World with their assumptions; who have arrogantly claimed superiority of race and civilization; who have heaped all manner of abuse upon the Free States and their citizens; to know and feel that they have been completely defeated, utterly subjugated by the stout hands and brave hearts of the people they had affected to despise!

Where now is all that rant about the impossibility of conquering eight millions of free people born on horseback, and destined to rule? Where is the last ditch? Where are all the men, women, and children who were to die so delightedly and so melo-dramatically before they would submit to the "Yankee" yoke?

Tell me, gentle shepherd; tell me where!

Very glad ought we of the loyal North to be, that we are not Rebels; that we are this day spared the galling consciousness that we owe our wretched lives to the magnanimity of the Nation we have sought to destroy. I should think our foes would seek some remote corner of the world and hide themselves from the public gaze, and from private scorn; that they would beg the earth to swallow, and the mountains to cover them.

Never was so vast a bubble as that of the pseudo Chivalry pricked before; never was such pompous assumption so effectually extinguished; never was such lofty arrogance so deeply humiliated. Give the Rebels their wish at this final hour—all but the prominent leaders—at least, and leave them alone. If they do not go and hang themselves—and they wont by any means—they are as devoid of sensibility and a sense of fitness as they are of chivalry and shame.

The end of the War has been obtained. The Republic has fullfilled its destiny. Slavery, the plague-spot upon the fair body of our Country, is dead, and no trumpet, though it were an angel's, can awake it to resurrection.

America for the first time is truly free. For the first time her people can sing her national songs without a blush; and the poorest of her sons can declare: "I am an American!" with, not uncovered head, but with mein erect, and a glow of purest satisfaction before the proudest potentates of the admiring world.

THE END.